THE BIG BOOK OF WOODEN BOAT RESTORATION

THOMAS LARSSON

THE BIG BOOK OF WOODEN BOAT RESTORATION

Basic Techniques, Maintenance, and Repair

SKYHORSE PUBLISHING

Skyhorse Publishing books may be purchased in bulk at special discounts for sales promotion, corporate gifts, fund-raising, or educational purposes. Special editions can also be created to specifications. For details, contact the Special Sales Department, Skyhorse Publishing, 307 West 36th Street, 11th Floor, New York, NY 10018 or info@skyhorsepublishing.com.

Skyhorse® and Skyhorse Publishing® are registered trademarks of Skyhorse Publishing, Inc.®, a Delaware corporation.

Visit our website at www.skyhorsepublishing.com.

10 9 8 7 6 5 4 3 2 1

Library of Congress Cataloging-in-Publication Data is available on file.

Cover design by Frida Sthlm
Cover photographs: Christer Ulvås, Malcolm Hanes

ISBN: 978-1-5107-0476-3
Ebook ISBN: 978-1-5107-0475-6

Printed in China

Contents

Preface

I've always been interested in boats and the Swedish Archipelago. To cast off from it all and go out and sail a few weeks each summer has been a delight and a driving force. In order to do this as a student with little money, an old wooden boat was the only option. Restoring and maintaining the boat then gave me a winter hobby, and I connected with like-minded friends. When the hobby evolved into a profession, I decided that if my interest in the archipelago, sailing, and boats ever had to suffer because of my career, then it would be time to change careers. There was no need: the work is varied, it's creative, the constant problem solving provides stimulus, and the sea still appeals to me.

I hope you who read this book will refurbish and maintain your boat with curiosity and persistence, more for the joy to get out at sea than to count the hours of work done.

Shortly after the commercial building of wooden boats largely died out forty years ago, I started working on wooden boat restorations. At that time, those of us who were working in this new profession of refurbishing wooden boats tried to learn as much as possible about a disappearing craft. Through renovations and repairs, we gained knowledge of various construction methods and of what were good and bad practices. I would like to pass on to a new generation what I learned. Trade language is included in the book to preserve it, but also because it is often more accurate than paraphrasing. Now, in the early 21st century, the availability of boats to renovate has declined, and they are building more new wooden boats, both replicas and new designs. The pendulum seems to swing back, and, because of this, there are also new methods in this book.

This book covers maintenance, knowledge of material, tools, and instructions, based on my own experience. One important lesson is that maintenance is important. It is maintenance rather than restoration that gives a boat a long life.

The descriptions in the book are given not only to answer the question how, but also to answer why. It can be equally interesting knowledge for those of you who are generally interested in wooden boats and for those who are interested in trying out wooden boat renovation as a profession.

The Big Book of Wooden Boat Restoration is an update of the book *Wooden Boat Renovation*, which was published in 2002. The basis for the book *Wooden Boat Renovation* was a series of articles that the Swedish Museum Boats Association encouraged in the 1990s.

When I say "we" in the book, I am referring to my teacher and colleague, Harry Johans, and my co-workers and apprentices from various renovation projects.

Many thanks to Susanna Höijer for her involvement as an editor.

Björn Melander and Wolfgang Johansson helped with fact-checking and proofreading.

Last but not least, I would again like to thank my family, Lena, Kristin, and Olle, for their patient support during my work on the book.

Nacka in October 2010
Thomas Larsson

Introduction

Sailing and boats have been my passion since childhood. For the past thirty-five years I have been working to repair wooden boats while sailing my own wooden boats. This means that I have had experience in both construction and maintenance and have been able to follow up on the results. At work, I have come into contact with most types of boats and have been able to see which construction methods have worked well and which really don't. On my own boats, I have been able to try out new ideas. Bad ideas and poor maintenance have quickly made themselves known. The good solutions I have used over and over again.

I have been asked to bring together my experiences in a book on wooden boat care and renovation.

Anyone who has had a boat in a boat club knows that there are as many ways to maintain a wooden boat as there are boat owners. My own experience is my starting point. You should all stick to the methods that have worked well for you over the years.

INCREASED INTEREST IN WOODEN BOATS

When I started with wooden boat repairs, most people had wooden boats for financial reasons. They could not afford to buy a plastic boat and kept up their wooden boats as well as they could. Today, there are plenty of pre-owned, inexpensive, and easy-to-maintain plastic boats, many of which also provide better comfort. Those who acquire wooden boats these days are making a conscious decision; there is a special kind of feeling to owning a wooden boat, a wooden boat culture.

The maintenance of a well-kept plastic boat and a well-maintained wooden boat takes about the same amount of time. However, a plastic boat is forgiving; a wooden boat is not. If you have no time for a plastic boat one spring, it only takes a little more thorough waxing the following year. The corresponding neglect of a wooden boat results in rigorous maintenance for years to come, and some damage may be permanent. Mass consumption of leisure has resulted in those who are looking to go out for boat rides acquiring plastic boats, while wooden boat owners often are interested in boat history and think of boat maintenance as a hobby.

The developments in this direction have gone further abroad, where a lot is also written on the wooden boat as a hobby. In the United States and England, there are several lavish magazines focused on wooden boats. Here in Sweden, there has been a lack of recent literature on the subject, despite the fact that Sweden has one of the largest wooden boat fleets. There are several reasons for this large fleet. We have been spared from war. Because of our climate, the boats are on land half the year and get a chance to dry out, and we have time for maintenance. Rot and fungal infestation do not spread in the cold. Our boats are not subject to worm attacks. Our unique boat club system makes it possible to have your own boat at a low cost, and fellow club members will share their experiences.

When the boats were built neither the customers nor the builders counted on the longevity they have attained today. This means that boats have a great cultural and historical value, while they often are in a condition that requires repairs, which are sometimes as demanding as new construction.

Today it seems like the interest is not on par with the availability of objects. Smaller boats with poor livability are chopped up at a fast rate at marinas and boat clubs; they represent so little economic value in comparison to their annual costs and labor that they are too expensive.

Boats that are in good condition are sold in large numbers to other countries. This may in itself be good since there don't seem to be enough people interested in caring for these boats in Sweden. The best way to keep our unique vintage wooden boat fleet is to increase interest and, through increased demand, to try to raise prices for well-kept boats so that people cannot afford to neglect them. This would also help set insurance values high enough so that they can cover repair costs, even for major damage.

WOODEN BOAT: UTILITY OR VINTAGE BOAT?

In Sweden, the wooden boat and the vintage boat have become synonymous concepts. It is all about an interest in carrying a tradition forward, primarily for older wooden boats. We have vintage boat festivals, while similar events are called wooden boat festivals in Norway and Finland. In Norway, the wooden boat is also continually built as a utility boat that is in competition with the plastic boat. English vintage boat publishers write about the old plastic and aluminum boats. Here in Sweden there are several clubs within the sailing world that have both plastic and wooden boats competing on equal terms. As interest in wooden boats increases while the supply of old wooden boats in need of restoration decreases, it may perhaps spark an interest in new construction in Sweden as well. I use the term "utility boat" for a boat that is used primarily for transportation or as a racing or vacation boat, as opposed to a vintage boat whose history and appearance are its highlighted characteristics.

TO PRESERVE OR RESTORE

Boatbuilding is a labor-intensive craft, which led to new construction coming to an end in the 1960s when quality-minded builders could no longer get paid for their work. Hiring professional help is expensive; however, I am noticing an increased interest in renovations instead of simple patchwork. It is more economical in the long run to invest in a long-lasting result.

An old wooden boat represents, in addition to its utility value, a piece of history. A constructor's ideas have taken shape and been preserved for posterity; talented boatbuilders have put their knowledge and craft tradition into the boat; various owners have worn out the threshold. The more of this that is preserved during a renovation the better.

Sweden has a tradition of continuous good maintenance by boat owners in boat clubs. As a result, we have many boats still in their original condition. An original boat is the most valuable vintage boat we have, and it is important to encourage careful maintenance. A completely renovated boat can never be an original boat again, but of course it becomes a wonderful, beautifully renovated boat. Abroad, there is a tradition of complete restoration—taking a boat in for a total overhaul, picking it up, wearing it down for a number of years, and then taking it back for repairs again. This is harder on the boat than continuous maintenance would be.

CARRYING ON THE CRAFTS TRADITION

When I renovate a boat, I try to make the new pieces of such quality that the repair can be as long-lasting as the boat was. Making a repair on a sixty-year-old boat that only lasts ten years feels wrong. Patching up on a provisional basis is sometimes necessary to keep "an old boat afloat," but it is not the same as renovating. When I describe procedures in this book, I want to reflect both the old tradition of craftsmanship and the best of the new methods.

SAILBOATS ARE UTILITY BOATS

Sailboats are now largely utility boats: they have auxiliary engines and rigging, sail handling is made easier, the deck layout is altered, and modern sheet rails and winches are bolted on. In a sailboat built for racing—built at the limit of durability—all the structural components must work together to make it able to be pushed hard into the wind. Structural repairs are therefore the most common, such as strengthening the mast step, mending broken frames, and splining damaged seams. Varnish maintenance is secondary. A sailboat does not do very well when left on land; it cracks and easily loses shape. The great logs that make up the backbone—such as the Wood keel—may crack. If you are unlucky, it will crack right in the middle of the keel bolt row. You could say that it's better to forget the boat in the water one winter than on land one summer.

USE THE BOAT FIRST, THEN RENOVATE

A structural renovation of a boat is almost insurmountable for an amateur and is not something I usually recommend. An enthusiastic new boat owner will find it difficult to prioritize if he buys a boat that has been taken apart to restore but that stays on land. It is better to buy a boat that can be launched and try to keep the boat going; if you have sailed it one summer, it is much easier to prioritize. Perhaps you will put a temporary sheet of metal over the rough parts at the bottom while you focus your interest on sealing the cabin so that you can go to sleep and stay dry even in the rain. That might keep you going until you fix the bottom after the summer. In order to continue working on a fixer-upper, you need to be able to concentrate and do what you're doing right from the beginning. At the same time, you have to be able to ignore some things or you will be eternally repairing and patching. It is satisfying to finish a partial renovation and know that that part is ready for the foreseeable future.

If you have both a genuine interest in sailing as well as an interest in wooden boats, then this is the only way for most of you to cope with it. Of course there are many examples of fine complete restorations, but it's rarely the person who started the project that gets the pleasure of using the boat. Either he got tired and sold it, or his sailing interest received a blow due to a lack of time to sail, and his boat is sold for that reason when it is completed.

INCREASED INTEREST IN COLLECTING

With motorboats, things are a little different. There is a different kind of vintage boat interest that lies closer to the the hobby of collecting vintage cars. The real enthusiasts sometimes have more than one project going on at the same time. Smaller boats are set up for a total renovation, but with an emphasis more on appearance—such as filling in damaged wood, renovating surface treatments, supplementing and re-chroming hardware and installing a new engine. The owner is often keen to keep up the finish, to have a full boat cover or even storage on land. An unglued mahogany speedboat can stand to be on land if one accepts that the seams between the planks will crack and will then have to be filled with varnish. Several fine examples of complete renovation of large motorboats have been conducted in recent years. Such renovations will increase if we are to follow the trend in the United States and England.

MAINTENANCE IN THE WATER

TOPSIDES

Spring surprises us every year. Snow and sleet are all of a sudden replaced by a hot sun and warm winds. To avoid having to discover new dry cracks each time you go see your boat, it should be launched at the end of April or early May in central Sweden. Spring is often the driest time of the year. To avoid having the topsides crack while in the water, you need to use your boat a lot.

If you do not have time to sail, then bed sheets are great protection from the sun. Attach the canvas to the railing and let it hang down a few inches into the water. The canvas absorbs the moisture, which evaporates with the heat and helps keep the topsides planking tight.

LEAKAGE FROM BELOW

Wooden boats often leak when launched, especially if they have been on land for a long period of time. To avoid the risk of your boat sinking, you need to tape the worst cracks. The easiest way is to use regular transparent tape on top of the bottom paint. Don't put too much tape on, as the boat must leak a little in order to swell up. Otherwise it may leak a lot on the first trip when the tape is taken off; it has happened more than once that boats have sunk for this reason. I usually check on the seams from the inside after a few hours in the water; I stick out a gauge through a pair of dry open seams to perforate the tape and allow water to penetrate and wet the seams so that they swell and close up. The highest water level possible inside the boat will accelerate the swelling. The floors will then have a chance to swell and tighten the keel bolts.

You can also use a soft, wax-based sealant or sheep's tallow. Then tape both sides of the seam and apply the sealant with a putty knife. When the planks swell, the excess of soft sealant will squeeze out from the seams and the excess will stick to the outside all summer. Small leaks can also be fixed at sea with a wax-based sealant.

If the leakage problems continue after the boat has finished swelling, then you should try to find the problem in order to fix it for the following year. Close up a few limber holes at a time with modeling clay and use a sponge to dry out the closed-up frame slots. If the water level doesn't rise, then there are no leaks in that compartment. Continue until the leaks are found. I often get questions about repairing leaks on boats that are already on land. If the boat owner is not sure where the leak is, I ask him to come back next year. Boats may well be leaking in different places in water and on land, depending on whether they float or stand on a pallet on the keel.

Beware of using a boat before it's finished swelling. Vibrations from the engine or subsidence from mast pressure can lead to permanent damage if the seems are not tight.

PUMPS

For safety reasons, a boat needs to have a manual pump. If the boat has a constant leak, it may be necessary to use an electric bilge pump with a float switch in order to leave the boat unattended, even if that means a big risk. With less leakage—and in open boats where rain falls into the boat—the water should also be kept as low as possible with an electric bilge pump with float switch. It drastically increases the life of both the frames and the planking. The limber holes need to be at such a low level that no water can remain; it is also important that they are clean so that the water can have free access to the pump.

The disadvantage of the float level pump is that it is not very reliable. One way to improve it is to ensure that cable connections are as far above the water as possible, and another is to take the parts home over winter so they don't freeze. Another disadvantage of having electricity in the bilge is that more than one boat has had its steel floors and steel frames damaged by corrosion from stray currents off bad cables and from terminal blocks that have been placed too low.

KEEP THE BILGE CLEAN

It is amazing how quickly it gets messy under the floor boards. If a boat leaks, at least the water will be fresh (at least that's one advantage of leaks). But if a boat has no leakage, there will soon be microorganisms in the dirty water, which eventually lead to rotting. You have to scrub and wash it clean a few times per season. It's always hard to get to, but rinsing it with a few buckets of clean water (preferably saltwater) is often quite simple. All parts of the bottom where bilge water will remain should be painted with oil-resistant paint to prevent water penetration and the growth of microorganisms. Many people surface treat the outside of their boats carefully to avoid water coming in, but on the inside they leave the wood bare, only oiling it, but oil does not prevent dirt from getting a hold on the wood or microorganisms from growing.

LEAKAGE FROM ABOVE

Fungi that cause rotting quickly attack moist, unprotected wood. Fungi need moisture, heat, and oxygen. At temperatures below 40°F (5°C), rot does not develop. Between 68–77°F (20–25°C) is the most favorable temperature range. Wood submerged in water hardly rots at all. This means that leakage from above is more serious with regards to the boat's life than leakage from below, and the damage will show up faster. Wood needs a moisture content of over 28% for rot to occur. If the wood is varnished or painted in good condition, it falls below 20%, while untreated wood easily surpasses 28%. If the varnish is in good condition, moisture leading to decay will only come through cracks, joints, seams, and old screw holes. If the openings have clear passage for the water to go through, then the joints will dry out quickly, such as with deck seams, which seldom rot. This means that you should only seal from the top—for instance, only the top edge around the hatch frames—or otherwise perfect pockets for rot are created. The worst areas for rotting are at the transom and between the deck and cabin, especially in the corners. If you discover moisture in those areas, you must seal them at once from the outside with a sealing compound or tape.

BOAT COVER

A boat cover is the easiest way to simplify maintenance. Time between surface treatments can be more than doubled, especially for the cockpit. The cockpit contains boat carpentry that are more susceptible to moisture than woodwork found in the hull and deck. Where the end grain of the wide benches meet bulkheads, cracks are more prevalent and form crevices that are hard to clean, which leads to rainwater collecting in them and then to rot. Rainwater will cause rot while salt water seems to make wood more rot resistant. Some Swedes who were in the salty waters of Norway considering purchasing a boat told me about how they were out test-sailing it when the owner happened to spill drinking water in the bilge. He quickly fetched a bucket of salt water and immediately pumped the mixture out. Fresh water is thought to rot wood.

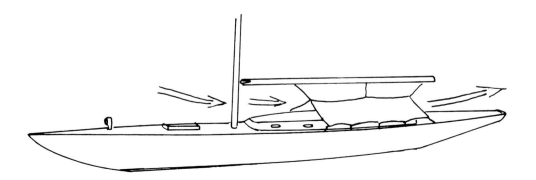

FIGURE 1 } A cockpit cover stretched under the boom provides good aeration of the boat if the hatches are left open.

Rainwater, which falls into a boat without a cover or a self-draining cockpit, will easily remain and penetrate into the wooden stucture of the inside of the boat, which is often less coated (with paint) than the outside of a boat. It allows the frame ends to rot and lapstrake boats to get waterlogged in the laps.

When I leave my boat at my home port, I always put a cover over the cockpit. The best is a simple V-shaped cover without ends that hang under the boom, tightened with rope to the railing. Air that blows in under the canopy pulls the warm, moist air out of the boat if the hatches are left open or if it's self-ventilated. More air can be supplied with a large vent on the foredeck. Motorboats often have covers as well, but they are usually poorly ventilated. There should be rain-protected openings to let air pass through. A cover is an expensive investment but will last a lot longer if you add simple protective covers for dirt and sun over the horizontal surfaces of the ordinary cover when the boat lies in its home port. The cover must be made of a well-ventilated material so that the condensation will dry quickly, otherwise there may be mildew on the underlying cover. Motorboats sometimes have covers that lie directly on the deck to prevent leakage and fading of mahogany, but the temperature under a dark cover can reach up to 140–158°F (60–70°C) and can cause cracks. A lighter cover is kinder on the boat.

Sails also have to be protected with covers against UV radiation, which shortens their life span considerably.

VARNISH HAS A SHORT LIFE SPAN

Alkyd varnishes, which are the most common, must be sanded and revarnished each year to maintain their elasticity and avoid cracking and blisters. One season's life span is almost too long for the most exposed areas, which are horizontal surfaces subject to wear and sunlight—for example, the cap of the rail. Another difficult area is the lower 4–6″ (10–15 cm) of the topside that reflects sunlight through a layer of dried out salt water. You have to wash this off with fresh water. Salt deposits, soot, pollen, and guano should be rinsed off with fresh water and then dried in order to increase the life expectancy of the varnish. It is practical to use the morning dew for wiping. A touch-up of the worst areas during the summer will save a lot of work the following spring. (How odd that it never happens.) Damage to the varnish must be touched up, otherwise moisture will penetrate and lift the surrounding varnish. As an example of the life span of alkyd varnish, I will mention that in warmer and sunnier climates around the Mediterranean, people only have two to three months between reapplications of varnish. When the first cracks appear, you have to sand and varnish all exposed surfaces within a few weeks to avoid having to scrape everything clean.

By fall, the humidity rises, and the wood does not have time to dry out during the day. If you have cheated on maintenance, your varnish may begin to crack now, and the air will be too humid for it to be improved. The moisture that penetrates worn varnish, cracks and joints will freeze and lift the varnish from the wood if you do not get the boat under a roof in time. It will increase the need for more maintenance. I like to say that every week without coverage after mid-October adds another weekend of work in the spring.

In the next chapter we will look at the season in a wooden boat owner's life that begins as the boat comes up on land.

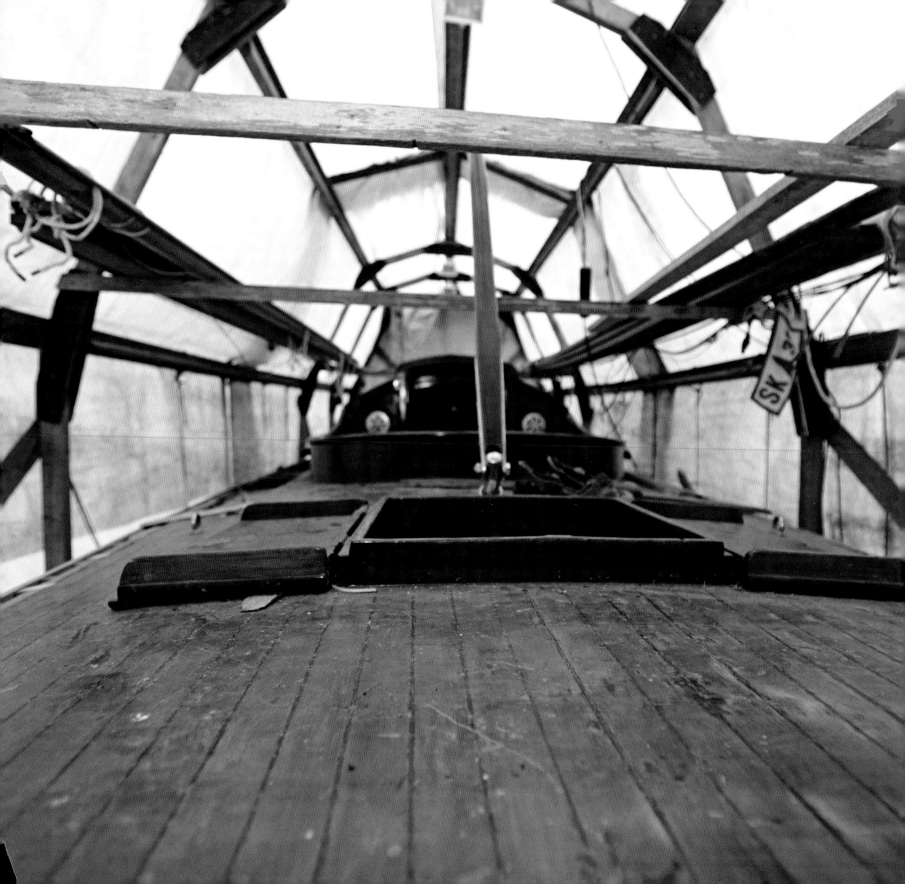

WINTER MAINTENANCE

The longer part (about seven months) of the season begins when the boat comes up on land. Even if you don't have any major repairs to do on your boat, it will still be a couple of weekends of work before your boat can be put away for the winter. Even if you have planned some winter maintenance, you might want to take a break: November is usually full of nothing but moisture and condensation anyway. This chapter will focus on maintenance during the winter months. The renovations will have to wait a little bit. It is annual maintenance that gives boats a long life span, rather than renovations. There is a saying: "You are not the owner of a wooden boat; you are just its keeper."

MAINTENANCE AND HAULING OUT

Cover up the boat as soon as possible when it comes ashore. It is more likely to have moisture and freezing damage on land as the temperature varies more than in the water. Humidity is high throughout the day, and the moisture works its way down through the worn finish. If the wood doesn't get a chance to dry before the cold sets in, the frost in the wood will lift off paint and varnish.

Wash the boat. Many clubs have access to high-pressure washers, but use them wisely. Soft antifouling comes off easily with any plant growth, but it is also easy to break splinters of wood off if water hits at an uneven angle, such as with poor joints. Teak decks should not be pressure washed as the seam sealant can come off from the water pressure. Instead, they should be washed with a soft brush across the grain so that as little as possible of the soft sections of growth rings will wear off, which might make the deck uneven. High pressure washing of the inside of the hull is very effective when you want to remove flaking paint and dirt, but it is not something you want to do in the late fall, as pressure washing will force a lot of moisture into the wood, risking freezing and paint lifting. The topside, waterline, and deck require washing with detergent and rinsing to remove traces of grease, dirt, and soot, which will otherwise clog the sand paper and diminish paint adhesion.

Lift floors everywhere and wash beneath, making sure there is no water left anywhere. Remove the garboard drain plug; it should be at the lowest point of the bilge with the lower edge of the hole at the height of the wood keel. On motorboats, there needs to be a drain plug on each side of the garboard. The garboard drain plug is also needed to drain out water that may come in if the cover stand breaks during the winter. Many boats have been completely ruined after having been filled with water during the winter. Damage caused by water that has been allowed to remain and freeze in hard-to-get-at areas is also common. On motorboats, you should be especially vigilant under the chain locker and bureaus and on the sides of the engine bed. The same goes for a sailboat; you should also look under the mast step and in the almost inaccessible compartment between the floors under a self-bailing cockpit.

Take home as much equipment as possible; textiles will only retain a bad odor, and they can rot if left in the boat. If you bring home valuable accessories, the boat can be left open and ventilated. Remove drawers and place them flat to air them out so that they do not swell, and leave doors ajar. Drawers and cabinets can be wiped with a vinegar solution to prevent mold. Wooden parts from the boat cannot be stored in warm and dry areas of your home, such as boiler rooms. They will dry, crack, and warp.

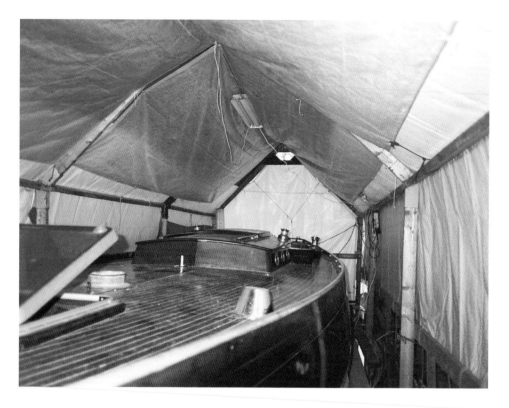

FIGURE 2 } Cover stand with inside tarps to prevent condensation. Note the ventilation hole at the ridge. The rack is built out of studs with bracket tubing. The truss has an angle of 90°, so most of the snow will slide off. The most common hardware has a 60° roof angle and requires snow removal, or it may break from wet snow.

Preserve the engine, replace filters, and clean up any spillage. You need to paint underneath the engine with oil-resistant paint, especially if the spill tray is missing; this way you may degrease the area without leaching the wood. Diesel leakage goes straight through the wood and creates characteristic greasy spots on the outside of the hull. The wood becomes brittle, and you can't glue on it; furthermore, it is harder to get paint to adhere.

Make sure the batteries are fully charged and in good condition. They must be stored in acid-resistant boxes that will collect any possible leakage, like that caused by freezing, for example. Battery acid will corrode the planks; they may look intact but will be quite brittle.

Take home or grease the chrome accents. Chrome ages rapidly in the damp, and by removing the hardware you will save a lot of time when sanding and painting. Keep

the screws from the removed hardware in separately labeled bags. You will appreciate this when you reassemble in the spring.

Scrape the bottom in places where the paint usually comes off in the spring anyway, usually where there is moisture trapped behind the paint that has to be vented. This is particularly true of boats built from African mahogany after World War II—this type of wood is not very appropriate under the waterline. African mahogany is porous and absorbs moisture from the end grain, and as the wood has interlocked wood there is end grain going straight through the planking at some places. On these types of boats, the planking should be scraped to the bare wood every fall in all areas where there is more wood on the inside—meaning along the garboard and stem—so the moisture can be vented out; otherwise you risk the planking suffering from frost damage.

COVER

- A wooden boat should have a stand-alone cover.
- It should be easy to set up.
- It should not be attached to the boat anywhere.
- It should not be in the way for spring maintenance.
- It will allow control of ventilation depending on the season.

A good cover is a matter of convenience. Arrange it so that when you get down to the boat you can plug in the power, put your toolbox down on your bench, and get started immediately after having greeted your fellow boat friends at the club. After a few hours, maybe it will be time for a coffee break with those friends. This is when boating becomes more leisure than work, but it's no fun building a stand for a cover in the rain during the fall.

Different materials for the stand. Steel pipe scaffolding with Burton couplings is sturdy but requires welding skills; otherwise it is difficult to avoid sharp corners from the joints where normal wear and tear will have its course. Aluminum tubes, which are commonly used, are too weak;

a freestanding aluminum structure is often too light, and the wind might blow it over, or it might rub against the boat. Wood is a suitable material for these boats. Studs 1¾ × 2¾ or 1¾ × 3¾″ (45 × 70 or 45 × 95 mm) are a good material to start with. Connections can be made out of plywood or square-section steel. They make it easy to install and disassemble, and you don't have to discard as much timber as when you demolish a nailed stand. Make sure to carefully store the cover timber over the summer, as rot and mildew from the stand may spread to the boat. Store it up off the ground with a tarp on top.

Tarps are available in different qualities. Transportation and rental tarps are heavy, so the cover stand will be stable, but the weight, about 700 g/m², makes them difficult to manage. If the boat is larger there will be too many overlapping seams, since those tarps are generally about 13 × 20 ft (4 × 6 m) and it would take too many tarps. Lightweight or Japanese tarps are inexpensive and easy to handle but time-consuming to tie, and the cover might be too light and might move around with the wind. The sun breaks them down; after one winter and one summer, they usually tear the following winter. It is possible to special-order tarps made out of tent canvas (500–600 grams) with drawstrings at the joints. Such a tarp may last up to twenty years unless you leave it out during the summer. The cloth size can be chosen so the joints are few and so less canvas will be needed; canvases larger than 430 sq. ft (40 m²) will, however, be difficult to manage.

In the fall, wind should be given an opportunity to dry out the boats. Leave a 3-ft (1-meter) air gap between the boat and the ground for ventilation and a triangle at the top to reduce condensation. Do not leave the ends open, as the wind that blows in will not go past the boat but it may lift the cover stand. After New Year's, when the air becomes drier, it is time to cover the boat all the way to the ground to maintain soil moisture under the boat and prevent it from drying out and cracking.

Inner tarps will prevent condensation. When you scrape the boat to the bare wood, the scraped surface becomes susceptible to condensation and dirt. To avoid this, rig up a hanging tarp of the Japanese type underneath the roof to divert condensation. The water will condense on the external tarp and drop down on the one underneath, which will lead the water outside along the hull sides.

Lighting is often so poor under boats that you cannot see well enough to try any carpentry or surface treatment. I heard of a half-way builder who just had one power outlet, one lamp, and one electronic jigsaw. First, he drew up where he would cut, then he turned off the lamp, plugged in the jigsaw, sawed, turned the light back on, and cursed.

It is difficult to get good results without a good workbench. Unless the parts you are working with can be secured well while you work on them, you cannot achieve a good handcrafted result.

INDOOR WINTER STORAGE

Today, when we have so little time, being the busy urban people we are, the demand for indoor winter storage has grown. People want to use the days spent taking care of their boats doing something else. A wooden boat is best stored in cold storage with a dirt floor. The environment is still damp, so the boat must be taken out in the same manner as if it had been under a tarp. For larger boats owned by full-service customers of a boatyard, a storage area that stays a few degrees above freezing is money well spent, as paint will not freeze off. Textiles and equipment can also be left on board. However, it is important that moisture in the storage area is monitored. For winter storage, a relative humidity of 60–65% is appropriate.

PREPARATION FOR LAUNCHING

After February, no exterior hull surfaces should be left untreated—mere linseed oil is not enough; the oil does not prevent moisture from seeping out of the wood. Keeping the humidity at a constant level throughout the year is one of the keys to easy maintenance. If the timber is prevented from moving then the planking will not crack and the paint will stay on.

Prior to launching, the bottom will start to become so dry that just a little sun is needed for it to open. I usually do not take my covers off until the night before launching. The boat can be kept moist the last week with wet rags inside or by water left in the bilge.

I have to warn you about leaving running water unattended inside the boat. As long as the boat is leaking like a sieve, it is not so bad, but when the boat seals itself, then debris or leaves can settle in the garboard drain plug. If the boat is filled with water, the best-case scenario is that the planking breaks—it is not designed to withstand water pressure from within—and the worst case is the whole boat breaking apart.

If the boat has been on land for a long time and has dried apart, it won't be worthwhile to do any maintenance work; the movement of the wood will make it worthless. Oil and prime the boat, but don't put a hard topcoat on, as it cannot tolerate great movement in the wood. Do not fill in seams, but launch it and leave the boat waterlogged (put it in shallow water and let it get filled with water) until it is resealed; then take the boat out for surface drying before doing the finishing coats.

MAST AND RIGGING

Masts are glued with adhesives that are not boil-proof. If a mast that is scraped to the bare wood is left outdoors in the rain and sunshine, it won't take long before it is destroyed. Rain weakens the glue, and the sun causes dry cracks. Masts should not be heavily oiled; oil is thought to reduce the stiffness of the wood. After rot protection, you should varnish with a very diluted (50%) varnish coat on the porous wood (masts are often made of sitka spruce or whitewood, which are light and have soft fibers). The varnish must also be of a soft type, in order to not crack easily. If the mast has a bolt rope groove, it can be surface treated with varnish applied to the gutter with a knotted rag. The mast should be stored in a mast shed over the winter. If you don't have a mast shed, the mast should be covered on the top; do not wrap it in plastic, as it will easily rot. If you store the mast outdoors, make sure to keep the butt end at the lowest point so that the mast can drain if it is hollow. All masts should have drainage down to the mast butt, otherwise they tend to eventually rot where the cavity ends (often just above the boom fitting). Do not forget to varnish the spreaders; spreaders tend to rot behind the tape at the spreaderheads, so change it occasionally. Check all sprints and shackles before mast stepping. Rub the halyard wire with wax so that it won't get so worn by the blockseaves. Galvanized wire can be treated with linseed oil against wear and rust.

SUMMARY

The key to easy boat maintenance is to keep the wood as evenly dry as possible throughout the year. Unless the wood swells and shrinks excessively, the coating won't crack, the glue will stay intact, and it will make it difficult for moisture to penetrate.

In the water, the bottom is kept dry with a good coat of paint. The inside of the boat is kept dry with covers, the bilge water level is kept low, and the boat is ventilated. Topside can be protected from excessive drying with fabric on the side exposed to the sun.

Cover your boat with a well-ventilated stand as soon as it is up on land; in central Sweden this would be in early October. Leave your boat clean and well ventilated. Let the boat air out until next year; then let the cover go down to the ground to prevent the spring sunshine and spring winds from drying the hull apart. Do not leave exterior hull surfaces without surface treatment after February. Launch in late April to May.

Cracked paint and varnish are nothing more than symptoms of moisture penetration; take care of what is causing them and do not just patch up.

If you follow these rules, your boat will age slowly and maintenance will be minimal.

FIGURE 3 } Limiting the scope of work is one of the greatest difficulties with renovation. Repairs to the stem in conjunction with replacing the wood keel.

SCRAPING DOWN TO THE BARE WOOD

FIGURE 4 } Extremely cracked oil paint. Saved as a color sample in the renovation of a steam sloop from the 1800s.

What will determine the life of a wooden boat fleet is scraping down to bare wood. Boats that change hands often are the worst; the scraping bug often affects recent wooden boat owners. Varnished mahogany surfaces are the most fun to scrape—it makes such a difference in appearance. To get a smooth, reddish brown mahogany you have to scrape down a considerable amount of wood; when only the varnish is taken off and the wood is scraped unevenly, the sun-bleached yellow mahogany that is left presents a mottled result. Yet the work is perishable; after a few summers, the wood will brighten again (raw linseed oil, stain, or glaze extends the redness, see the chapter on surface treatment). When the planks are so thin that the plugs come undone and the rivets start coming to the surface, then all that remains is painting or glazing. If a boat is being ruled out, it is usually because its planking has become too thin; damaged or rotten parts are easier to renovate.

A recent wooden boat owner should wait to embark on scraping down to bare wood on the deck and the superstructure in particular until he has gotten to know the boat over a couple of years. Some places suck in moisture, which will result in the varnish coming off, and the problem will return the year after scraping down to bare wood unless the underlying problem of moisture penetration is fixed. The deck, or part of the deck, may need to be re-seamed first. Tenons on the windscreen might need to be glued, and some wood might need to be replaced. After this, it may be time for scraping down to the bare wood, which should then not have to be repeated for another ten to fifteen years.

A bleached mahogany that has gotten an even honey color over the years is, to me, a sign of both a hull in good condition and a boat owner who knows his boat and knows what he is doing.

With good priming and maintenance, you should be able to at least follow the time intervals below before scraping down to the bare wood again.

PERIOD OF TIME BETWEEN SCRAPING DOWN TO BARE WOOD

• Varnished hull and bridge	15–20 years
• Varnished deck	10–15 years
• Bottom made of pine	10–15 years
• Bottom made of mahogany	15–25 years
• Painted topside	30–40 years

Painted surfaces above the waterline that are sanded and painted can be kept without scraping down to the bare wood for thirty to forty years unless the paint layer is allowed to become so thick that it cracks. Scraping down to the bare wood of surfaces that are to be oiled with raw linseed oil is work that should be done in the fall. The more drying time for the oil, the better.

TIPS ON SCRAPING

Do not dig pits. Do not scrape the wood in an area where the boat has a scratch or is just worn; it's better to replace a piece of wood or just plug it. Worn areas can also be filled with clear epoxy or be left to be filled with varnish over the years. A pit is clearly apparent on a glossy surface; a filled-in scratch is less visible.

Use inner tarps. When the wood is scraped bare it is susceptible to condensation and dirt, so it is a good idea while scraping to hang up a lightweight, free-hanging tarp underneath the roof trusses to divert condensed water. It is effective and saves a lot of irritation.

Remove the paint with heat. I never use paint strippers but prefer a heat gun on varnished surfaces and a gas burner on painted surfaces. Check whether you can use the burner at your boat club, have fire extinguishers on hand, stop burning at least an hour before you go home, and use a mask with a gas filter—gas is toxic.

There are various kinds of scrapers. The sharpest are hardwood floor scrapers or a Skarsten scraper that you sharpen with a file (you need a single-rated file or a saw file—file rates are just on the diagonal, not double cut; see Figure 6). However, if the paint layers are thick, the heated paint will easily clog those kinds of scrapers. In that case a triangular scraper will be a better choice. When the paint is heated, the scraper doesn't need to be that sharp; however, you should round off the corners of the scraper blade so they don't cut into the wood if you slip. In recent years, I have come to use a paint scraper with replaceable carbide inserts (made by Sandvik). It has a cutting angle that works well on paint but protects the wood. It can also be used for dry scraping, especially when it's really cold outside. If the temperature is below freezing, don't hesitate to dry scrape two-component varnish; the cold will help it come off.

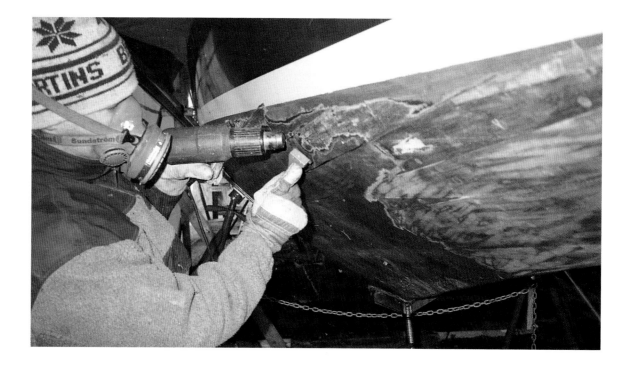

FIGURE 5 } Scraping the paint using a heat gun.

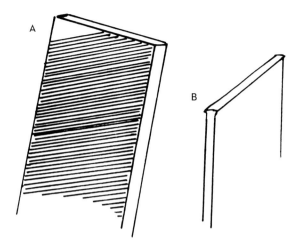

FIGURE 6

A Single-rated file for sharpening scrapers and cabinet scrapers.

B The card scraper's edge is obtained by folding the edge of the scraper with the file.

When the coat is removed, the wood surface has to be prepared, and this can be done in several ways: by scraping, planing, or sanding.

Scraping down to bare wood after the paint has been burnt off is best done with a hardwood floor scraper or a Skarsten scraper. They should be sharp, so they need to be sharpened frequently; if the sharpness only lasts for twenty scrapings, you may need to sharpen it (see Figure 7). A scraper blade can be filed off completely in one day. This type of scraper works well on bare wood, but requires an experienced hand on the surface in order for it not to become wavy and scratchy.

You mostly use a plane on newly fabricated pieces. When scraping down to the bare wood, a plane is used to remove uneven surfaces—sometimes to fair the deck and topside and to get a smooth, fine color on mahogany. For a surface to be easy to maintain, it needs to be even so that you can easily sand it with a machine, and it cannot have grooves and scratches or the sander won't be able get to the surface coating. New surface coating won't stick to glossy paint areas.

The card scraper is a piece of hardened steel that is sharpened with a file and is used to smooth wood and paint. The edge of the card scraper is made of steel, but since I mostly work with old wood, paint, and toxic solutions, all I do is file the card scraper, as the edge quickly becomes dulled.

The card scraper is a tool that can take a while to get used to, but once you do it will have its place in your pocket, ready to be used for many purposes. In addition to smoothing bare wood and coated surfaces, it can be used to erase pencil marks and remove dirt, polish off smaller repairs, and even smooth out the grain that rises after a first coat of varnish or epoxy.

Sanding is the most common method to get a good smooth surface before coating. Abrasives come in all shapes and forms; the grains are made out of silicon carbide (silicone paper) or aluminum oxide. Silicon carbide on gray and white paper is mixed with zinc stearate to prevent clogging from paint dust, and it is used for glossy surfaces. For bare wood, use wood-sanding paper, either machine-sanding paper with a more even grain size to avoid circles from the machine, or hand-sanding paper with varying grain size, which will be more efficient. This paper is used when you hand sand along the grain so scratches will not be as visible as when you go against the grain. Varnish-sanding sheets are usually gray and white, but other than that, the paper manufacturers usually pick different colors for their papers. The numbering of the papers is based on the number of grains per unit area—the higher the number the finer the paper. Sixty or 80–100 is coarse sandpaper for wood, 120–180 is finer for wood or coarse grinding of varnish, 240–280 is finer for paint, and 320 is finer paper that is used just before the final coat, but beware—this begins to border on polishing rather than sanding; when sanding with finer-grained paper, you might see a negative effect on paint adhesion.

The various machines for sanding are rubber-sanding pad, belt sander, sheet palm sander, and random orbital sander (Rotex or PEX).

A rubber-sanding pad on a drill or an angle grinder work well on dry wood, but the high peripheral speed allows oil and paint to attach to the abrasive paper,

FIGURE 7 } Sharpening the scraper. Push the file diagonally away from yourself, and from the edge of the scraper. Hold the scraper on a steady surface.

FIGURE 8 } Gas nozzle, heat gun, hard wood floor scraper, and scraper with carbide inserts (cannot be filed), and don't forget the facemask with a gas filter.

which clogs it. An experienced auto body repairman can make a boat look sleek and smooth with a rubber-sanding pad, but the amateur should not even try it.

A belt sander could possibly be used on the deck, but then it needs to have an adjustable frame so that the wheels can't dig into the wood. Apart from the fact that you often see boats with horrible sanding marks from the belt sander, it does have the advantage of removing saw dust very efficiently, which can be essential in preventing the wood from getting stained by saw dust from caulking sealant when sanding decks with seams.

Sheet palm sanders and random orbital sanders with dust bags are efficient; the dust extraction makes the sandpaper not clog up as quickly, and it makes your work area cleaner. I use them on coated surfaces and on bare wood surfaces that are to be painted. On bare wood surfaces that are to be varnished they create sanding circles, so for that I prefer using hand sandpaper. Random orbital sanders often have smaller sanding pads than sheet palm sanders, so a topside

can get a little wavy in the long run if it is sanded with the orbital sander. Here, I prefer an orbital sander with a large plate, 4 × 7″ (100 × 180 mm) (see Figure 9).

Hand sanding has the advantage that you do not have to lug around a heavy machine that can also cause vibration damage on your hands, which might affect your blood circulation. I like to hand sand areas that are smaller than the hull and deck; a machine is more difficult to control and sands through the edges too easily and will make marks in the inner corner. There is an American saying: "Leave the corners to themselves"; corners wear off by themselves, so leave them alone when sanding. Use a sanding block when sanding flat surfaces.

To get a nice surface result with a high-gloss lacquer or varnish, you need to have a smooth and even surface. To create a hull surface that is even, you need a long block (see Figure 10). A long block is a piece of plywood as wide as your sandpaper, 4–5″ (10 or 12 cm), and 20–30″ (50–80 cm) long, that has two handles on top. The correct thickness for

FIGURE 9 } Sheet palm sander and random orbital sander.

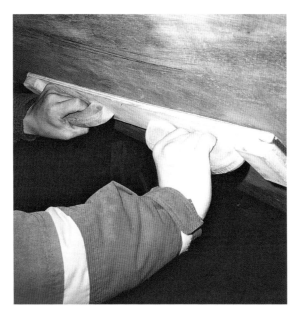

FIGURE 10 } Long block on a bare wood bottom. The length of the plywood sheet depends on your own arm strength and the thickness of the curve of the hull.

sanding flat surfaces such as decks is about ⅓–½″ (10–12 mm) and for topsides about ¼″ (7 mm). If the hull surface is concave transversely, then the block will be easier to work with if it's fitted with a softer layer (e.g., a piece of foam, such as a camping pad) between the plywood and the sandpaper. For the long block, use sandpaper on a roll (sold by the yard or meter). If the surface is already smooth, you can just skip the long block.

If your sanding job is a mahogany topside with bare wood that you will varnish, then you should start with 60-paper on a long block; the hull may need to be sanded on the diagonal to be smooth vertically as well. Then switch to 80-paper on the block and then to 120-paper—both are used to sand along the grain—until all the yellow wood and all rough sanding scratches are gone. If the hull just needs oiling, it should be done now, as is necessary when using an oil-based stain or glaze. If you are going to stain it with boat stain, all the sanding streaks will be much more apparent and you are better off moistening the surface with a sponge to get the fibers to rise; all the fibers and scratches that would otherwise appear with the stain will rise and can be sanded with 180-paper.

If you are going to stain the surface, you should do it before oiling, as the stain won't settle evenly on top of the oil. To avoid having to sand yourself to death, you should always think about how visible the piece is when it is in place. Things that are near your eyes require a more detailed sanding job; if they are down by your feet, they require less work.

If the hull or deck is to be painted, start with a long block with a 60-paper, then use the sander with a 80- to 100-paper; after that, the surface is ready for oiling. Some sanding stripes from the block can be left; the rough surface gives the paint a better grip. The surface will smoothen as you sand in between coats.

SUMMARY

Don't scrape away wood for nothing; every time you scrape the wood bare, it's another nail in the coffin. Scraping determines the outcome of the surface treatment that follows; the wood surface needs to be flat so that the finish will be smooth.

It's hard to get smooth surfaces with a rubber pad and a belt sander, and they do not belong in my tool collection for scraping wood bare.

SURFACE TREATMENT

Writing about surface treatment is like going into a hornet's nest; most boat owners have formed strong opinions from many years of trial and error. We really know how it should be. There are many ways that are right; the chances of success are greater than those of failure as long as you know some basics. The basics are simple: be careful with the preparations, sand carefully, wash and dry thoroughly, keep an eye on the weather, read the instructions on the paint can, and follow recommendations consistently. The products on the market are so good that they will protect your boat. If the finished look is not what you expected, then you will get another chance next year.

The degree of treatment will be decided by the boat owner himself; different types of boats are given different amounts of treatment. The difference is great between a rowboat and a Riva. The end result of the surface treatment is most affected by the sanding and the number of coats, and that is where you can save some time if you settle for less.

I have chosen to write about the methods and products I have experience with.

WEATHER

It's probably just boaters that paint outdoors in the winter. If the air is dry and the cover is good, it's usually fine. Inside the boat, there is no problem at all with painting, as you can heat up smaller areas. Oiling and priming the exterior is fine just as long as there is no condensation on the hull. Likewise, it works to varnish, just as long as the varnish has been thinned out and is warm enough that it doesn't get choked by the cold hull. All paint and varnish should be warmed to room temperature (68°F/20°C) when it is applied.

The weather must be even; the temperature shouldn't shift between above and below freezing, and the air should be dry. If the temperature rises from below zero to above freezing, the air moisture will cause condensation on the cold hull.

Final coats with undiluted paints are made later in the spring. What you have to think about then is not to paint too early in a day with rising temperatures; the hull will be colder than the air, and the paint will be difficult to apply and will dry first on the surface and create a dried top layer that air cannot penetrate to dry out underneath. At noon on a cloudy, calm day after a rain, when there is no dust in the air, it's time to attempt to put your final coat on. Weather conditions are more important to the outcome than the choice of varnish. On a calm, cloudy day, you can get twice the amount of varnish on the hull without any problems compared to a sunny or windy day. During the same coat, you might have to thin out the varnish depending on whether it is drafty or if there is sun on one side and not on the other of the boat.

When applying a coat uncovered, the paint and varnish have to be applied early in the day to allow them to dry before the evening dew. Moisture can cause a matte finish or milky stains. Avoid any surface treatment in bright sunshine.

IMPREGNATION

Impregnation may protect against rot as well as have a water-repellent effect.

Mold protection with the help of biocides (i.e., substances that eliminate living organisms) are now more restricted according to the EU Biocide Directive from a couple of years ago. Products that have been banned in recent years include red lead, black varnish (Hydroline);

Intertox; lead oxide as a drying agent in paint, copper, and tin compounds in antifouling; and copper salts as mold protection (Cuprinol). However, there are some pesticides still allowed in primers, but their main function is to prevent paint from becoming moldy in the can. Pine tar was also on the verge of being banned but wasn't. This means that we have, in principle, no mold protection to use for boatbuilding. Oils have a water-repellent effect, and paints prevent water penetration, but they have no protection against rot, except that wood does not rot as long as it stays dry with a good coat of paint.

Once damage has occurred, there are some products to use: mildew and other lesser problems on the surface can be treated with vinegar. More severe fungi infestations can be treated with a Boracol solution.

Which areas should be treated against moisture penetration? Obviously all wood underwater and all exposed end grain—preferably by dipping into the solution. Joints, cracks, and seams where moisture can work its way down should be treated several times. Larger homogeneous areas, such as glued topsides, are well protected by their varnish layer. Plywood should not be treated, but the plywood end grain should be saturated with epoxy to prevent water penetration.

Raw linseed oil is a treatment that has long had a special place among boaters and is used partly below the waterline to prevent water penetration and partly above the waterline because it gives the wood an unrivaled color and luster. Oxidizing oil in the wood, combined with sunlight, provides a beautiful dark tone to Honduras mahogany; the wood should be left alone for at least three weeks before any further treatment so that the oil is allowed to oxidize.

During the first half of the 1900s, many quality shipyards applied linseed oil to boats throughout the construction period; linseed oil has small molecules that penetrate far into the wood. A pine boat that has been leaking and that has resealed a few hours after launching could take a few weeks after being scraped bare and oiled during the winter to reseal again. The oil will even penetrate damp wood and replace water gradually; however, it won't prevent the hull from drying out further as additional moisture evaporates.

In the mid-1950s, there were some tests with linseed oil that indicated the oil had little effect on water penetration, and the use of raw linseed oil decreased. It was around that time that they started to glue and mass-produce wooden boats, and linseed oil did not quite fit into either of these styles of production. It deteriorated adhesive bonds and took too long to dry. They also concluded that the oil did not give any rot protection, and if it was impure, it could contain sap and contaminants that fungi would thrive on. Boats were built at this time with lean anti-rotting solutions instead, such as pentachlorophenol and copper naphthenate, but these boats had major problems with freeze damage due to water penetration. Boats that were built during this time have also swelled to a point where they burst their ribs if they were sunk and salvaged.

Today, there has been a major boost for linseed oil in house building. Linseed oil—and the soft paints that it is used for—follows the movement of the wood; it penetrates the wood and gets good adhesion and ages by chalking, not by peeling. Interest in flax seeds has led many growers to begin to press their own oil. We'll probably get to see a great deal more of linseed oil products for wooden boats in the next few years. There are some exciting experiments being conducted with pure linseed oil, which is said to be good protection against rot.

Below water, I use Swedish cold-pressed oil. There are various ways to apply the oil. Linseed oil boils at 465°F (240°C) and can be heated to 300°F (150°C) when applied. The oil is kept warm with an immersion heater, and a heat gun can help warm the oil into the cold wood. It is time consuming but gives good results. You have to consider the risk of fire, so the oil cannot be diluted with any solvents.

Cold oil is applied in a fatty mixture, about ¾ raw linseed oil and ¼ turpentine; oiling is done first wet on wet, then once a day so that the oil doesn't have time to start to solidify due to the oxygen intake. On fresh wood, you will soon get greasy stains, which tells you to stop; older wood will soak longer and require more coats. The oil penetrates quickly if the air is warm, but it's fine to apply oil in the winter as well; the oil might need to be diluted even more to penetrate the wood. An old rule of thumb is that there should be a real cold snap that freezes out the worst of the moisture from the wood before you oil in the fall.

After finishing oiling, you have to wipe off the hull before the excess oil has created a skin; in the winter, it takes a week, in the summer, two to three days. Skin that has hardened on the surface is hard to sand and may impair the adhesion of subsequent layers of paint. If you have this situation, the card scraper is the best tool to remove the oil. Used oil rags should be kept in a tin can with a tightly fitting lid; otherwise there is a high risk of spontaneous combustion—a lot of boat clubs have been ruined this way.

Applying oil can be done on both the inside and the outside of the hull. On varnished topsides, I use oil mostly for the sake of the color richeness of the wood, and I give it only one to two coats. If I have time, I prefer raw oil here as well, and I wipe away the excess just as if I were oiling below the waterline. It might be safer to surface treat dry topsides from the inside; too much raw linseed oil on the outside underneath varnish or paint can cause blistering of the coating. This is due to the solar heating of gases discharged from contained oil that could not oxidize and solidify due to lack of oxygen.

Boiled linseed oil is used to lock raw oil into the wood so that it will not bleed through and blister varnish in the sun. Some varnishes will not work well directly on top of the raw oil. The excess of the boiled oil must be cleaned off in a few hours to avoid a skin. If you don't do this you will have to scrape the hull. I have often oiled with raw linseed oil, skipped the boiled oil, waited three weeks, and started surfacing with a 50% thinned top coat without getting any of the above problems, so there are, as, I said earlier, many different ways to do this. One of the advantages of having boats on land half the year is that time-consuming methods can be used as long as you plan the job right.

Owatrol oil is another petroleum product that penetrates the wood deeply. It penetrates so well that the manufacturer warns against using it on dried out boats, which then may fail to swell again. Owatrol is applied wet on wet until it penetrates the wood or until there are bright spots. It's very difficult to glue previously Owatrol-treated wood. In Norway's humid climate, they use oils more than varnish as a clear finish.

China wood oil, or tung oil, as it is known, can be used for oiling, although it is more common as a part of quality varnishes. It is believed to have smaller molecules than linseed oil and will penetrate the wood better, but I have no personal experience of using it to oil bare wood.

Red lead is a treatment that prevents both water penetration and wood rot because of its toxicity. Red lead has been, by far, the best finish of the boat hulls but is now banned because of its toxicity. It is still possible to buy red lead powder from traditional boat supply shops in the UK, not in North America. While writing this book, there has been an issue with which materials to recommend instead of red lead, both when it has been used as paint as well as when it has been used as putty, while assembling planking, for example.

Red lead paint for wood was based on lead oxide and raw linseed oil. You could have, depending on interest and ambition, either mixed it yourself or bought it ready mixed. If you mixed it yourself, you stirred the red lead pigment in water, 2 cups (½ liter) of water to 4.4 lbs (2 kg) of pigment. The pigment swelled in water, and the mixture had to be stirred vigorously every day for one week; then you stirred 2 cups (½ liter) of raw linseed oil into the jar, at which point water rose to the surface and could be poured out. Red lead was diluted with raw or boiled linseed oil and turpentine to a paint-like consistency and was applied thinly; a second coat was applied after one week if the first had had time to settle. After that, it took at least six weeks for the red lead to harden and result in unsurpassed water protection of the bottom for many years. Red lead is so hard that it has to be sanded in order for the next finish to adhere. Red lead is highly toxic. People who lived by the ocean knew that a stick with red lead on it could kill a cow if it chewed on it. If you are going to sand and scrape old red lead, be sure to use a facemask and vacuum up all the sanding dust; wet sanding is a good alternative. The dust should be considered hazardous waste.

THINNERS AND CLEANING
Thinners used for dilution and cleaning.

Balsam turpentine is extracted from distilled sap from pine trees and is considered the best dilution for fatty oils. Turpentine leaves almost no residue after evaporation. Turpentine is more harmful when inhaled than mineral spirits are. Mineral spirit is a mineral product and contains some impurities that may remain on the surface and reduce adhesion. Many paint products have their own thinners; check the can. Plant-based products are considered best for wood while mineral products are thought to break down lignin—the chemical compound that holds wood cells together.

Dirt and grease are to be washed off in the fall. Wash with a mild detergent and rinse well.

Before and between surface treatments, you can wipe with clean rags and paint thinner; keep cloths clean and leave no solvent puddles—paint does not stick to greasy stains. If it is humid outside, you can clean with methylated spirits, which will force the moisture out before surface treatment. The methylated spirit will also dissolve the surface of the old varnish and let the next layer adhere better; too much methylated spirit can cause your paint surface to become milky.

Greasy wood and diesel spills should be cleaned with acetone.

For wiping between coats, I often use a tack rag; it is pretreated so that it effectively takes care of dust. Microfiber cloths can also be used.

Do not use solvents for washing your hands; it will cause paint to seep into your pores. Grease your hands with a good hand lotion, use disposable gloves, and wash your hands with a mild hand soap afterward.

PAINT AND VARNISH

It is easy to get confused among different names and concepts. Surface treatment of a boat can be done in many ways. Old fishing boats have always been treated with tar and linseed oil, or any locally produced oil, such as seal oil or herring oil. The tar may have been wood tar or coal tar. Vessels were treated to reduce the water penetration of the wood, which would result in swelling, and to prevent rot and decay.

Pleasure boats have mostly been treated with linseed oil. They called it varnish when they added resin and a solvent to linseed oil in order to create a hard surface. In the Swedish language, it is not uncommon for boiled linseed oil to be called varnish. However, I should use the clear coating or varnish for the varnishes we use today that are not oil-based. If linseed oil is added to a pigment, you obtain an enamel. A shiny paint made from a factory-mixed, finely grated pigment and synthetic resin will make an enamel. Back in the day, we made most paints locally by grating a pigment, such as metal oxide, in a paint mill into tiny solid particles and then mixed it with boiled linseed oil, for example. In the second half of the 1900s, paints based in alkyd resin, which is synthetic, were dominant for boat paints.

BASIC INGREDIENTS

Below are the most common basic ingredients in our boat paints. They are combined to obtain various properties for the products.

Raw linseed oil is a drying oil, which hardens taking in oxygen from the air. It has been the dominant drying oil for centuries. It penetrates into wood well and dries slowly. It is used in the production of some varnishes and linseed oil paint.

Boiled linseed oil is obtained when linseed oil is boiled. It can also be further finished into stand oil that was the basis of paint production in the beginning and middle of the last century.

Chinese wood oil, or tung oil, is produced from the nuts of the tung tree that grows in East Asia. Tung oil is considered the finest oil for varnish production; it dries quickly and adheres well, darkens slowly, and is elastic. But it becomes brittle faster than linseed oil does when exposed to sunlight.

Phenolic resin is the oldest form of synthetic resin; it is used in some paints and provides good water resistance but crumbles down relatively quickly.

Alkyd resin is an adhesive prepared by condensing carboxylic acids with alcohols. It has excellent adhesion, gloss, and water resistance but cracks as it ages. Sunlight accelerates the aging process, and the more expensive varnishes have UV filters.

Urethane resin is a synthetic resin that has a high gloss, is durable, and is sunlight proof. It dries at low temperatures but has poorer adhesion to bare wood. Paints of this type do not work well on linseed oil surfaces.

Polyurethane, a two-component varnish, has a long life and is flexible, high-gloss, durable, and UV stable. It requires immobile surfaces without seams and joints. It is more difficult to touch up and repaint, and it is difficult to repair dents and cracks with it. It cannot be combined with linseed oil.

OIL DYE

Old mahogany fades quickly, and without being treated with linseed oil treatment it can only last a couple of seasons. With raw linseed oil treatment, you might get five seasons. Honduras mahogany that is oiled with raw linseed oil darkens with sunlight; it darkens more the longer it is left unvarnished.

If your boat is well stained the paint can last for ten years, but the tone will be very dark, almost black at first. Stain is best applied with a sponge; be generous and go

FIGURE 11 } Glossy topside at launching. The long sanding block gives smoothness; the sanding gives the glossiness. The surface has been obtained with a roller and a foam brush. Total varnish used for the final coat was 1.2 qt (1.2 liters) to 172 sq ft (16 m²) of topside.

back in about ten minutes to wipe off the excess. You may want to have a second person—one who applies the stain and one who wipes away the excess. Use rubber gloves. Treatment may be repeated until you have the desired color tone. A varnished surface can be improved by applying stain with rags on top of last year's varnish; just check first to make sure the stain doesn't dissolve the varnish. Never put a stain can on board the boat—the solvent is strong and the can will always drip a little; the stain will dissolve the varnish and leave dark circles. Mahogany stain is not at all forgiving but will highlight the dents and sanding marks in the wood; staining requires fine sanding of all surface treatment, at least with a 180-paper and, on the end grain, 240-paper. Raising the grains by wetting the wood with water before the final sanding is recommended prior to staining.

Regular powder stains will get paler outdoors.

Glaze will last longer but will kill some of the luster of the wood and the depth of the lacquer. There are readymade glazes that are alkyd- and oil-based, or you could make your own glaze from linseed oil and pigment; you can also experiment with art supplies. Glaze is applied to bare wood. This is a classic method that has been forgotten in Sweden, while it is still popular in the rest of Europe. It is very forgiving to old discolored wood and repairs that have mismatched colors. An old recipe I have is burned terra with a hint of English red and a touch of black mixed in boiled or raw linseed oil. The most even glaze will be obtained if the excess glaze is wiped off after a while.

A special form of stain is filler stain, which is used especially for American-built racing boats. It is a paste that is rubbed into the wood and gives a mahogany tone while it fills the pores of the wood and therefore results in a faster build-up of the varnished surface. Stain fillers are used in Sweden too, but because they fill the pores, you risk the varnish not adhering as well to the wood, and it is not recommended as we have boats on land for such a long period every year that we have enough time to do a proper, although time consuming, surface treatment.

If you attempt to stain old and new wood together, it is necessary to know that new wood darkens in the sun the first few years, while older wood already exposed to the sun quickly brightens again. Thus mahogany that is replaced should be selected at a brighter tone than you might think.

CAULKS AND SEALANTS

Fairing. Below the waterline I try to use a plane and sand the bottom as evenly as I can when I scrape down to the bare wood so that fairing won't be needed. I plug screw holes with wood plugs glued with epoxy glue. Otherwise, I use unthickened epoxy and then epoxy filler to fill damages in the wood, and this is of course done prior to oiling. A sparse, fine layer of spackle with epoxy putty is applied between the primer layers.

Dry cracks can be sealed with transparent tape on top of the bottom paint or filled with a soft sealing compound based on wax or tallow.

Above the waterline, you could fill with polyester putty after priming and sanding. Large chunks of plaster follow the wood's movement poorly and will easily crack and detach.

A thin filling can be made with alkyd or urethane putty, which in principle is thickened paint; putty is applied in several layers so that it has time to harden through the layers.

Sealing compounds come in all different types and brands. On wooden boats, don't use silicone rubber as it doesn't adhere well to bare wood, and when you sand it a dust is formed that may cause "fish eyes" in the following coating, as the particles' surface tension decreases.

Polyurethane products are the most common sealing compounds. They are used as seam sealant and structural adhesives. Sikaflex is the most common brand. Polyurethanes contain isocyanates, which may be carcinogenic, and the products have changed in recent years to reduce the levels of isocyanates. They adhere better to primed or surface-treated wood, and generous impregnation with linseed oil can dissolve them. It may also be difficult to get alkyd varnishes to dry on seam sealants.

In recent years, we have used seam sealants and structural adhesives based on silyl modified polymer—SMP; it is marketed as MS Polymers, such as Simson Deck Splining. They have worked well and can withstand both linseed oil and alkyd varnish. But they require a surface treatment, such as a primer or varnish, in order to adhere to the wood.

TOOLS AND ACCESSORIES

Brushes come in many different styles; the ones made of natural bristles have the longest life expectancy and are the most expensive. That kind of brush will last for many years. I let that kind of brush stand in a mixture of raw linseed oil and turpentine during the season; white spirit may ruin the brush. During the rest of the year, I keep them clean and dry. All kinds of primer are worked into the pores of the wood with a brush. I apply paint and varnish for the topcoats with a roller, and then I finish it off with a foam brush. To get an even paint layer, I like to use a shorthaired fleece roller or a foam roller. Don't forget to wash out a new shorthaired roller with soap and water to remove any lint found in the roller with the purchase and dry it for one day before using it. A foam brush can't be used with solvents, but can be stored in a plastic bag overnight.

Masking tape comes in a variety of types; tapes of better brands release more easily from surfaces and leave no sticky residue. Don't let the tape be left in the sun or rain, as it will be impossible to remove. There is a thin plastic tape used for the waterline, which provides a sharp edge.

A tack rag is used to wipe dust. A good quality tack rag will last longer and provide a dust-free result. I prefer to use tack rags between coats instead of using solvents. A dust-free surface is crucial for a high-gloss varnish.

PROCEDURE FOR "PAINTING THE BOTTOM"

There has been so much development in primers and antifouling in the last ten years that it is difficult to come up with any recommendations. Plastic boats are treated with two-component products that protect well against osmosis and the solvents in primer, and antifouling bottom paints are adapted for bottoms that are stable and difficult to sand. Paint manufacturers count on people not having the energy to sand the bottom properly, so they add strong solvents instead to ensure that the new paint will adhere to the old paint. Some products with up to 80% xylene (a strong solvent) will dissolve the varnish on the waterline and even year-old primer on the bottom. Follow the guidelines and drying times on the cans. If you use xylene-rich paints they

A

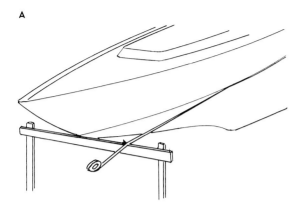

FIGURE 12 ⟩ A Taping the waterline.

B The waterline is usually made a bit higher in the bow. It is vertical height that is marked; the actual width of the waterline mark varies with the slope of the hull.

should be applied in the wind and so that the solvents evaporate as fast as possible.

The bottom does not need to be scraped down to the bare wood unless the paint has begun to flake off down to the bare wood. If it has, however, it is important to scrape it bare and give the bottom a new good primer treatment. The antifouling is just a protective layer that self polish and it cannot be counted on as a waterproofing layer.

After scraping down to the bare wood, you have to sand it with 80-grain sandpaper. This is followed by oiling with raw linseed oil; see the section on raw linseed oil.

When the excess oil is wiped off and the oil has had time to oxidize (at least three weeks), it will be time to apply two or three coats of an oil-based yacht primer to the bottom. Then paint with a antifouling that has a low content of xylene (less than 20%) so that the primer doesn't dissolve.

If the bottom is in good condition, wash it in the fall. Any flaking paint is scraped off and areas of bare wood are fixed with yacht primer. Thin antifouling can be painted over for many years without the layers becoming too thick. Self polishing antifouling can create a too-thick layer, which must then be sanded before recoating with new bottom paint.

Waterline

A nice looking waterline mark emphasizes a boat's appearance. A moderately high painted line gives the boat a light impression; if it's painted too high, it gives a bobbing and unstable look, and a low line gives a feeling of heaviness and being overloaded. The waterline is usually made wider fore and aft to make sure that it gets an even look from above, as the hull often leans outward at the fore and aft. It also makes it easier to trim it without being submerged in water. The waterline on a clinker-built boat can be painted to make it look straight when seen from above, which is how it's usually looked at.

A quick way to tape a straight waterline—if you know where the waterline is located amidships and by the bow and stern post—is to attach a plank perpendicular to the boat at the waterline in the bow. The plank should have a smooth top surface and be level with the waterline amidships. When you are satisfied with the plank's position, secure the tape amidships and then let it follow the plank edge with the glued side up. The tape will be stretched out and pulled out into the hull. The tape will stick in a nice curve against the hull. Repeat the maneuver on the transom. See figure 12A.

PAINTING TOPSIDES AND DECK

Generally speaking, the shinier result you want when it comes to painting and varnishing, the more labor is needed, and the more durable, hardier paints are needed, which in turn creates a higher demand for a healthy hull so that the paints stay on.

An old oak or pine boat: Annual maintenance includes scraping loose paint off in the winter so that the wood dries, oil and prime any bare wood, sand the entire surface, and apply a final coat.

An unglued mahogany or pine boat in good condition: Annual maintenance is the same as with an oak or pine boat. If the topsides do not have moisture issues, you can apply a single-component urethane and won't need to repaint every year.

Canvassed decks: To maintain a deck painted with pure linseed oil paint, it is enough to just wash it once with boat cleaner prior to applying the new coat; linseed oil paint should be applied thinly, and the top layer will wear off so much during a season's use that the paint won't ever get too thick over the years.

A glued mahogany boat can be surface treated just as in the paragraph above, but it can also be treated with a two-component paint that will keep for many years without needing any improvement. That kind of coating of polyurethane paint is, however, difficult to touch up and paint, as it may be difficult to obtain good adhesion to old two component paint. The two-component paint becomes hard and is used on laminated wood (plywood and cold baked boats) that does not move as much. When the polyurethane gets old, you have to redo it completely by scraping the wood bare and surface treating it.

In my experience, a traditional one-component paint that is kept elastic by sanding and with a fresh coat of paint each year may be retained indefinitely, as long as you sand so much that the paint never gets too thick. One trick to achieve this effect is to add a different color to the primer and the first paint layer, and then the surface may be periodically sanded down until the odd tone begins to show.

If you spend a lot of time in ports and rub fenders with other boats you may need to repaint your topsides every year, if the topsides are in good condition it shouldn't take longer than washing and waxing a plastic boat.

Plywood decks are finished without oil and with hard paint; cracks on plywood joints are sanded down with an abrasive pad and built up with epoxy and fiberglass. Pine plywood easily cracks in the top layer; use fairing first, then sand and coat the deck with glass cloth and epoxy.

Anti-slip treatment consisting of small sand or glass particles can be applied on the deck in both paint and varnish and will provide a slip-resistant surface on the deck.

Maintenance of a painted surface is as follows: washing, sanding with 180-paper, filling dents and areas sanded smooth with 280 to 320-paper and a final coat.

Use a facemask with a charcoal filter for oiling, painting, and varnishing with turpentine, alkyd, and urethane products. I have several friends who cannot be in a room where there is solvent-based paint without getting headaches. It has developed over the years, even though they haven't exposed themselves to any more paint fumes than is normal when you own a wooden boat.

COATING AND VARNISHING

What has been said about paint also goes for different types of varnish. Soft varnishes that can withstand movement are used on slatted decks; hard and glossy ones can be used on glued topsides. The coating film that is formed must have an elasticity adapted to the movements of the surface underneath. A high-gloss, thick varinsh or clear coating adheres well to the homogeneous panel that a glued mahogany topside provides, but it can begin to loosen in the joints of unglued planking and in the seams on a ribbed deck. The thick varnish film begins to have a life of its own, and the adhesion is insufficient when the edge of the varnish film is broken at the seams and moisture finds its way into the wood.

PROCEDURE FOR USING OIL AND ALKYD VARNISH

For a good result with varnishing bare wood, the wood surface should first be smooth and polished along the fibers, and the surplus from the oil should have been rub-

FIGURE 13 } Foam brush, foam roller, and tack rag.

bed into the wood fibers before the oil has solidified due to oxygen.

The first three varnish layers must be thinned considerably; follow the instructions on the can and thin it out even more. This is what allows for good penetration and adhesion. Sand lightly against the raising grain with a fine sandpaper in between coats.

If the surface is stained then apply coats with the shortest possible interval in between coats and sanding won't be needed; it is easy to sand too much and damage the stained surface otherwise. Apply thinly so that the varnish won't dry on the surface but has enough air to dry through. If there is a lot of raw linseed oil in the wood, it may be that the dryers in the first thinned varnish layer is not sufficient to dry the surface; then the second layer tends to provide enough dryers to dry the surface. After these three thin layers, you need to wait a couple of weeks while the varnish sinks in, then sand the surface to make it smoother and for better adhesion. Drying time for the varnish varies considerably for different varnishes. If you apply new varnish too soon then the underlying layers may have a hard time drying and the top layer will float on top of the softer varnish underneath.

Next apply three undiluted coats with light sanding in between. Then wait as long as possible; the varnish is now easing into the fibers, and the surface will develop more pores each week.

Then sand it well with a cork sanding block and 240-paper so that the surface is completely matte and smooth. Apply two coats with light sanding in between. Wait until the surface has sunk. Dry or wet sand it with 320-paper. Clean off the sanding dust from the cover and tarps. Vacuum the boat and then wipe the surface.

It is the smoothness of the wood surface and the surface of the sanded varnish finish that give it its high glossy result. In an article from the 1930s about surface treatment, they compared sanded varnish surface tops to the foil on the back of a mirror, with the end result being the actual glass of the mirror.

Next put the finishing coat on. It will be nine layers in all, but a lot of coats are sanded off. If you are not that particular with the sanding, then six layers will suffice; that's the minimum, and then the surface won't remain porous until next fall. A couple of more coats will be needed the following year, which will be when the surface will be porous for the first time.

Maintenance of a surface in good condition includes washing, sanding with 240- to 320-paper, dusting, and varnishing once or twice. Sand as much as needed every year so that the thickness of the layers remain constant; if the thickness increases then the varnish layers will begin to have a life of their own and start to release from underneath.

INTERIOR FINISH

The inside of the hull finish will not wear as much. This is fortunate because interior sanding is among the most time-consuming things you can do. Many people prefer oiled planking to just improve the oil in intervals, but the surface is difficult to keep clean and turns black over time.

The humidity is high inside boats; the vapor pressure is high when many people sleep in a small area, and this type of moisture in the form of steam penetrates wood more easily than water in its liquid state does. The outer surface is coated in several layers, but internally, more-or-less bare wood is exposed to water vapor and bilge water.

The boat should be painted below the floor boards, but the bilge should not be maintained each year. After scraping down to the bare wood, you need to oil it and apply a coat of oil-resistant paint. The bilge will be maintained by simple washing and touch-ups only as needed. If you repaint you will keep building up paint on hard-to-reach rough nooks and imperfections; this will only lead to a complete scraping down to bare wood as thick layers of paint easily crack and loosen.

I usually treat other hull surfaces with oil (linseed oil or a waterproofing oil), then an oil varnish.

If the boat has glued planking then I try to create as low and constant a moisture level as possible in the wood by varnishing the inside as well. The planking's moisture level stays less than 18% year-round in that case. This applies to the homogeneous panel that glued carvel strip planking represents. On an unglued planking and, above all, on clinker-built boats in which moisture can penetrate in between the planks, there should be one side of the hull that allows moisture to evaporate.

The best interior climate can be obtained if the deck ribs are just oiled underneath. It will suck up condensation from exhaled breaths at night and release it during the day. The warm, moist human breath turns into condensation droplets on the underside of a plywood deck. Therefore, there is often mildew and mold underneath a plywood deck unless it is painted to a glossy finish and well ventilated.

Interior carpentry is difficult to sand to a high gloss finish; there are so many nooks and crannies, and a semi-gloss varnish for the last coat is more forgiving to a lesser job of prepping underneath. All surfaces on the new interior must be sanded lightly so that the varnish will stick. The interior does not fade with the sun, so there is no need for staining.

FIGURE 14 } Moisture meter. Measures the moisture content in the wood by the wood's conductivity, which increases with increasing moisture.

SUMMARY

The basics are simple: be careful with preparations, sand carefully, wash and dry thoroughly, keep an eye on the weather, read the paint can, and follow the recommendations consistently. It is poor economy (and a waste of your own time) to not use good materials for surface treatment.

- Weather conditions are more important for the outcome than the choice of varnish.

- If you attempt to stain old and new wood together, it is necessary to know that new wood darkens in the sun for the first few years, while old, previously sunexposed mahogany quickly brightens again.

- Used rags with linseed oil should be kept in a jar with a tight-fitting lid, otherwise there is a high risk of spontaneous combustion.

- Do not use solvents for cleaning your hands.

- Use a facemask with a charcoal filter for oiling, painting, and varnishing with turpentine, alkyd, and urethane products.

TO GLUE OR NOT TO GLUE?

As far as I am concerned, the renovation of old boats is about replacing or repairing parts that are damaged and that no longer measure up. It can be rotten wood or freeze-damaged wood or an otherwise weakened structure. Often in renovations, you have to remove poor repairs and find your way back to the original structure and build on that. Bolting, screwing, or other fastening has to be checked. You strive to recreate the boat lines and the way it floats in the water. All this without any unnecessary removal of original parts and repairs that show decades of use and bear traces of its former owners. To scrape a boat down to the bare wood and give the boat a new surface treatment is more like maintenance than restoration.

When I restore different boats, I can see how designers and boatbuilders solve the various problems. Over time, I learned to see who designed the boat and who built it. Making that visible with a renovation is an interesting task. If a person interested in wooden boats can say that this boat was built by Henning Forslund at the *Sjöexpress* yards, or designed by Erik Salander in the late 1910s, then the renovation is a success. Motorboats are often renovated to return to their original appearance, while sailboats are often given functional changes. If there are major changes to an original boat, then there will be a true loss of cultural history. If a restored boat is kept in the style in which it was once made, then there is no loss of culture or history. A previous owner could have requested solutions that were not well designed by the designer—solutions that just do not fit the current owner.

Glue was not used as a structural reinforcement of wooden boats until the 1930s. Today, I glue a lot when I renovate. It can be to avoid having to replace entire pieces of old wood or because the old parts of a boat, such as the sanded-down planking, are too thin to withstand the loads that the hull is exposed to without gluing the seams. Glue also effectively prevents moisture from penetrating the structure. When older boats were built, putty caulking, linseed oil, and red lead was used below the waterline, and various resins and linseed oil were used over the waterline, to prevent moisture penetration of joint surfaces. When I dismantle an old design, I can often take whole pieces apart in order to copy them. When the structure is glued, you lose that opportunity. With boats from the second half of the 1900s that were glued from the start, it is, on the other hand, often just sufficient to router or pane away the damaged area and glue in a new piece of wood.

There aren't many wooden boats built in Sweden today. The construction of the type of boats that dominate the wooden boat fleet with which I usually work—i.e., carvel-built boats with frames, lightly built—has ceased. New boats constructed today follow two paths: one is rustic clinker-built with traditional methods, and the other is cold moulded boats out of epoxy. Most of the boatbuilding schools focus on rustic building, and it is used mostly for small open boats. Epoxy construction on strip planking or cold moulded are used as an alternative to plastic vessels for one-off constructions.

Epoxy adhesives can be used as glue as well as being a means to fix inferior wood. So it is a way to get old parts to stay together for another few years. But to cover bad wood in epoxy is not really renovating; rather, it is a method to use the boat for a while without having to renovate.

When renovating, epoxy can be used not only as an adhesive and as a filler, but also as a surface treatment of the planking. This can be done after replacing old wood, refastening the screws, and seam gluing. It is a relatively expensive method that provides a waterproof surface—one denser than that obtained after oiling and applying red lead. A well-ventilated hull that is properly surfaced, with red lead on the outside and oil and varnish on the inside, will keep, even below the waterline, a wood moisture content of 12–18% during the year; this is below mold and frost damage levels. The same can be achieved with epoxy on the outside. The epoxy treatment on the outside does not make a drier hull. The dryness of the hull depends on whether the wood on the inside has been affected by relative humidity.

Epoxy on the outside is not a miracle cure; it requires good ventilation, a dry top, and a boat owner who carefully looks after the boat and keeps it dry and clean on the inside—thus the same care that is required to keep a conventionally treated wooden boat well maintained. A boat that leaks through the deck and whose cushions and sails have a musty smell is definitely not suitable for an epoxy treatment; rot would thrive. A traditionally maintained boat can stand a period of abuse much better than one with external epoxy.

Full epoxy treatment of traditionally built wooden boats should only occur with new construction and renovations in which the boat is taken apart entirely and reassembled with glue in all joint surfaces. This is very complicated to implement consistently; it's a bit like building the boat twice. But it makes for rigid boats and minimal maintenance during the first twenty years.

A strongly built boat with good fasteners (screws, nails, rivets, etc.) hardly needs such help as seam gluing and an epoxy layer on the outside, but a six-meter yacht or a Skerry Cruiser that has a weak construction to begin with and then has been scraped down through the years could, with seam gluing and epoxy treatment with glass cloth, gain the strength that rule makers generally once intended but that later designers altered in pursuit of speed and weight.

Wooden boats have been treated with plastic or epoxy sheathed for 60 years. Planking, especially pine, has

FIGURE 15 } This kind of planking would need to be exchanged without the ability to seam glue and glue in old plugs.

fared well. However, bigger timber, such as stems and oak keels, have not. Oak and epoxy do not work well together. Therefore, on an old boat with an oak backbone, I would limit myself to treating the planking with epoxy and surface treat the exterior parts of the stem and keel and oak parts with oil and yacht primer.

Wood that is bonded and dimensionally stable, such as mahogany, can get by with a finish of pure epoxy. Wood that has moved more and hulls that have become thin and weak can be reinforced with fiberglass or veneer. Glass cloth may be easier to work with; you do not need to use wood as reinforcement for the epoxy resin. For better homogeneity and strength of the hull, I would recommend seam gluing the planking prior to any epoxy.

Leaky timber requires such a thick layer of epoxy and Glass cloth that it will restrain the movement of the wood. Trawlers have been GRPed since the 1950s; it has worked well when the plastic has been so thick that it has been able to keep to the wooden hull from moving and not vice versa. A common example of a too-thin plastic coating is a coach roof with ribs treated with plastic or epoxy and just one thin cloth; it buckles and often bends. A bottom planking that is becoming thin and poor requires a thick epoxy coat to distribute the loads—at least two to three thick fiberglass matts.

TO GLUE OR NOT TO GLUE? 45

I use total epoxy treatment on all surfaces on plywood. And when a stem or a keel is laminated with thin slats and glued to the planking.

For new construction, cold moulded or stripplanked, I would obviously isolate all surfaces with epoxy. If the wood can be given a low constant moisture level through surface coating, the glue joints will receive a minimal level of stress.

The actual epoxy treatment of a boat is something for the warmer season; the moisture content of the wood should have dropped below 14%, and the temperature of the wood and the air should be above 59°F (15°C).

Epoxy has advantages in terms of maintenance, but on a well-maintained wooden boat, sanding and painting the topsides are hardly more time-consuming than the waxing and polishing of a plastic or epoxy hull.

What is written here applies to epoxy treatment of the hull with subsequent painting. I have little experience with transparent epoxy treatment of old boats above the waterline; however, I have experienced difficulties with the adhesion of the new UV protective polyurethane when recoating old epoxy. Epoxy must be protected from the sun's damaging effect with a varnish with UV filters.

Thirty-five years ago, when we bought the old gaff-rigged boat *Oberon*, built by August Plym in 1901, we exchanged a lot of the bottom, but from garboard down she was covered with plastic; the wood was still very bad, and the replaced iron keel was to be replaced with a newly cast lead keel like in the original drawings. Plastic allowed her to sail the first summer, and we could continue to do the fun job of changing the covering board and cockpit. The plastic covered planking was changed only a few years ago.

In my experience, those who sail an old boat keeping it afloat with plastic and an electric bilge pump, can focus on getting the boat tight from above. Perhaps that can give them the courage to work on the bottom after a few years. There are many boats that have just been cut up after a new owner gutted the bottom and then got tired and gave up.

GLUING
Different Types of Glue
The oldest adhesives for boatbuilding are animal-based glue, more like bone glue, and the oldest adhesive

applications I've encountered are glued coach roof beams from 1911.

Among the first parts to be glued were masts. Gustav Plym describes in his book *En seglare minns* (*A Sailor Remembers*; Nordstedts 1972) how one of the first major wooden masts was glued together with bone glue in 1918:

> I think that, to begin with, these masts had their lower part drilled hollow, and the upper curved portion was massive. In any case, I know that the masts were spliced with a galvanized steel pipe where the curved portion began. Later, they made them in two pieces, which were hollowed out and glued. How that all started, I remember well, and I think the first time I saw it was when they glued the mast to the 2,368 sq ft (220 m²) *Miranda*, which was built in 1918 and was the largest skerry cruiser ever built.
>
> The only glue that existed at that time was so-called carpenter's glue that was sold as hard cakes that we boys thought looked like chocolate bars. Before you used it, the adhesive had to be heated into a liquid.
>
> The adhesive power of the glue was destroyed or deteriorated if it was done too fast or at too high of a temperature, and it was therefore done in a double boiler. The time of bonding could only be as long as it took for the glue joint to reach room temperature, and to extend the time, you had to heat up both the pieces worked on, as well as the surroundings.
>
> In the workshop, there was a dryer, which was heated by steam from a central boiler that went through several rows of pipes that extended along the entire dryer. This was primarily used for drying the planking timber, but in order to also use it for gluing masts, it had a length of about 100 ft. (30 m).
>
> In the drying room, they would put two mast halves on trestles and put glue buckets all along the mast. Custom-made clamps were attached at approximately every 20″ (50 cm). Then the temperature in the dryer was brought to its maximum, about 100°F (40°C) as I recall, and then the adhesive was warmed up to 212°F (100°C) in double boilers. When the "master builder," as August Plym was called by the workers, checked that everything was in order, everyone who was available at the

yard was put in two rows on each side of the mast elements. *Miranda*'s mast was about 75 feet (25 m) long, and it took two men every 3 ft (1 meter), so there were about fifty men in the hot dryer. At a given signal, everyone took their glue brushes, coated the joints, put the mast halves together, and attached the screw clamps. The faster it went, the better the result was, and if it took more than about five minutes, the gluing would fail. It was a sweaty bunch of workers that came out of the dryer.

Ruben Östlund used carbamide glue for planking and structural reinforcement in the construction of *Sea Song III* in 1939.

Zake Westin's R-6 *Lillevi* from 1938 is the oldest boat with glued planking that I worked on.

World War II brought on a rapid development of chemical and technical products, and they began to use carbamide glues in the aerospace industry. They are used even today for gluing masts. An example of such an adhesive is Aerolite. From the 1940s on, many boats were constructed with glue; the shipyard in Neglinge built several large offshore cruisers designed by Sparkman & Stephens—including *Ballad*, *Refanut*, and *Anitra*—with glued frames and glued planking. The glue used was carbamide glue, either Aerolite or a Swedish version from the company Hernia. Carbamide glues are not boil proof and require a surface coating to withstand moisture. Glue in the planking that was glued fifty years ago is beginning to come apart now.

Phenolic glues dominated in the 1960s; the most common phenolic glue, Cascofen, made a red glue line. Phenolic glues were boil proof but became brittle over time. Within the glue industry, as well as in plywood manufacturing today, they use the closely related resorcinol glue, which is boil proof and ages better but is also red.

In the 1970s, epoxy adhesives were introduced. I fixed a mast with epoxy in 1971, and it is still in use.

Polyurethane foam adhesives have been used for twenty years; they have changed them in recent years to reduce the levels of harmful isocyanates. I myself have little experience with polyurethane glues and have not come across them as much in renovations.

There are adhesive sealants with good adhesion; the most common ones—such as Sikaflex—are based on polyurethane. It adheres well and is elastic, but for that elasticity to function, the seam must have a certain thickness. If the seam is clamped together to almost nothing, then the ability to stretch is close to zero.

FIGURE 16 } Here, the bow has been replaced below the waterline; the ability to glue joints has made it possible to replace the planking, which had frozen apart, without replacing the entire bottom.

Increased Strength with Adhesives

The adhesives of the 1950s are starting to fall apart now. We do not know if today's adhesives will survive longer. If I am renovating a boat from the 1920s and large parts of the boat are still in good condition, then I want the renovation to be just as durable. I usually glue joints, but at the same time I use the old construction and the same number of screws and bolts as the original. The adhesive provides increased strength and density, but the construction will not break down if the glue fails.

The ability to laminate-glue the frames and deck beams puts less demand on the timber used; knots and deformations can be shifted among the laminates. The need for curved timber is also reduced. If you retain the dimensions of the pillars and beams, they will be glued stiffer than the originals. Planked deck can be glued onto plywood; the design gives a stiffer, denser boat. Boats that already crack in the topsides when the crane lifts them into the water in the spring can be sailed hard against the wind after gluing the seams.

Dry wood is stiffer than wet wood; if the wood is treated with epoxy, it could stay dry. Wood with a moisture content of 15% has a stiffness that is 30% higher than the wood fiber saturation point (at 25–30% moisture).

Limitations on Adhesives

"Today's adhesives are stronger than the wood they glue" is a common saying among people who prefer epoxy. It is a simple statement about a complex reality. There are many different forces that attack a structure: pressure, pulling, bending, shearing, and peeling. It is the glue adhesion to the wood—the interface between wood and glue—that is interesting. It has been observed that glue has a difficult time adhering to the hard and acid-rich surface of oak. Wood cannot be wetter than 14% during gluing. Adhesives are also susceptible to peeling. Peeling is when all the power is deposited in one place in the joint, such as when you tear off a glued carpet from a floor. In a glued wood construction, peeling occurs when wood swells and shrinks. If damp and untreated, but glued, construction dries in the sun, the surface of the wood will shrink, and large loads will attack the joint edge. If the plies are thinner than ¼" (6 mm), then the glue joints can withstand the pressure. But if the wood is thicker,

it is my understanding that the glue joints will give up eventually. The Gougeons brothers' philosophy on West brand epoxy is that wood surfaces should be encapsulated in epoxy to prevent this moisture movement, and in these circumstances, that may be true. The gist of this is that glued wood must be protected with surface treatment so that the joints will keep long term. This is also why glued teak deck is never given a thicker layer of teak than ¼" (6 mm).

This is also why I do not laminate glue stems and knees in structures below the waterline if they are being jointed and surface treated in the traditional way.

EPOXY ADHESION

I have used epoxy adhesives for most adhesive applications for the last thirty years. Using the same type of adhesive is practical, and the ability to succeed increases with more experience. There have been whole books written about epoxy construction and epoxy renovations, so here I will only describe the procedure when gluing.

Low Molecular Weight Epoxy

I use low molecular weight epoxy adhesives, of which the most common brands are West, Epiglass, and SP. Epoxy adhesives bind primarily mechanically—meaning it is the penetration of glue into the wood fibers in the joint surfaces that provides strength for the joint.

These adhesives penetrate well; they are fluid and saturate the wood well. Here, temperature is important for good saturation. At temperatures lower than 53–59°F (12–15°C), the glue and wood need to be heated in order to ensure good saturation. Upon curing, the molecules in the adhesive bind to each other; the temperature is too low, and the molecules move so slowly that the molecular chains are not capable of binding to the same number of other chains.

Advantages of Epoxy

- Epoxy fills well. It does require great clamping pressure or tight joints.

- It is easy to dispense with pumps.

- With different hardeners and fillers, epoxy can be used for different purposes, ranging from surface treatment to splining.

Disadvantages of Epoxy

- Oak is difficult to bond.
- The epoxy softens at 140–180°F (60–80°C), depending on the brand. (Which means that it is not boil proof.)
- It may be difficult to find your way among the variety of products.
- The adhesives can be allergenic.

PROCEDURE FOR GLUING

1 *Prepare the surfaces.* Always wear gloves when the adhesive is hypoallergenic. Wash greasy wood (teak and pine heartwood) with a solvent recommended by the epoxy manufacturer or with acetone. Roughen the surface of the hardwood with sandpaper for better adhesion. At low temperatures, heat the wood surfaces with a heat gun.

2 *Mix the adhesives.* Pumps on the bottles make it easier to mix; the ratio is usually one part curing agent and five parts of a base. Stir until you think that the adhesive is mixed, and then stir another minute just in case. The adhesives arc exothermic, meaning that a larger volume of mixed adhesives generates heat when it is cured. At temperatures above 64°F (18°C), curing may be so fast that the mixing vessel melts in smoke. Pour the adhesives into a plastic container with a large diameter to avoid overheating (it will give more surface area for the heat to be dissipated from). Do not mix more adhesives than you need. If the container with adhesives has been stored in a damp place, you may have a deposit around the tip of the curing pump; take that off in order for the pump to dispense the right dosage. The adhesive should always be stored at room temperature.

3 *Spread glue on both bonding surfaces.* I use a disposable brush for small gluing and a notched trowel or roller for large adhesive applications. I often use a slow curing agent when I want as long an open wetting time as possible (at 72°F or 22°C for two to four minutes and at 59°F or 15°C for about twenty minutes). At low (approximately below 54°F or 12°C) temperatures, the adhesive can be heated into the wood with a heat gun;

FIGURE 17 } Containers of adhesives with pumps simplify mixing and handling of the adhesive.

use low heat and keep the nozzle at a distance from the glue such that you, at the same distance, could blow on the top of your hand without burning it (max. 122°F or 50°C). Just make sure that moisture does not evaporate from the wood and mix with the glue, which will become milky and will get ruined. This is avoided by heating the wood properly before the glue is applied.

4 *Thicken the glue.* If the applied adhesives bond together and are subjected to excessive compression with only a thin adhesive on the surfaces, then the excess adhesive will get pressed out of the joint, and the adhesive left in the seam will continue to be drawn into the wood surfaces. When the clamps are removed, the joint is being "starved," i.e., is without glue. To avoid this, mix Microfiber (cellulose, cotton fibers) in the adhesive into a syrup-like consistency (up to 50% by volume). The thickened adhesive is applied on one surface before the joint is put together. The fiber will bind the epoxy to the joint during the curing. Even if I, a craftsman, struggle with it, the fact is a good epoxy is a visible epoxy.

5 *Keep the joint warm and dry during curing.* Glue, even preheated, that is left to cure without maintenance

heat at low temperatures (approximately below 36–41°F or 2–5°C) often weakens or fails. The molecular binding is poor, and the curing times are so long that they allow moisture into the adhesives, and moisture during the curing process is the biggest enemy for achieving any kind of strength.

6 *Epoxies are hard and difficult to remove after curing.* Surfaces that are not to be glued may be protected with masking tape. Masking tape and plastic sheeting will protect your workbench and other areas from adhesives. Warming gently with a heat gun may soften cured adhesives.

Health Hazards

There is a risk of epoxy allergies. The low molecular adhesives have no solvents, so the need for respiratory protection is not that great. The risk of contact allergy is high, so please use disposable gloves at all times. Use a dust mask when sanding and heating the epoxy.

SUMMARY

Miracle cures pop up from time to time; some will disappear when it becomes apparent that they do not measure up, but most manufacturers find their niche. Only time will tell. The first bonding from the 1950s and '60s are beginning to deteriorate now. How will epoxy constructions look fifty years from now? It may not be interesting; if the boats have worked well and have been sturdy and easy to care for thirty years, then that is perhaps enough. But it should be compared to our historical craft, which can be in excellent condition even after seventy to eighty years. If they are being renovated today, they are worthy of proven methods that may give them the same length of life span for the future.

WOOD FOR BOATBUILDING

Choice of wood is, along with quality craftsmanship, the key to great boatbuilding, so it's foolish to try to skimp on wood quality.

Restoration of a boat and the "patchwork" are extremely laborious. The material costs for the type of work that we do is usually between 10 and 20%, and the rest is labor costs. During thirty-five years of renovation, only once have I had a client come to me with a finished drawing. In all other cases, the effort is to solve a task that is composed of a problem-solving part, a design part, and a labor part. Usually, both the customer and I have a more difficult time estimating the time needed for the first parts.

Replacement of one plank of the topsides on a varnished mahogany boat can take up to a week of dismantling the plank and possible ceiling and interior, purchasing materials, shape the plank, mount the plank, fair and finishing. The result is never better than the quality of mahogany used. That is something that some lumberyards don't understand when you are standing and looking through a woodpile for a suitable piece of wood; they then, and perhaps rightfully so, think that you are downgrading their lumber.

QUALITY OF BOATBUILDING WOOD

There are few other uses for wood that puts so many and such varied demands on the timber as boat construction does. Boatbuilding is a matter of strength, durability, and good quality, not only on the surface but also on the inside.

The perfect boatbuilding wood should be light, strong, rigid, tough, durable, impervious to rot, dimensionally stable against moisture movement, uniform in quality, easy to finish, pretty, available in long lengths, and economical, and should also come from ecologically-correct forest management. This means that you always have to compromise.

Although the head of the distinguished Neglinge shipyard, Bengt Plym, is said to have once listed in a lecture to the Shipyard Association all the bad characteristics a boatbuilding material could have and then summarized them under the concept of wood, modern thought in composite construction is focused on fibers and low weight in relation to strength and durability. Wood matches these criteria better than most other materials. The construction of Sweden's prestigious fleet of vintage boats has largely been based on the availability of an old and not easily renewable forest resource. Our children may only experience the large trees from tropical rainforests through our wooden boats. The cultivated options—teak can be grown, but mahogany is more difficult—will probably not be able to deliver naturally mature timber. A planned regeneration of oak that produces mature timber continuously is hardly possible. Pine for boatbuilding should grow on north slopes and not in rich soil; it provides a high percentage of heartwood, and the trees must be mature until their growth slows so that the percentage of heartwood will increase. There is hardly time for that kind of growth in today's forest plantations.

Oregon pine and spruce from North America come from older forests, and larch comes from Russia's sensitive northern forest belt.

As a wooden boat enthusiast you have to be satisfied with what you can get, and that is another reason to really appreciate fine timber. As a restorer and boatbuilder you get the opportunity to do something lasting and handmade from a good material.

Trees are individuals of their own species, and just like us humans, their features differ and have many variations. A mahogany tree grown in Africa may be more similar to a mahogany tree grown in South America than to one that has grown right next to it in the same forest. The ability to distinguish between good and bad specimens of one species is as important as knowing the overall characteristics of a wood species.

ENVIRONMENTAL CERTIFICATION OF WOOD

Today, the tropical timber imported to Sweden should be FSC-labeled—for the Forest Stewardship Council. It means that the wood comes from ecologically sustainable forest management. These rules have changed the wood industry in the last few years, and it has become increasingly difficult to get a hold of boatbuilding lumber. For example, there is a ban on exporting teak from Burma, spruce is only taken down depending on road and power line construction, and Brazilian mahogany is almost never brought to Sweden. Let's hope that the environmental certification will create a more sustainable forest management for the future with regular supplies of timber through controlled tree felling. The FSC also proposes the use of other woods, such as those felled with organic logging in rainforests; the wood we use for boatbuilding today is just a small part of what is harvested. There are other types of rot-resistant wood used, but they are usually heavier and less dimensionally stable than mahogany.

THE STRENGTH OF OAK

We can describe a timber's ability to absorb forces by looking at the strength values of oak at a moisture content of 12%.

- Pulling in the direction of the grains is 90 Mpa.
- Pulling across the grain is 4 Mpa.
- Oak thus is more than 20 times as strong along the grains as it is across them.
- Pressure in the direction of the grain is 60 Mpa.
- Pressure across the grain is 10 Mpa.
- Oak thus takes up pressure six times as well along the grain as it does across.
- Oak is 1.5 times stronger when it comes to pulling with the grain than pressure along the grain. This means that cracks due to bending first appear on the pressure side (inside of the bend).
- Oak is 2.5 times stronger when it comes to pressure across the grain than pulling across the grain.

Oak is one of the strongest types of wood used for boatbuilding, but on account of its weight, spruce is sturdier. It can often be beneficial for the rigidity and weight to make a thicker beam of a lighter wood than a thinner one of a heavier wood.

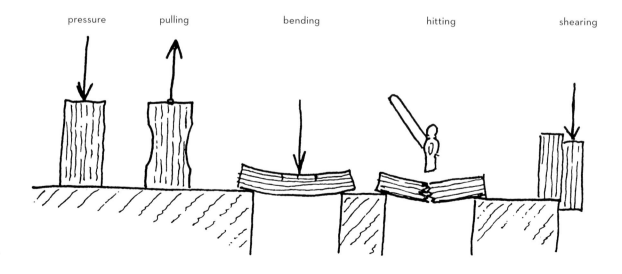

pressure   pulling   bending   hitting   shearing

FIGURE 18 } Various types of durability.

ASPECTS OF BOATBUILDING WOOD STRENGTH

The grains of the wood provides both the strengths and the weaknesses of the material.

Their strength is that the material, when used correctly, provides superior strength and toughness for a boat. Examples of this are masts, beams, and the structure of a hull that is built correctly with planking, frames, stringers, keel, floors, and stem that together distribute the strength in the best way.

Their weakness is that the wood is not strong across the grain, and it may be difficult to achieve good diagonal strength in the construction without gluing; careless renovation can easily destroy the structure.

The strength of wood is highly dependent on the timber's humidity. When the timber is newly felled, the wood is rough because it contains two types of moisture: the free water in the wood cells and hygroscopic bound water in the cell walls. The free water does not affect the strength of the timber; when it has evaporated, the levels of humidity drop to about 25–30% of the fully dehydrated weight. This is called the fiber saturation point. Air-dried lumber has a moisture content of about 15% weight, and the reduction in moisture content from fiber saturation point down to this level leads to a strength increase of up to 30%. Because of this, to maintain the strength of the hull the wood needs to be kept as dry as possible. I have previously concluded that the key to an easy-to-maintain boat and a comfortable boat ownership is based on keeping the boat moisture as low and as uniform as possible over the year. In saturated, poorly surfaced-treated boats, the structures are often easily overloaded with deformations as a result.

The part of today's boatbuilding that uses epoxy technology is based largely on the fact that you can use the strength of the wood better if the wood is kept dry by being sealed with epoxy.

THE STRUCTURE OF THE WOOD

A tree trunk consists of bark, sapwood, and heartwood. The bark protects the trunk. The sapwood is the living part of the trunk; it is the part that transports water and nutrients up and down the tree. The heartwood is the mature portion of the trunk that has stopped transporting nutrients. Sapwood is more susceptible to rot and should, in principle, not be used for boatbuilding.

The annual growth of a tree can be seen in its growth rings; the broader, often lighter, part is called springwood; the smaller, often darker, part is called fall wood or summerwood. Fall wood is stronger and harder than springwood; it also contains more resins. Wood species that live in year-round green forests closer to the equator often have no marked growth rings.

The appearance of growth rings reveals a lot about wood quality. Pine should grow tightly; the width of the annual rings are about $^1/_{32}$–$^1/_{16}$" (1–2 mm), and the proportion of fall wood is as large as possible. On trees that have matured until the growth has slowed, the proportion of heartwood is greater. The situation is a little different with hardwoods such as oak. Oak will still have a high percentage of fall wood, but oak will have grown faster, with a distance between growth rings of $^3/_{16}$–$^5/_{16}$" (5–8 mm) for the wood to be as strong as possible. This requires a warmer climate and more fertile soil.

DRYING WOOD

As we have seen earlier, dry wood is stronger than wet wood. Wood can be dried in various ways. Different considerations must be made so that no timber rots or gets cracks when it dries. Airdrying at a slower pace can give the timber a further chance to mature. An artificial drying (steam drying, condensation drying) may dry the wood more rapidly and with less risk of rot. If the logs dry too quickly, they crack first at the end. To reduce this risk, the tails of the logs are often painted. If the log first dries on the surface, it will shrink while the core will still be moist and retain its old volume. In this case, the surface won't reach around the heartwood, but a wedge-shaped crack will form on the outside going inwards.

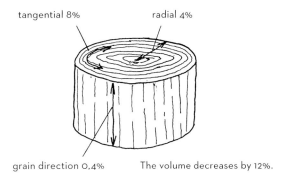

tangential 8%   radial 4%

grain direction 0,4%   The volume decreases by 12%.

FIGURE 19 } Wood dries differently in different grain directions; it dries tangentially—along the growth rings—the most. Drying across the growth rings, in a radial direction, is about half that amount; that is why planking and deck should preferably be made of wood with standing growth rings (quarter sawn). The percentages show the drying of pine from fresh wood to an absolutely bone-dry wood. There are other drying rates that might better describe how much boat lumber dries. For pine: from fresh to 12% moisture: radial 3%, tangential 4.5%. From 20% to 12% moisture: radial 0.9%, tangential 2.1%.

HUMIDITY RATIO IN WOOD

HUMIDITY RATIO	FRESH WOOD	WOOD IN THE BOAT	WOODWORK
Over 30%	Fresh cut wood. Fresh oak will sink.	Keel and dead wood. An old oak garboard will often sink if it is launched after disassembly.	Untreated wood on the ground outdoors during the fall.
25–30%	Free water gone.		
25–20%	New oak keel plank at renovation. In order to be suitable for old bottoms and stems and to not squeeze out the garboard while swelling.	The bottom planking when hauling out. Outside of stems.	Construction outdoors in the fall.
17–18%	Air-dried lumber in the fall.	Bottom planks in the spring. Topside in the fall.	Wood construction outdoors under a roof in the fall and winter.
14–15%	Upper level for adhesives.	Topside during the summer.	Wood construction outdoors under a roof in the spring and late summer.
10–12%	Dry enough for woodworking, accurate enough for assembly, drier than the boat's wood. Lower level for air drying, late spring.	Deck during a heat wave.	
6–8%	Artificial drying. This is how dry mahogany and teak are when imported to Sweden.	Wooden parts that have been taken home and put in the garage or boiler room for the winter.	Woodwork in centrally heated houses in the winter.

If bark is kept, it will reduce this risk but will instead increase the risk of rot and insect infestation.

Wood dries best under a roof in the shade. It should be laid with cross battens between plank layers. The timber cannot have any contact with the ground.

There is no reason to dry boat timber too much as it adapts to the humidity. For a new bottom plank to work well, it should be slightly drier than the bottom is in the spring before launching in order to not crack. But the plank should not be so dry that it presses apart adjacent planks at the joints when it swells.

Warm air can hold more moisture than cold air can; look at condensation on a cold windowpane, or dew. In winter, this means that the cold outdoor air that vents into a house and gets heated up becomes very dry. Therefore, it is devastating for a rudder or old shutters to be taken home and stored in a garage or boiler room during the winter for renovation.

This is good time to clarify a few things:

Moisture content or humidity ratio is the percentage of weight change as water in wood is compared to bone-dry wood.

Relative humidity is the amount of moisture present in the air. The relative humidity outdoors varies throughout the year between about 50 and 90%.

Equilibrium moisture content is the moisture content wood will retain if it is exposed to a certain relative humidity for a long enough period that the moisture in the wood has time to even out. The equilibrium moisture content at 90% relative humidity is about 20–22%, and at 60% relative humidity, the equilibrium moisture content is around 12–13%.

Density is the weight per volume of wood. It is common to specify kg/liter or dm³; the values will then be around 0.5–0.7 kg/dm³. Water weighs 1 kg/dm³. According to the standard, density should be expressed as kg/m³; the values are about 500–700 kg/m³.

MOISTURE MOVEMENT IN WOOD

Different types of wood will swell at varying levels when exposed to moisture. I think the biggest reason why so many quality boats are built of mahogany is that it is dimensionally stable compared to other woods. Topsides remain tight even if the sun is hot, and the boat can stay on land without anything but very thin lines appearing between the bottom boards. This stability means that all structures and joints are subject to less stress from drying and swelling, and thus they become more durable.

Oak is one of the woods that moves the most—at most nearly twice that of the Honduras mahogany. Oak is known to rupture with moisture movements, and the adhesive bonds will break down, as they are unable to resist great moisture movements.

ROT

One of the key requirements of boat timber, on the one hand, is that it is rot-resistant. Different wood species are sensitive to rot; teak is the most durable. On the other hand, the quality of the selected piece of wood matters just as much. Pine is available knot-free with a density of 0.6—it is then rich in resin and tight-veined—and for some construction grade wood that has a density as low as 0.35, it is almost white in color. This type of wood is so porous that it is hardly possible to screw a drywall screw in them, and if they lie on the ground, they soon turn blue. Blue-stain fungus is a common problem with Swedish coniferous wood, but it lives on the sapwood and does not affect the strength of the wood. It will turn blue when the wood moisture content is around 30% or higher.

The most common and severe rot grips on boats come from the decaying fungi that live on cellulose, known as dry rot. The fungi thrive in dark, damp wood, and the largest growth occurs around 68°F (20°C). The fungus requires oxygen to thrive, so it cannot develop in water.

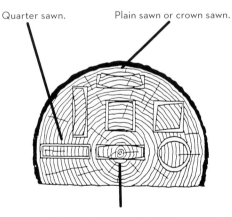

FIGURE 20 } This is a common illustration of how wood changes as it dries.

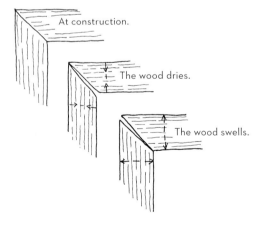

FIGURE 21 } 45° joints are not boat-worthy. They are sometimes used for deck framing, but the seams should be filled right away in that case.

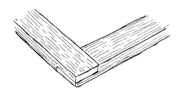

A better joint, particularly if the lower piece is jointed in half with the upper and the joint is then glued.

FREEZING

The bottoms of boats freeze apart; they do not rot because, when the temperature is right for rotting in the summer, the boat is in the water and rot cannot develop in water. In the winter, when the boat is not in the water, it is too cold for rotting fungi.

Some species of wood will freeze apart more easily than others; a common view is that wood that has grown in a cold climate can withstand freezing better than tropical wood. But, as usual, it depends on the quality of the timber. Wood that is uniform in structure and contains a lot of resin will not absorb as much moisture as an unsettled, more vibrant wood.

Surface treatment provides us with the possibility of influencing the result. Impregnation provides protection against blue stain. Linseed oil and a good coat of paint give the wood a better resistance to moisture penetration.

TYPES OF WOOD

Here is an overview of different types of wood used for boatbuilding. Remember that the quality of the individual piece of wood can be as important as the wood's theoretical properties, which are estimated as an average and vary a lot.

CONIFEROUS WOOD

Pine

Pinus sylvestris, Scotch pine. The English trade name is Red or Redwood.

Pine is the wood that, along with oak, is used mainly in traditional clinker-built boats. Pine planking is elastic and tough, but screws and nails come out of the soft wood easier when compared to the harder woods.

Pine was also used a lot for caravel planking in the first half of the 1900s. For planking they used heartwood, but it was in short supply. With a decreasing proportion of heartwood, the discarded amount was so substantial that African mahogany became more financially viable during the serial construction of boats in the 1950s and 1960s.

Pine moves twice as much in the tangential direction as in the radial direction. In all the older literature on boatbuilding, it says that the planking should be quarter-sawn blocks (with standing growth rings). In reality, I have rarely encountered planks sawn in this way. In most cases, the planks are sawn through on each side of the core in order to use the log more economically and efficiently.

Having the core on the outside is also an old rule in planking, but even on the old boats made by Plym you can see exceptions to that rule that probably mostly apply to clinker planking. There are a few Plym-built pine boats from the late 1800s in use. The pine in Plym boats is yellow and nice on the topsides, but on the bottoms all the wood that is not heartwood has darkened. The bottoms are leaky and require a lot of raw linseed oil in order to not move too much. The wood moves so much that the seams cannot be filled in, and splining only accelerates the leaking. Uniform moisture and early launching is the best method of care. It is more devastating to leave an old pine boat than a mahogany one in the same shape on land over the summer.

There are some old boats made by Pettersson that are built with resin-rich heartwood that have been maintained with oil. The pine is almost transparent, and you sense the sunlight through the wood.

Pine resists corrosive attacks from steel much better than mahogany does, and old poor pine planking is much tougher than corresponding mahogany planking.

Pine is used to a large extent for beam shelf and deck beams, but also for the frame and beams in the interior. Other uses include ceilings in the superstructure and for canvassed decks.

Pine, and especially its sapwood, should be protected from blue-stain fungi with some kind of rot protection.

Appearance: Heartwood is, in freshly cut condition, yellow and darkens upon drying to a reddish brown, and sapwood is yellowish-white. The growth rings are distinct and should be around 1/32–1/16″ (1–2 mm) in good boat timber.

Norway Spruce

Picea abies. The English trade name is White, or White Wood.

Spruce is Sweden's most common forest tree and makes up half the stock of wood. It is used commercially as structural timber and is, therefore, considered to have the same characteristics as pine. Spruce is more difficult to impregnate than pine and lacks the more resistant heartwood that redwood may have. That is why spruce cannot replace the resinous and more heartwood-rich pine for boat construction.

Spruce is a light, tough wood that is used for canvassed decks and masts. The disadvantage of spruce compared to sitka spruce for masts is that it is harder to get a hold of knot-free lengths and it turns blue easier, especially behind damaged varnish.

Appearance: Both heartwood and sapwood are yellowish white, and it is difficult to distinguish between them. Spruce twigs are generally more slender than pine twigs.

Spruce

Picea sitchensis, also known as Sitka spruce, is imported from North America.

Sitka spruce is a light, tough wood that comes in long, knot-free lengths and is therefore well suited for masts. The wood is easily glued, but because of its softness it may be difficult to get screws to attach.

Sitka spruce was the predominant mast timber for finer pleasure boats during the 1900s. Sitka spruce is more resistant to staining than Norway spruce, and I've mended cracked masts from the 1920s in which both wood and glue have otherwise been in excellent condition. The wood has also been used for decks and deck beams on racing yachts.

Appearance: The surface is relatively thin, and only the yellow-white heartwood is used. Spruce has a characteristic sweet odor.

Oregon Pine

Pseudotsuga menziessii—with the trade name Oregon pine, British Columbia pine, or Douglas fir—is a North American wood. The tree is neither spruce nor pine.

Oregon pine is the premier deck material above all others. Varnished pine deck has set the measure for elegant-looking decks in Swedish boatbuilding. Even to this day, you can get straight-grained, knot-free timber in lengths over 20 feet (6 meters). The wood is, like other coniferous wood, tough, and in addition to being used for decks it is also used for enforcements such as beam and bilge stringers. Masts for cruisers are another use. Oregon pine planking is more common in Norwegian and Danish boats than in Swedish ones. The wood is corrosive when placed against steel, as it contains acetic acid, so discoloration of iron rivets is a problem in Oregon pine planking.

Wounds from splinters in your fingers will irritate and fester.

Appearance: Oregon pine has clear growth rings with a high percentage of fall wood. The fall wood is hard and rich in resin and provides durability. The wood can be golden to reddish-brown, varying between logs. For a good-looking deck, you may want to sort by color and choose either a yellow or a red-brown deck. The wood has a pungent sweet smell.

Larch

Larix decidua, European larch. *Larix russica*, Siberian larch.

Larch is a wood that is well suited for boatbuilding. The larch boats that we usually come in contact with are the Folkboats. Here, the quality of timber may vary quite a bit; resin-rich larch is a heavy wood and was chosen by the sailor who wanted a strong boat with a good resale value for long trips. Those who wanted a fast boat to race with chose a lighter wood, often the fast-growing Danish larch.

Today there is a major import of Russian larch. That timber is a good option for renovation of pine boats. What you have to watch out for is the connections across the growth rings, which are weak and make longitudinal cracks very common. Even if the heartwood is much better than pine heartwood, a lot of wood is discarded due to cracking.

Appearance: Larch has a small amount of sapwood. The heartwood is pink when cut but darkens to reddish-brown. The annual rings are clear, and the northern-growing larch has a high proportion of fall wood.

DECIDUOUS WOOD

Oak

Quercus robur, English oak. *Quercus alba*, American white oak.

Swedish oak has been used for ships since ancient times. Oak is strong and rot-resistant. But oak is also the wood used for boatbuilding that moves the most during drying. Oak volume changes around 14% between fresh and dry wood. For teak and mahogany, which are the woods that move the least, the change is 8%.

This large change in volume makes oak hard to dry without cracking. Wood larger than 3″ (75 mm) is seldom dried and kept, except for shipbuilding where ample dimensions are forgiving to cracks. Swedish oak does not often grow in large groups but more as solitaires that are able to grow large crowns.

This makes it difficult to find oak without knots. All this means that the proportion of waste is greater for oak than for other types of wood, but its branches and roots are suitable for knees and frames.

The sapwood is not at all rot resistant; even if pests haven't dug paths in the surface during drying, it will still be decayed and rotten within ten years. If you build for long-lasting value, you want to avoid sapwood.

For repairs, oak that is as dry or drier than the oak frame around it should be used. If the timber is a lot drier, it will be difficult to prevent the explosive effect that hard oak has when it swells. Pine is softer and deforms at the edges and becomes leaky instead if it is not allowed to swell freely.

If you use a damp oak tree, it must be protected against dehydration that is too rapid; during the work, this can be done by wrapping the piece in plastic overnight; if it will sit for several days, then it is advisable to varnish with a plain old tough varnish.

Oak is used for backbone, knees, floortimbers, and frames. Here we use a crook. When it comes to planking, oak is suitable for clinker planking, where moisture movements are not of great importance.

Oak contains tannins. Tannins are corrosive, and the wood blackens rapidly on contact with iron. If you forget a fresh green oak plank on the planer overnight, it can be devastating both for the lumber and for your machine planer. Oak, due to its tannins and hardness, is difficult to bond. Here it may be better to use ash, even though it rots easier; bonded structures should, in any case, not be exposed to too much moisture.

Eastern European oak, such as Slavic and Polish oak, were used extensively during the 1900s. It was imported in long, knot-free lengths and generally contained fewer tannins than Swedish oak.

Japanese oak was used for frames. It was both straight-grained and easy to steam bend, but today it is expensive and difficult to get hold of.

American white oak has now taken over the role of imported timber; it is imported very dry—at 6–7% moisture level. Before steaming, it must be soaked; it can be moistened quickly by placing it in water for a week or so.

Appearance: Fresh wood is yellowish-gray, and dried wood is light to dark brown. The sapwood is yellowish-white. A characteristic of oak is medullary rays; they are about one millimeter wide and an inch (2 cm) long and are deviating radial lines without pores. Its flavor, especially Swedish oak, is acidic.

Ash

Fraxinus excelsior, European ash. *Fraxinus americana*, White ash.

Ash is a precious deciduous wood used for boatbuilding even though it is not regarded as rot-resistant. Ash has superior tensile strength compared to oak and is sometimes used for deck beams.

Traditionally ash was used for trim details like lintels for railings and ledges on mahogany boats to break up the color or highlight the lines. Mostly, however, it is used to frame because ash is easy to steambend. Although ash is not rot-resistant, many frames of boats from the 1920s and 1930s have done well, but they have taken a beating where, for example, interiors have been mounted against them. Ash does not like stale rainwater. Despite the trouble it means to glue hard wood, ash is easier to glue than oak.

Appearance: The wood is yellowish-white; its heartwood is slightly darker than its sapwood. Since ash thrives in good soils with humus, the growth rings are relatively wide, and there is a color difference between fall and springwood.

Elm

Ulmus glabra, Wych elm. Elm is easy to steambend and is sometimes used for the frame. I recently worked with a Norwegian racing boat from the late 1920s where steamed ribs of ash, oak, and elm had been used together.

Teak

Tectona grandis.

Teak is, alongside American mahogany, the wood that is most dimensionally stable, with a change in volume of 8% compared with 14% for oak and 12% for pine.

Teak is a heavy wood, rich in resin, and contains a high level of silica crystals. The wood is extremely resistant to rot. The silica crystals make tools dull quickly when working on teak. The teak surface feels greasy and is difficult to surface treat.

For boatbuilding abroad, teak is used for the frame, planking, and decks. In Sweden, it is only used for decks—mainly due to its high price, weight, and the risk of freeze damage. Despite the high price and excellent durability, teak is a more robust rather than elegant wood, which is accentuated by the difficulty of getting surface treatment to last.

Today, much of teak is farm grown; it comes from smaller trees and is difficult to get in knot-free lengths longer than 10 feet (3 meters); the resin content is often lower, and the teak wears down faster.

Appearance: There are probably many carpenters who have returned teak to the lumberyard after the first time they came into contact with it. The newly cut timber is namely a mottled greenish-yellow, but when it is oxidized in air it becomes brownish—from golden brown to dark brown—with hints of black streaks and chalky lines. The sapwood is gray and is not used.

Iroko

Chlorophora excelsa and *regia*.

This is one of the heavy, rot-resistant, and dimensionally stable tropical wood species. Iroko is well suited for wood keels. In Swedish boatbuilding, Iroko was used relatively infrequently, while the Norwegians used it more. Iroko is considered, along with teak, to be more freeze-prone in boat hulls, but while renovating I have noticed that Iroko backbone have often been in better shape than oak backbone.

Iroko has a structure similar to that of African mahogany, with short grains, and is less suitable for structures subjected to the stress of bending.

After World War II, Iroko was launched as "African Teak" for use in floor boards and decks; the name is botanically incorrect and based instead on where it was used.

Appearance: The sapwood is yellowish-gray. The heartwood is gray to greenish-yellow in a fresh cut; drier and more mature wood is golden brown to olive green. The wood often has a marked interlocked grain, i.e., it spirals and reverses direction regularly.

Mahogany

Mahogany has been the most important species of wood in yacht construction, particularly in racing boats and high-speed motorboats. In the United States and in Europe, they speak of yachts built "the Scandinavian Way," which means that boats are built with dry wood and perfect fits so the seams do not need to be filled. That kind of boatbuilding requires dimensionally stable wood, such as mahogany.

It is said that even the invincible Spanish Armada in the 1500s was superior because its boats were built of mahogany from Cuba and not the oak that the British naval vessels were made of. The ships of the invincible Armada were thus stiffer and lighter.

There are many varieties of mahogany; there are said to be over 150 varieties. An attempt to survey them has to start with the botanical family Meliaceae, which is called mahogany and mahogany-like. In that family, there are several genuses, such as Swietenia, Khaya, Entandrophragma, and Cedrela.

Swietenia mahogany is the almost-lost Spanish or Cuban mahogany. *Swietenia macrophylla* is the Honduras mahogany, and various South American varieties such as Brazilian mahogany, also known araputanga.

Khaya ivorensis is African mahogany, such as Grand-Bassam (named after a shipping port, which is common among African varieties). There are more varieties of khaya, such as *Khaya granola*, which is heavier and more rot-resistant.

Entandrophragma utile is an African mahogany marketed in Sweden as Sipo and in England as Utile. *Entandrophragma cylindricium* is a cedar-scented African mahogany, which in Sweden is called Sapeli (after its shipping port).

Cedrela is a Central American genus called Spanish cedar or cigar box wood and is used for light racing boats.

Honduras Mahogany Today, this wood is mostly imported from Brazil. In recent years, export restrictions and requirements for sustainable forest management with certificates of origin on the timber has caused the supply to decrease.

Very small quantities reach Sweden. The mahogany that does comes here as cut and edged planks, so it's hard to find wood with the same color and texture, and thus it's hard to build good-looking and uniform varnished hulls. The wood is dried hard; 6–7% is not uncommon.

Unfortunately, sometimes the wood parts have already been mold-damaged when they arrive in Sweden. Mold is visible as dark spots that can go deep into the wood.

The quality varies in wood of the same weight and texture, such as old Honduras—on the one hand, a lighter wood both in color and weight with poor rot resistance, and on the other hand a heavy darker wood with fine rot and durability levels. The dimensional stability is that of old Honduras.

Appearance: The wood is reddish-brown and darkens when exposed to light. The wood has no distinct growth rings; flat-sawn lumber has less defined structure than quarter-sawn lumber that might have a tendency of interlocked grain.

African Mahogany Khaya varieties began to be used just before World War II. They were not considered to have the same quality as the Honduras.

The timber is sawn from logs here in Sweden, and the logs have lengths of up to 50 feet (15 meters) with a diameter just above 3 feet (1 meter); the structure is uniform, so waste is minimal. Thus the timber is appropriate for new construction. In 2010, the Bohman Company in Oskarshamn stopped cutting logs; thus it is possible that the era of processing tropical timber in Sweden has come to an end. Hopefully it will be possible to import sawn wood in the future, but it becomes even more difficult for individuals to get a hold of good mahogany.

Quarter-sawn timber has an interlocked grain and is difficult to plane.

Khaya ivorensis is relatively light and has transverse grains in the spiraled wood, allowing the timber to easily absorb moisture. Fairly new bottoms that froze apart were not uncommon, especially during the 1960s when linseed oil was out of fashion. Transverse cracks, caused by wind, for example, are relatively common.

Heavier Sapeli and Khaya and Sipo are more resistant to moisture if they do not have too many interlocked grains; they may prove a bit too heavy for hulls though.

Appearance: Heavier wood is often darker than lighter wood. The color goes from yellow-brown to reddish-brown; on Sipos, it is dark red with hints of violet. The lighter sapwood is worthless as boat timber. Mahogany often has interlocked grains and is then very difficult to plane.

Philippine Mahogany

During the 1900s, wood of the genus Shorea has also been marketed as mahogany, although these woods are not of the family Meliaceae. Dark red Meranti is a durable wood; it is dark brown and relatively heavy but has greater moisture movement than the Honduras. The Lauan is another timber that is mainly used for plywood manufacturing.

On page 61 there are two tables outlining properties of wood. The values vary in different books on wooden boatbuilding. Values in the tables are taken from *44 träslag i ord och bild* (44 types of wood in words and pictures) by Julius B. Boutelje and Rune Rydell, published by Trätek, the Institute for Wood Technology Research.

SUMMARY

The strength and weakness of timber is that it isn't a homogeneous material. Wood is, along the grain, a very strong material in relation to its weight. Across the grain, however, it is not very strong. Poor timber, cracks, and twist grains will impact the strength significantly. Boat construction puts great demands on using the wood's own strength for the construction.

The quality of the particular piece of wood is more important than the wood's theoretical properties, which are estimated averages that in reality vary a lot.

In general, you could say that the strength is dependent on the density of the wood; a heavier block of wood has a better strength than a lighter one. The situation is the same with the durability; a heavy piece of wood resists rot better than a lighter one as the heavier piece contains more resin. The reasoning applies for the same kind of wood.

Air-dried wood has about 30% greater strength than fresh wood. Sapwood is in principle not used in boatbuilding.

SHRINKAGE OF DIFFERENT TYPES OF WOOD

TYPES OF WOOD	DENSITY AIR DRIED	SHRINKAGE IN % FROM FRESH TO COMPLETELY DRY				SHRINKAGE IN % FROM FRESH TO 12% MOISTURE		MOVEMENT AT A CHANGE OF MOISTURE QUOTA FROM 20% TO 12%	
	12–15 % | KG/M³ %	RADIAL	TANGENT	ALONGSIDE	VOLUME	RADIAL	TANGENT	ALONGSIDE	VOLUME
deciduous wood									
ash	550–800	3, 8–5	5, 4–8, 4	0, 2	8, 5–13, 6	2, 3–4, 5	4, 9–7	1, 2–1, 5	2–2, 5
oak	690–760	4–5	7, 8–10	0, 4	12, 6–15, 6			1, 5	2, 5
teak	610–700	2, 3–3	4, 2–5	0, 3–0, 6	7–9, 4	1, 5	2, 5		
iroko	610–780	3, 7	5, 4	0, 6	10	1, 5	2		
mahogany and mahogany like woods									
honduras	500–560	3–3, 7	4, 2–5	0, 1–0, 2	7, 5–9	1, 2–2	1, 8–3	1	1, 3
khaya	500–620	3, 2–5	5, 7–8	0, 2–0, 4	9–13	2, 5	4, 5	0, 9	1, 5
sipo	610–640	5	7	0, 3	12	3	3, 5	1, 4	1, 6
sapelli	640–710	4, 8	6, 5		11	2, 5	4, 5	1, 3	1, 8
meranti	580–770	3, 3–4	7, 1–8			3	5, 5	1	2
coniferous wood									
pine	480–530	4	7, 7	0, 4	12, 4	3	4, 5	0, 9	2, 1
larch	550–640	3, 3–4, 3	7, 8–10, 4	0, 3	11, 8	2, 3–3, 3	4–6	0, 8–1	1, 7–2, 8
oregon pine	500–550	4, 3–4, 8	7–7, 5	0, 2–0, 5	11, 9	2, 4–2, 5	3, 8–4	1, 2	1, 5–1, 9
norway spruce	390–480	3, 6–4, 2	7, 8–8, 8	0, 2–0, 3	12	1, 9–2, 2	4–5	0, 7–0, 9	1, 5–2, 1
spruce	390–450	4, 1–4, 6	7–7, 8	0, 4	11, 7–12, 6	3	5	0, 9	1, 3

WOOD'S STRENGTH AT 12% MOISTURE QUOTA

TYPES OF WOOD	STRENGTH								HARDNESS NUMBER	
	TENSION ALONG MPA	TENSION ACROSS MPA	PRESSURE ALONG MPA	PRESSURE ACROSS MPA	FLEX MPA	SHEAR MPA	BEND KJ/M²	E MODULE MPA	END JANKA	ALONGSIDE JANKA
deciduous wood										
ash	165	7	38–58	11	80–120	13–16	70	8 300–13 400	760	400–610
oak	90	4	53–65	11	90–100	11–14	60–75	10 000–13 000	690–715	450
teak	119	4	55–72	7–8	90–145	8–9	50	10 000–13 000	450–500	400–450
iroko	79	2–3	50–60		85–130	10–12	30	9 500–11 000	600–670	490–560
mahogany and mahogany-like woods										
honduras			43–50		74–84	8, 6–12, 7		8 800–10 600	430–630	290–530
khaya	61	2	42–46		72–87	9–11	30–40	9 500–10 000		380–420
sipo	110	2, 5	50–60		90–115	10–15	28–49	11 000–13 000		560
sapelli			50–60	11	94–140	6–7	35–63	10 000–12 000	760	625–670
meranti			53		92	7–9		10 500–12 500		350
coniferous wood										
pine			45–47	7, 5	85–89	10	70	10 000–12 000	300	250
larch	105	2, 3	47–54		92–94	9–12	70	9 900–13 500	370	340–360
oregon pine	103	2, 3	50–52		80–93	8–9, 5	60	10 500–13 500	300	280
norway spruce	88	3, 3	35–44		66–84	9–9, 8	50	8 300–13 000	270–290	160–230
spruce	85	2, 7	33–42		60–80	6, 8–8, 7	50	9 000–11 000	310–340	220–250

SCREWS AND NAILS

FASTENINGS

A boat is composed of many parts; they cannot stand alone, but together they form a strong unit. What keeps the parts together is called a fastening. The fastening can be done with bolts, screws, nails, or glue.

Most of the really old boats that remain in Sweden today are quality built by August Plym at Stockholm's Båtbyggeri AB (Stockholm's Boatbuilding Inc.), first located at Liljeholmen and, after the fire at the shipyard in 1904, moved to Neglinge. What really distinguishes a boat by Plym is that its wooden backbone was held at the minimum dimension, while the fastening with bolts and screws was made with shorter intervals than other boats. This, plus careful adjustments, made the Plym boats last. *Aziza, Naima, Gandul, Aj, Alca, Gundog, Eel, Foam, Ariella, Gerd, Estrella, Elvin, Tarantella*, and *Gandul II* are all still there even though they were built the 1800s. Some other shipyards used large oak logs for the backbone, but that means that the bolted joints cannot manage to remain tight to the wood when it swells and dries, so the boats leak, the moisture penetrates, and the boats rot and lose their shape.

Do Not Tighten Too Hard and Do Not Screw Too Loose

A screw is often relatively much stronger than wood; a mechanic who is accustomed to working with steel often tightens the screw so hard that the head of the screw goes right through the planks. You have to listen to the sounds and stop when the wood starts making noise. In a wooden boat, place the screws close together so that each screw only needs to take a limited load. The screws will fit so tightly that they will manage to keep the joints tight even when the wood moves. The distance between the screws in a rabbet should, according to the old rules, be 2.3″ (60 mm), and the screws through the covering board into the sheer strake should be at a 5-inch (125-mm) spacing. A lot of restorers break this rule, with leaks as a result.

Adhesives

Nowadays we can use good adhesives, but my experience of how glued boats age has made me look at adhesives as a complement to regular screwing. I have written about adhesives in Chapter 6, but with a little exaggeration you could say that if the adhesive is to last below the waterline the wood must be protected by a thick surface coating.

DIFFERENT TYPES OF SCREWS

Regular wood screws. The screw has a head, shaft, and thread with a core, which is usually slightly conical. This type of screw is almost like it's designed to screw onto boats. The shaft has both spiral stiffness (will not break when tightened) and takes up lateral forces (shear). The shaft works as a filler and seals the drill holes that are required for the thread to move freely through the first piece of wood (see Figure 22).

Lag bolts with a hexagonal head. The screw has a shank and thread, like wood screws. It is used for larger dimensions of screws (5/16″, or 8 mm, and bigger) when one slot is not strong enough and is, in these dimensions, cheaper than regular wood screws.

Sheet metal screws. They are fully threaded with a cylindrical core (the core is of uniform thickness) and tip. This kind of screw is suitable to screw sheet metal hardware into wood. The thread has a large area and is therefore better than wood screws. I use it to fasten sheet rails, for example, and for mast hardware.

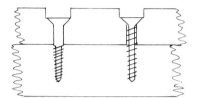

FIGURE 22 } In order to pull together two pieces of wood, you have to drill a hole in the top piece that is the screw's maximum diameter; otherwise the screw will attach to the top hole and the screw won't connect the pieces.

FIGURE 23 } Today there are some stainless wood screws manufactured that have poor, shallow threads. Compare it with the threads of the old bronze screw from the 1800s. It is easy to understand which screw attaches better to wood.

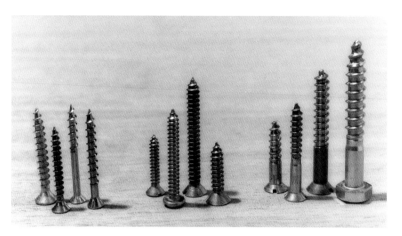

FIGURE 24 } On the left: Self-tapping screws, fully threaded and partly threaded. In the middle: Sheet metal screws with countersunk heads and one with a rounded head. On the right: Wood screw, first a stainless steel screw with poor threading, then one with a better thread, next a bronze screw, and finally a lag bolt.

Self-tapping screws. Examples of self-tapping screw brands are Spax and Grabber. The screw has a cut in the lead and stronger pitch (longer in between the threads). It is fully threaded or partly threaded, but the shaft is not wider than the core. It is suitable for screwing plywood decks; the screw must not be threaded to the piece that is to be screwed down to obtain good contraction. Partly threaded stainless steel decking screws are an option that have been marketed in recent years. We often use this type of screw now, as it is significantly cheaper than traditional wood screws. For use in harder wood, you should only use the shortest length versus diameter or you risk the screw breaking when you fasten it, and it will also be almost impossible to unscrew.

Machine-threaded screw. For the nut, the thread standard used today is the M-thread (metric). In older boats (before the 1960s), Imperial-threaded screws were used. Keel bolts are usually Imperial threaded. The standard used for inches is Whitworth or UNC. The standard dimensions for threads at each millimeter go from M2 to M6, M8, M10, M12, M16, M20, M24, M27, M30, and M33.

M stands for metric thread and is the measure of the outside diameter of the thread.

Different Heads

Hexagonal head (i.e., nut shape) is used on larger screws; the head is better for the tool when tightening. It is coarse and clumsy and not suitable for plugging.

Square with a pan head-wagon bolt. Has a head with a large diameter and the square is pressed into the wood and prevents the screw from turning when tightening the nut.

Pan head and rounded head. Used for surface mounting, for example, for assembly of thin sheet metal hardware on a mast.

Oval head. Is sometimes used for hardware and for interiors that should not be plugged.

Flat head. Used primarily for plugged screwing—an all-round head.

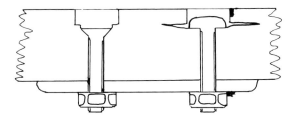

FIGURE 25 } A flat head that is too tight will split the wood with the grain, resulting in humidity and frost damage. A countersunk screw is pulled down into the wood without damage; the plughole does not need not be as deep but will still give a decent plug thickness.

Screw Drives

Slot is the classic type; it can be difficult to drive with a machine, and the bit will easily jump. The slot can be dug out if the screw is to be removed from a glued, plugged hole. Visible screws on a vintage boat should be made with slotted screws for the correct look.

Phillips head drives are difficult to loosen if there has been damage or if there is glue on the head, but are easy to drive with a machine. There are different types of Phillips drives, and the correct screw driver (bit) is a must for successful screwing. Phillips is only suitable for stainless steel screws; brass and bronze are too soft.

Hex drives have come more into use in recent years; I like using it. The drive is better than other types in driving with a screwdriver as well as when dismantling. The drive is also relatively easy to drill out if it has become filled with glue.

CORROSION

Corrosion will be discussed more fully in the next chapter, but a little bit on this problem may be in order now.

Galvanic corrosion happens when metals of various types interact in a damp environment. The "noble" metals will destroy the "base" metals. Stainless steel and bronze are examples of noble materials, and aluminum and zinc are base.

Electrochemical attacks describe what happens in damp wood when it is affected by metals exposed to galvanic corrosion. In such instances, the wood weakens around the noble metal and causes "nail sickness," which is very harmful to the wood.

Some Ways to Reduce the Attacks

- Do not mix metals.
- Insulate different metals from each other.
- Keep the wood as dry as possible.
- Keep the electrical system in good shape.
- Use zinc anode.
- Use marine grade 316 underwater.
- Never use copper rivets, brass screws, or bronze screws in galvanized steel frames.

VARIOUS METALS IN SCREWS AND NAILS

Bronze is considered to be the most stable metal. In the United States it is regarded as the only secure attachment under water. Bronze itself is not attacked, but when in contact with base metals it can result in corrosion of the base metal and nail sickness in the wood. Bronze has approximately the same strength as stainless steel. I have had good experiences with American silicon bronze that I have imported and used in hull renovations in recent years. You rarely have problems with broken screws, and in fresh oak, copper precipitates and has a preservative effect on the wood. Compared with a copper-clad bottom where water that contains copper is left sitting in the boat between the plates and the wood, preventing rot. (Such boats should not be on land during the winter, as they will damage when they freeze.) A bronze and tin alloy is also good, and today we import German screws made of it. The bronzes that are the least stable are those with zinc or magnesium.

Brass is an alloy of copper and zinc; the more zinc, the worse the quality of the screw. Red brass with 20% zinc lasts a long time, but modern brass screws with 40–50% zinc should not be exposed to salt water or tannins. However, they can be used under a sealed plug on decks and for interiors.

Brass screws in boats from the 1950s and later are often of poor quality, while older boats may have screws in better condition. The nickel in nickel-plated brass screws protects the screws but will result in nail sickness with deposits and discoloration of the wood. The most severe attack of nail sickness I have seen was in the planking around brass bolts mounted in a galvanized steel frame. The wood around the screw was completely ruined after only twenty years.

Copper is almost too soft for screw manufacturing but is used for rivets and nails. Do not use copper rivets in steel frames; they will cause nail sickness. Older boats sometimes have keel bolts of copper; they do not seem to be affected by time but will stretch a little too much, so they may need to be tightened. I've reinstalled ninety-five-year-old keel bolts of copper after changing the wood keel.

Stainless steel is the most easily available material for screwing with strength and durability. Below the waterline, you need to use acid-proof screws A4 Marine Grade (AISI 316). Underneath the plugs above the waterline, you may use A2 (AISI 304).

The worst environment for stainless steel is a damp, salty one with a low oxygen content (stationary salt water). In that one, the stainless steel may corrode and create so-called pinch holes. Polishing or surface treatment reduces the risk, and it rarely happens in the brackish waters on the Swedish east coast. I have seen signs of nail sickness in poorly plugged screws below the waterline but no severe attacks, possibly due to the fact that stainless steel has not been used for long but more likely because stainless steel is not a good electrical conductor (see the chapter on corrosion). Stainless steel will easily "cut." If there is a grain of sand or any other damage to a machine thread of stainless A2 or A4 steel, then the thread and bolt will likely bind together through friction. The threads of the turnbuckles and bolts that need to be drawn tightly should be lubricated.

Galvanized steel is the most common material for fastenings on old boats. It is also the material that wears out first. Today there is no need to use galvanized steel if you're striving for a long-lasting restoration. For heavier bolts, the price difference is not that different compared to stainless steel. The wood screw and machine screw with smaller dimensions than the M10 are not available in hot-galvanized steel anymore, but are now zinc-plated; it provides less protection that disappears in a few years in moisture.

Re-screwing Steel Frames

During the first half of the 20th century, the majority of larger boats were probably built with galvanized

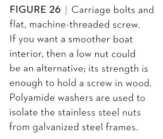

FIGURE 26 } Carriage bolts and flat, machine-threaded screw. If you want a smoother boat interior, then a low nut could be an alternative; its strength is enough to hold a screw in wood. Polyamide washers are used to isolate the stainless steel nuts from galvanized steel frames.

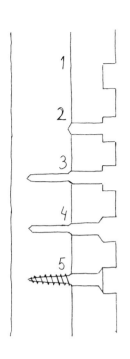

FIGURE 27 }

PROCEDURE FOR SCREWING

Example: Screw an 18-mm planking to a frame. The rules (Lloyds) say that the screw should be a number 9 and that at least half of the screw should be screwed into the frame.

Measure the screw with a caliper; a number 9 screw has a $5/16$-inch (8.3-mm) head, a $1/18$-inch (4.5-mm) shaft, and a core in the middle of the thread of $3/32''$ (3 mm). If the screw is plugged $3/16$ inch (5 mm), the length of the screw will be $1/4''$ (13 mm) in the planking, and $1^1/16''$ (17 mm) in the frame if a $1^1/4$-inch (30-mm) screw is used.

1 Drill the plug; a $5/16$-inch (8.3-mm) head requires a $3/8$-inch (10-mm) plug bit; drill approximately $3/16''$ (5 mm) deep.

2 Drill with a $1/18$-inch (4.5-mm) clearance for the shaft; drill through the plank so that you have a center marking so that no thread will pull on the board. The center marking will make sure that the hole for the core is in the center of the shaft hole.

3 Drill 3 mm for the core; tape the drill at $1^1/4''$ (30 mm) from the end, and drill all the way. If the frame is made out of hard wood (ash, oak), then drill with a bit that is a couple of tenths too big rather than with one that is thinner than the core.

4 Countersink the plughole; if you don't, there is a risk that the planking will crack.

5 Attach the screw. To decrease the friction when screwing into hard wood, you can dip the screw in tallow, grease, linseed oil, or glue to make it go in smoother and not break off.

6 Plug, glue the plug, and put the plug in so that the direction of the grain is the same in the plug and the planking.

Please note that the screws will not attach any better if you drill smaller holes. On the contrary, the shaft should go in easily—the core as well; it is the thread that should hold the screw. This is especially important when it comes to sheet metal screws with their cylindrical core. Self-tapping screws (Spax, Grabber) are self-drilling in soft woods.

(hot-galvanized) steel frames. The rivets are beginning to rust now, so changing them is a common renovation need. I use flat stainless steel A4 screws as replacements. Mixing metals can cause corrosion in the long run, but hot-galvanized rivets cannot be found anymore. The galvanizing on the frame was enough to prevent the rivets from rusting when the boats were built, but in re-riveting today, the frames do not have enough zinc to prevent rivets from rusting. You can minimize the mechanical connection by dipping the screws in paint or glue and using plastic washers under the nuts, and it is particularly important not to scratch the frame with the nut, as that will create a very good mechanical contact.

Cost Aspects

Screws are expensive and it is tempting to choose an inferior, less expensive screw. Wooden boat restoration is an art and handicraft that will take time and cost money. An invoice from a restoration performed by a professional often has a cost for labor representing 80% of the total; thus cutting down on materials is a bad idea. For an amateur, it may feel more important to keep costs down, but you waste your own time when you use materials that only last a few years.

Under the Waterline

The best screw is the most expensive; below the waterline I use A4 or bronze wood screw. Self-tapping screws are cheaper than wood screws and have a better thread. However, to get good pull in a screw joint the hole in the piece to be screwed must have clearance, and a gap is formed with self-tapping screws that must be filled with epoxy adhesive. For a larger project, you may order cheaper bronze screws from abroad. For screws with nuts, use A4.

DIMENSIONS OF WOOD SCREWS

LENGTH			NUMBER OF SHAFTS: 5	6	8	9	10	12	14	16	18
			DIAMETER: 2	3,5	4	4,5	5	5,5	6	7	8
			HEAD: 5,6	6,5	7,5	8,3	9,2	10,2	11	12,5	14,5
Stainless	Brass	Bronze									
12 mm	½″	12,5 mm	x								
16 mm	⅝″	16 mm	x	x							
20 mm	¾″	19 mm		x	x						
25 mm	1″	25 mm		x	x	x	x				
30 mm	1¼″	32 mm			x	x	x	x			
40 mm	1½″	38 mm				x	x	x			
50 mm	2″	50 mm						x	x		
60 mm	2½″	63 mm							x		
70 mm	2¾″	69 mm							x	x	
80 mm	3″	75 mm							x	x	x
100 mm	4″	100 mm								x	x

Above the Waterline

Here, a stainless steel deckling screw could be a better alternative to brass, but when it comes to precision mounting, you need a wood screw with a shaft for good control. Compare on Figure 22.

Dimensions of Wood Screws

The numbers on the screws and the lengths in inches dominated up to the 1970s, when the length was changed to millimeters. The numbering is still available on some packages and on imported screws.

A standard range of appropriate length/diameter ratios where the screw fits well and does not break during installation can be found in the table above.

COPPER NAILS

The Pros and Cons of Copper Nails

Copper nails are used mostly in Scandinavia; in North America, they have had a worse reputation, possibly because of the pioneer of yacht building, Captain Nat Herreshoff, known as the Wizard of Bristol. Before and around the turn of the 20th century, Herreshoff led the development of the type of boat that would dominate the 1900s. The boats were relatively lightly built and had a hull with an overhang and external ballast in a keel or fin. Herreshoff ran a great shipyard in Bristol, Rhode Island, and wrote the rules and regulations for the design of sailing boats that is still in use. Herreshoff thought that the copper nails would break the ribs and recommended wood screws.

Our experience in Sweden suggests the opposite; you can see cracked frames with both methods, but a nail with a washer keeps frames in place against the hull better in the long run. This is an additional advantage in laminated-glued wood frames when the ribs are held together by nails; even if the glue joints bursts, the risk of further tearing of the adhesive joint is minimized. Copper is also more stable in the face of corrosion than brass. The advantage of the wood screw is the smooth elegance it creates on the inside of the frames.

In the past, copper nails were made in the shipyards out of round annealed copper. The head was made in a tool that was fastened in a vise, and the washers were punched from copper plate. The washer, called a rove, was given—and still has today—a curved shape for it to "pull," or range better against the surface and the

28

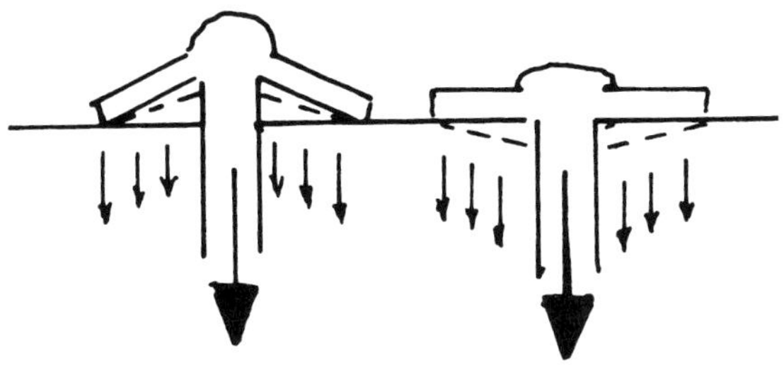

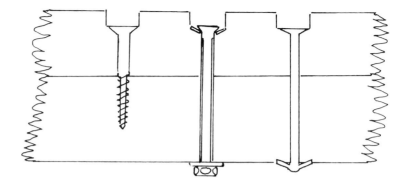

29

FIGURE 28 } The rove, i.e., the washer, is given a cupped shape in order to give proper tension to the surface and the nail, where a flat washer would turn and release the nail.

FIGURE 29 } Wood screws, machine screws, and copper nails—three different ways to join planking and frame.

Wood screws provide a smooth and stylish interior of the frame; they are easy to install, even when the interior is in the way. But they won't hold laminated frames together where the glue starts to release. Bolts and nuts can be easier than

riveting for the amateur, and in confined spaces where it's hard to rivet, e.g., in the bilge. The screw's head may be too weak in soft wood; a washer under the head that has been curved, like a copper washer, solves the problem. Copper nails are the best for newly steam-softened frames; it's quick to assemble and the nails hold the rib in place while it cools off.

nail, where a flat washer would turn and release the nail (see Figure 28).

They used to be called copper rivets in boatbuilding, but more than one boat owner has had to come out of the store empty handed after having asked for copper rivets; the next time the clerk admitted that he had copper nails. What the difference is I never really understood. Perhaps it has to do with the square shape and the pointed end.

Previously, copper nails were cheap, but for the last few years some of the manufacturing moved abroad, the distribution changed, and thus prices have soared. Today, nails and washers are more expensive than stainless machine-threaded screws with nut and washer.

Equipment for Copper Riveting

Some of the tools for copper riveting are hard to buy over the counter. What is needed for riveting is a ball-peen hammer, wire cutter, set, bucking iron, rivet puncher, and fastener.

Anvils are made of a piece of round steel with an approximate weight of 11–13 lbs (5–6 kg); it may also have a body-friendly shape; see Figure 30.

FIGURE 30 } Riveting. The rove is applied to the nail with the help of the rove set and a ball-peen hammer. Note that the bucking iron is made to fit the thigh.

FIGURE 31 } Tools for riveting. Homemade sets and fasteners and a combination tool that was previously sold in hardware stores. Round copper rivets and square copper nails and roves, i.e., cupped copper washers.

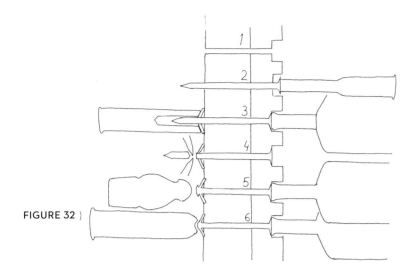

FIGURE 32 }

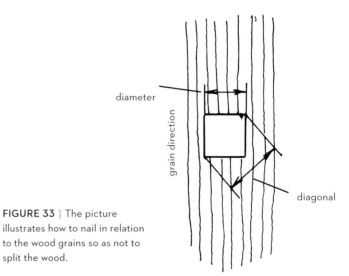

FIGURE 33 } The picture illustrates how to nail in relation to the wood grains so as not to split the wood.

PROCEDURE FOR COPPER RIVETING

(See Figure 32.) Attaching a 1-inch (28-mm) frame to ¾-inch (18-mm) planking with ³⁄₃₂-inch (3.5-mm) nails (e.g., regulation for a 320 sq ft (30 m²) Skerry cruiser). The diameter is ³⁄₃₂″ (3.5 mm), and the diagonal is ⅛″ (4.5 mm); see Figure 33. The head is approximately ⁷⁄₁₆″ (10.5 mm).

1 *New planking, old frame.* Drill through the old frame and through the planking with a ³⁄₃₂-inch (3.5-mm) bit. If the planking is made of hard wood, you can use up to a ⅛-inch (4-mm) bit. Plug drill ½″ (12 mm) for the head.

   Old planking, new frame. Drill the plughole to a suitable dimension to get clean edges and drill through the hole in the planking through the frame. If it's a dry-laminated frame of ash, then drill from the inside with a ⅛-inch (4.5-mm) drill (the diagonal measurement of the nail is ⅛″ or 4.5 mm) so as to not crack the frame.

   New planking, new frame. Drill in a suitable place through the frame and into the planking. (For the number of rivets needed, check the Square Meter Rule.) Newly steam-softened frames can be drilled with the measurement of the diameter, but if you drill too narrow of a hole, you may experience cracks later as the frame dries and ages.

For the rest of the work, you need two people— one on the inside and one on the outside of the hull.

2 The nail is attached from the outside, the last bit with a drift.

3 The anvil will be used on the outside; a plug-drilled hole is almost necessary in order to hold the anvil in place; a flanged out tip on the bucking iron will allow the hole to not get damaged around the edges. The set is used to attach the rove, i.e., the cupped washer; don't hit so hard that the rove is flattened.

4 Cut the nail one millimeter above the washer with pliers.

5 Make an edge on the rivet with small, quick movements with the ball-peen hammer; heavy movements can bend the nail and crack the frame.

6 Tighten and give the riveting a clean look.

A piece of round bar is drilled into the end of the steel and welded; the diameter of the round bar is chosen so that it fits into the plughole approximately ⁵⁄₁₆″ (8 mm) is a good all-round dimension to fit in a ⅜-inch (10-mm) plughole. Approximately a little more than 1¼″ (3 cm) may be just right for the protruding length.

The rivet set is made by a drilled out round bar or a thick-walled pipe, with an outer diameter of approximately ⅜–⅝″ (10–15 mm); the hole diameter is chosen so that the nail goes in easily, and the end is formed according to the cupping of the washers.

The fastener is also made of some kind of round bar. In one end you drill or grind a bowled shape suitable for the riveted nail; the fastener tightens the nail and rove, and cleans up the marks from the ball peen hammer.

Boatbuilding is a craft that has been handed down; during the apprenticeship period, apprentices made their own hand tools like the ones that existed in the workplace. Local varieties were developed, and if any tools were bought over the counter, they were looked upon as mediocre products and were adapted for the yard and its use. We also have to adapt to that tradition, as no market exists for these tools.

RULES AND REGULATIONS

Rules and regulations have always been around to provide sound boats; the most well known is issued by Lloyds, which is a classification company. Another classification society is Norske Veritas, whose rules have been the basis of Nordic boat standards and were used as the regulations for new construction in Sweden in the late 1900s. Nordic boating standards have a full section on the design of wooden boats but nothing that deals with fasteners other than keel bolts. The figure above and the one on page 73 show a pair of planks of screws rivets and bolts. For a major renovation, you may want to obtain the rules as a basis for dimensions. In the USA, there are also *Herreshoff's Rules for the Construction of Wooden Yachts* and *Nevin's Scantling Rules for Wooden Yachts*.

The Square Meter Rule

The Square Meter Rule was first adopted in 1908; the largest revision was made in 1925. On both occasions, the work was led by Karl Ljungberg at the Department

DIMENSIONS BY LLOYDS

DIMENSIONS FOR ATTACHMENT

PLANKING AND DECK	STEEL FRAME	GROWN FRAME	LAMINATED FRAME	BENT FRAME	DECK BEAMS
Thickness	Bolt	Wood screw	Copper nail	Copper nail	Wood screw
19 mm	5 mm	5 mm	4,5 mm	2,5 mm	4,5 mm
22 mm	6 mm	5 mm	6,5 mm	3,5 mm	5 mm
25 mm	6 mm	5,5 mm	6,5 mm	3,5 mm	5 mm
28 mm	6 mm	5,5 mm	6,5 mm	4,5 mm	5,5 mm
31 mm	8 mm	6 mm	7,5 mm	5 mm	5,5 mm
34 mm	8 mm	6 mm	7,5 mm	5,5 mm	6,5 mm
37 mm	8 mm	7 mm	7,5 mm	5,5 mm	6,5 mm
40 mm	10 mm	8 mm	9,5 mm	6 mm	7 mm
43 mm	10 mm	8 mm	9,5 mm	-	8 mm
46 mm	12 mm	8,5 mm	11 mm	-	8 mm

Source: Rules and Regulations for the Classification of Yachts and Small Craft, 1979.

of Solid Mechanics at the KTH Royal Institute of Technology. The most recent reprint of the rule is from 1996. There are still yachts built based on this rule.

Building descriptions are well adapted to Swedish conditions; the internationally renowned designer Knud H. Reimers considered it the best building regulation for other types of boats as well as for Skerry cruisers. On page 73 there is a facsimile of a page from the rulebook that talks about fasteners.

Skerry cruisers were classified according to sail area in different square meter classes. If every square meter class is given an average displacement, then the rule can be used for dimensions of most types of boats, including motorboats. (To clarify, I will mention that Li is the measured length that approximately equals the wave building length. It is measured as, for example, 15-yacht at 5″ (13 cm) and, for a 55, at 9.5″ (24 cm) above the design waterline.)

SUMMARY

A screw is often stronger than wood, relatively speaking. The screws are placed so closely together because the wood is only capable of holding a limited load per screw.

Close screwing also keeps the pieces of wood together better when the wood swells and dries.

In order for a screw to be able to connect two pieces of wood, the thread must have clearance when it first goes in.

Do not use copper rivets, or brass or bronze screws, in galvanized steel frames; they destroy both frame and wood.

Copper rivets are a great attachment for wood frames; they are corrosively stable and holds the slats of wood in a glued wood frame.

For major renovations, it is recommended that you obtain a suitable rulebook for sizing. If the boat is rated from the beginning, then the edition of the rule that the boat is built from will provide good support. If the boat is to be used for racing, then it is especially important that it be renovated after the correct rule; otherwise it may not measure up, and therefore may not able to race.

M2-CLASS	15	22	30	40	55	75	95	120	150
Displacement, tons	1–1.5	1.5–2.2	2.3–3.4	3.5–4.5	4.5–6	6–9	9–12	13–15	16–20
Deck and plank thickness, mm	14	16	18	20	22	24	27	31	35

(A reproduction of a page on attachments from an old edition of the Square Meter Rule.)

3.4.5 TABLE VI. BOLTS, RIVETS, SCREWS
(WITH THE EXCEPTION OF FRAME SPACING, ALL TABLES ARE SET AT MINIMUM VALUES.)

		CLASS SQ.M.								
		15	22	30	40	55	75	95	120	150
Bolts, of galvanized or stainless steel, through keel, stem and stern:										
in $^2/_3$ Lx, diameter	mm	8	10	12	12	12	16	16	20	20
above and below $^2/_3$ Lx, diameter	mm	6	8	10	10	12	12	12	16	16
Rivets through the planking and ribs, number of paths:	mm	2	2	2	2	2	2	2 (1)[1]	2 (1)[1]	2 (1)[1]
with 71–120 mm width	mm	3	3	3	3	3	3	2	2	2
with 121–170 mm width	mm	–	–	–	–	–	–	3	3	3
with 171–220 mm width										
Rivets through planking and steel frames, of galvanized steel, diameter	mm	3.5	4	4.5	5	5	5.5	6	6.5	7
Screw, stainless steel, diameter	mm	5	6	6	6	6	8	8	8	8
Rivets through planking and bent ribs of copper, diameter	mm	3	3.5	3.5	3.5	3.5	4	4.5	4.5	5
Rivets in steel structures, of galvanized steel:										
diameter[2]	mm	4–5	5–6	5–6	6–7	6–8	7–9	8–10	8–11	8–12
maximum spacing	mm	32–48	40–48	40–48	48–56	48–64	56–72	64–80	64–80	64–96
Rivets through stringers, steel frames, and planking, of galvanized steel, diameter	mm	3.5	4	4.5	5	5	5.5	6	6.5	7
Screw, stainless steel, diameter	mm	6	6	6	6	8	8	8	8	8
Rivets through stringers, bent frames, and planking, of copper, diameter	mm	4	4.5	5	5.5	6	6.5	7	7.5	8
Rivets through planking and wooden floors, of copper, diameter	mm	3.5	4	5	5.5	6	6.5	7	7.5	8
Rivets through planking and the arm angle of extra floors of galvanized steel, diameter[3]	mm	3	3.5	4	4.5	5	5.5	6	6.5	7
Screw, stainless steel, diameter	mm	5	6	6	6	6	8	8	8	8
Rivets through planking, wooden floors, and additional floors of steel, maximum spacing	mm	60	70	80	90	100	110	120	130	140
Rivets through vertical knees and beams and frames, number of each, see Figure 6.		3	3	3	3	4	4	4	4	4
Rivets through vertical knees and beams: of copper, diameter	mm	3.5	4	4.5	5	–	–	–	–	–
of galvanized steel, diameter	mm	3	3.5	4	4.5	5	5.5	6	6.5	7
Screw, stainless steel, diameter	mm	5	6	6	6	6	8	8	8	8
Rivets with horizontal knees and beams and respective stringers: number of each arm		2	2	2	2	3	3	3	3	3
of galvanized steel, diameter	mm	3	3.5	4	4.5	4.5	5	5	5.5	6
of copper, diameter	mm	3	4	4.5	5	5	5.5	6	6.5	7
Screw, stainless steel, diameter	mm	5	6	6	6	6	8	8	8	8
Wooden screws through the planking and keel, stem and stern diameter	mm	5	5	5.5	5.5	6	6	7	7	7
length	mm	32	38	38	44	51	51	64	64	76
maximum spacing[4]	mm	55	55	60	60	60	6	70	70	70
Wooden screws through the side deck: Diameter[5]	mm	5	5	5	5.5	5.5	6	6	7	7
length	mm	32	32	38	38	38	40	40	50	50

[1] Numbers in parentheses indicate the number of rivets in every two frames at the narrower width.

[2] The lower numbers apply to common minimum wall thickness (mean).
The higher numbers apply to common maximum wall thickness (mean).
With steel construction is meant building components of steel, e.g. plates with angle iron, angle iron with angle iron, etc.

[3] Near the keel, prow, or hedge, one may use a screw (brass, galvanized or stainless steel) at least 25% larger in diameter than the rivet.

[4] These screws should be located as far as possible from the zigzag.

[5] The side deck attached to the planking, stringers, and beams is shown in Figure 6. Screws through the side deck and planking may be taken with a smaller diameter and placed at shorter intervals than the figure shows.

CORROSION AND NAIL SICKNESS

CORROSION IS ONE OF THE WORST ENEMIES OF WOODEN BOATS

When we think of wooden boat restoration, sanding and carpentry probably immediately come to mind, but when the time comes for repairs, it is usually not the wood itself that causes the problems. Instead, it is the corrosion of metals that causes problems.

It is in the areas between wood and metal that damage occurs. The rust from the iron rivets forces plugs in the bottom out. The wood turns black and softens when in contact with rusty steel frames and stem bolts. Sometimes you come across mahogany planking in good condition in a 1.5-foot (50-cm) section, and then there's a poor section that is almost coming apart near the steel frame. Iron keels corrode and destroy the wood keel. Keel bolts rust. Propellers and shafts corrode, and support trestles and other parts of the propeller fold. This corrosion is a result of moisture and wear and tear, and progress is slow.

ELECTROLYSIS ONBOARD INCREASES RISKS

It is possible that we will see an increasing problem with galvanic corrosion on our boats since we have, for our convenience, increased the use of electricity on board. The last twenty-year period has been an electronic age when it comes to gadgets and accessories. We dragged more and more of our home environment onboard—electronics, stereos, TVs, refrigerators, pressurized water—along with what we already had: old lights and, for some wooden boats, the indispensable electric pump. In order to get these to work, we need land-voltage installations and sometimes solar panels.

This can lead to corrosion problems, which you can read quite a bit about in boating magazines. It is similar to electricity from the shore where there is poorly executed grounding of the pier's electrical system that can cause stray currents. There is talk of some marinas where the water is live with electricity from such stray currents.

GALVANIC CORROSION

The principle of galvanic corrosion is shown in schools with the experiment of lowering two metals into a bowl of salt solution and then connecting the metals with a cable. This created a simple battery (see Figure 34).

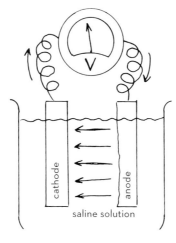

FIGURE 34 } Two metals are immersed in an electrolyte and form a battery. The metal that has lower electrical potential becomes the anode, and the one that has more is the cathode. When they are connected through the electrolyte, ions migrate from the anode to the cathode. A galvanic cell has been formed, and the anode is consumed over time.

But at the same time it means that this reaction doesn't happen with more noble metals. One can thus use a base metal as cathode protection.

The galvanic voltage chain shows the difference in potential between the metals. The greater the voltage difference, the stronger the battery.

In these days of plastic boats, you are advised to use zinc anodes to protect other metals on board. But in the case of wooden boats, you must remember that in the saline solution from the school experiment, other chemical reactions occurred.

ELECTROCHEMICAL ATTACK OF WOOD

Pure water does not conduct electricity well; lake water does slightly better, while salty ocean water is a good conductor—a good electrolyte. When two different metals, such as copper and iron, are immersed in salt water and joined with a pipe, you have a galvanic element. An electric current with a voltage of 0.3 volts (the difference between copper's 0.3 volt and iron's 0.6 volt) passes through the connection, and salt undergoes electrolysis. The more noble metal—copper—becomes the cathode, and the base metal—iron—becomes the anode. During electrolysis, sodium hydroxide, a "caustic soda," is formed at the cathode, and at the anode, chlorine ions are released and unite with the anode metal, which corrodes, and new metal salts are formed.

In a hull that is allowed to take in salt water, the wet wood works as the saline solution in the example from the school experiment, and the caustic precipitation is concentrated in the wood around the copper bolt, and iron ions are formed around the iron bolt. The caustic soda and the ions cause the wood to dissolve. The dissolution is faster on the caustic side.

NAIL SICKNESS

This problem is called nail sickness in England, and is often forgotten in the discussion of corrosion.

I have recently seen severe attacks on mahogany and oak where steel floors and steel frames have been attached with bolts or rivets of copper or copper alloys. It may be that the damage, exacerbated by zinc on steel, increases the voltage difference in the battery. The voltage difference between steel and copper is 0.3 volts, and between zinc and copper it is 0.7 volts. Corrosion damage from the caustic precipitation around the rivet makes the planking soft and porous, and on the surface you will see a white powder. In planking that is only twenty-five years old, I've seen corrosion holes about 1¼" (3 cm) across and 4" (10 cm) along the grain and straight through the planking. It made it easy to stick a knife right through a 1-inch (2.5 cm) plank.

Different woods have different resistances to electrochemical effects. Coniferous wood has greater resistance than deciduous. Among deciduous wood, teak is the most resistant, while mahogany and oak are worse; when it comes to oak, the attacks are also affected by the fact that oak is corrosive to metals—it has a low pH value and contains tannins.

WOOD'S CORROSIVENESS

Most woods contain acids; the most common is acetic acid, which ultimately seems to degrade metal

GALVANIC SUPPLY CHAIN
In reference to ocean water

	VOLTAGE
Titan	+0.06 to –0.05
Stainless A4 (passive)	0.00 to –0.10
Monel 400	
(70% Ni and 30% Cu)	–0.04 to –0.14
Silicon bronze	–0.04 to –0.14
Stainless A2 (passive)	–0.05 to –0.10
Silver	–0.09 to –0.15
Nickel 200	–0.10 to –0.20
Stainless A4 (active)	–0.18 to –0.54
Nickel bronze	
(70% Cu and 30% Ni)	–0.18 to –0.23
Lead	–0.20 to –0.30
Copper (Cu)	–0.30 to –0.40
Brass	–0.30 to –0.40
Tin	–0.31 to –0.33
Aluminum bronze	–0.31 to –0.40
Stainless A2 (active)	–0.46 to –0.58
Cast iron, steel	–0.60 to –0.71
Aluminum alloy	–0.71 to –1.00
Zinc, galvanized steel	–0.98 to –1.03
Magnesium	–1.60 to –1.63

Noble metals–cathodes–protects

Base metals–anode–corrodes

PH-LEVELS IN WOOD

Wood	pH value
Oak	3.35–3.9
Oregon pine	3.45–4.2
Larch	3.45–4.2
Pine	3.45–4.2
Teak	4
Elm	4
Spruce	4.65–5.45
Norway spruce	4.65–5.45
African mahogany	5.1–6.65
Iroko	5.4–7.25

Source: John Keaton/Mersey Side Maritime Museum, 1992.

attachments. Moisture increases corrosiveness. Most woods are, therefore, acidic, i.e., have a low pH.

As usual, when you are looking for context, try to understand by looking at its opposites and properties that counteract each other. Conifers that can withstand electrochemical attacks better cause metal corrosion because of their acidity. Oregon pine is well known for its discoloration with iron because it is corrosive to iron.

CORROSION PROPERTIES OF COMMON METALS

Iron and steel corrode easily; hot galvanization gives a longer life span. For a long time, iron was the most commonly occurring metal on boats and also the biggest source of problems. In older boats and in workboats, they often used forged steel, and it has better corrosion properties than today's commercial steel. If the forged steel bolts were burnt with tar, the result was a corrosion-resistant bolt, which had good properties in relation to wood.

Today, I use mostly stainless steel when iron needs to be replaced during a renovation.

Copper fares well; you rarely encounter bad copper rivets. In the 1950s and 1960s, they used mold protection with copper salts in the wood that corroded the copper rivet; the rivets weakened, and the wood around the rivets became greenish.

Bronze is an alloy of copper and one or more other metals. Bronze alloys of copper and silicon, nickel, or tin are good; magnesium bronze is worst, from a corrosion standpoint.

Brass is an alloy of copper and zinc, usually with 30–50% zinc. Over time, especially in ocean water, zinc and copper leach, and a weakened hollow copper remains. The screw heads come off when the screws are taken out.

Stainless steel has a unique position, and in England it is not recommended underwater in boats because stainless steel appears in two places in the voltage chain: first, as the most noble metal in its passive form, second, between iron and brass in its active form. The passive form is when the stainless steel has a protective oxide layer, which is obtained by polishing. The active form is obtained under the worst conditions for stainless steel, which are a damp, salty, deoxygenated environment, such as keel bolts that are trapped in humid salty wood—no oxide is formed here. The quality of the stainless is important; in Sweden, the quality used is A4 rust-free, acid-free steel with 3% molybdenum interference: SIS 2343. It is the best quality for these conditions. A2, SIS 2333, is used more abroad, but also sometimes here in Sweden.

At a test in England in which stainless steel was left in still-standing salt water 1/64-inch (0.66-mm) corrosion holes were found after 300 days in the A2, while the A4 had an average of 1/128-inch (0.3-mm) holes after 1,500 days. The Baltic Sea's low salinity should not be a problem for stainless steel; on the Swedish west coast, you have to be more attentive.

I recently worked on a forty-five-year-old boat that showed all the signs of electrochemical damage after sailing in saltier waters, but found that the stainless steel wood screws on the bottom, despite some corrosion, were in much better shape than the bronze or brass screws with powdered heads and threads that had corroded away.

Use A4 below the waterline, and on oak A2 can be used underneath glued plugs on the deck.

Aluminum is not a common metal in wooden boats. The metal requires very specialized knowledge to be used safely in corrosive environments. Aluminum masts are the most commonly used, so then the base metal is protected with anodizing.

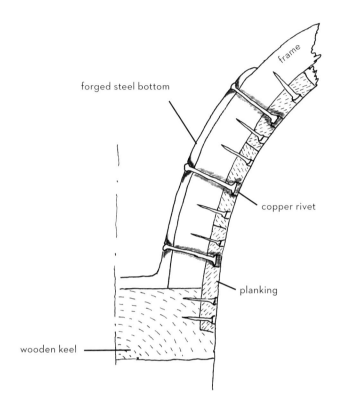

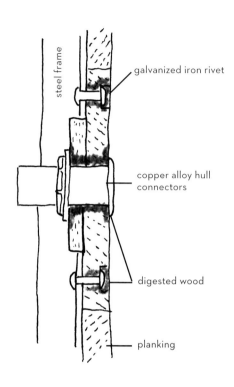

FIGURE 35 } Electrochemical attack on wood when different metals are joined. Moisture has penetrated through the copper rivet and has led to caustic precipitation of the copper rivet, as well as corrosion and iron salt attacks on the steel.

FIGURE 36 } Electrochemical attacks occur even if the metals are not joined. Even though the copper alloy hull connectors and the steel frame with its rivets aren't attached, there are still electrochemical effects when the wood becomes conductive via moisture.

AVOID MIXING METALS

Mixing of different metals should be avoided in order to avoid galvanic problems. During renovations, the appropriateness of using different materials—such as stainless steel screws in galvanized steel frames—is often discussed. But then it is almost impossible to get hold of hot-dip galvanized rivets of good quality, and the remaining galvanization in the ribs is not sufficient to prevent corrosion of the riveted end of the rivets. I think that A4 screws are the best option. If you use different metals together, you need to avoid direct contact by isolating the metals from each other; dip the screw in some kind of sealant and use a nylon washer under the nut.

Furthermore, the oxide layer on the stainless steel results in less galvanic corrosion in stainless steel when coupled to base metals in salt water than what the difference in power potential would allow. Stainless steel is, of course, a much poorer electrical conductor than copper.

Stainless steel in contact with a base metal is also subject to less risk of becoming active and corroding.

The poor conductivity of stainless steel may be one reason that, in practice, there are fewer examples of electrochemical attacks—meaning caustic precipitation on wood—with stainless bolts than with copper bolts.

A test of jointed metals that were placed in salt water shows that there is a potential difference in the voltage chain without stability and conductivity that affects the amount of corrosion.

	Corrosion of steel in mm per year	Difference in voltage according to the galvanic voltage chain
Steel on steel	0.79 mm	0 volts
Steel on stainless	0.91 mm	0.57 volts
Steel on titan	1.07 mm	0.48 volts
Steel on copper	2.54 mm	0.41 volts

Source: Nigel Warren, Metal Corrosion in Boats, 1991.

HOW ARE ELECTROCHEMICAL ATTACKS DISCOVERED?

Keep an eye on the galvanic and the electrolytic effects on surface treatment and wood. The initial signs are the varnish and paint softening and flaking over the copper rivets. When the damage has gone further, the wood whitens and becomes porous and cracks from the plughole. Rusty iron rivets with soft wood around them is also a clear sign. With litmus paper you can also detect the presence of lye and acid, which color the paper blue and red, respectively.

HOW CAN YOU PREVENT THE ATTACKS?

Keep the wood as dry as possible. Good maintenance with a well-oiled bottom and a dense layer of red lead paint or primer prevents moisture penetration. The bottom paint is not very dense and cannot be included in this layer. Touch up any cracks in the paint layer with primer each year.

Make sure the boat is well ventilated; let in air through the vents, and leave all shutters ajar when leaving the boat.

Keep the bilge water at the lowest possible level. Sometimes you may need a float switch for the electric pump.

Replace plugs that are coming undone. If there is a rusty iron rivet underneath then exchange it for a stainless steel bolt and nut at the same time. Glue the new plug with epoxy and allow the plug to be at least ³⁄₁₆″ (5 mm) thick. When boats were first built, rivets and screws on the bottom were often caulked over with putty, but the putty cracked over time. Polyester putty such as Plastic Padding is not very waterproof and should be avoided.

Do not use copper or brass in the steel frame in a renovation. If the boat is built or renovated with copper rivets or brass bolts, then replace them with stainless steel bolts; put the bolt in the sealant or epoxy and glue the plug.

Review the electrical system. Stray currents increase electrochemical attacks greatly. An electrical system in a wooden boat that is exposed to moisture will be safer if it is 2-polar. This means that all appliances that use electricity—everything from light bulbs to the

FIGURE 37 } Corrosion and burns in an eight-year-old stainless steel bolt and crystalline surface fractures of a forty-year-old stainless steel screw.

refrigeration compressor—should have insulated positive and negative wiring; the housing must not be connected to a negative charge. This is in contrast to a car that has negative charge on its body. Often you see discoloration behind old fixtures where the negative charge was on the cover against the wood, and then when the wood gets wet it allows a current to flow when the circuit is closed, and the light is turned on.

Car stereos installed in boats are also a source of problems. For the antenna to work the stereo has to be grounded, but if you use the negative pole as a grounder like on the car, you can get stray currents in the boat if the wood is wet. Electric bilge pumps are also a problem; often the cables that come with the pumps are so short that the joint ends up deep in the boat. There are waterproof connectors, but sometimes regular connectors are used. If the pump gets clogged, the water will rise to the connector and the water will become live until the battery is discharged.

Turn off the main breaker when leaving the boat. Set the electric pump to bypass the main switch.

There is a system called bonding that combines an entire large metal board with a ground wire that is "connected to" a zinc anode on the outside of the hull.

The zinc anode prevents corrosion of the other metals on board, but "if the contacts are broken, through carelessness or oxidation of the couplings, the electrochemical attacks will increase, as the dissimilar metals are no longer connected to the sacrificial anode."

The risk also increases if the boat's power system (usually on the negative side), due to ignorance, is grounded.

FIGURE 38 } Nail sickness in wood from a copper nail in contact with a galvanized bolt in the rib.

For many zinc anodes relative to the need also increases the voltage differences and thereby increase the electrochemical attack on wood.

SUMMARY

Take this with a grain of salt. Boats will not disappear because of electrochemical attacks on wood that result from mixing metals, but their life span decreases. A metal construction or a rail of aluminum, however, under unfortunate circumstances, can corrode and collapse in a relatively short period of time if a proper sacrificial anode is not provided. An increased knowledge of problems with electrochemical attacks allows you to avoid unnecessary mistakes.

TOOLS

In boatbuilding there are some special boatbuilding tools used, along with the usual tools for working wood and metal and for measurement. These tools are not that hard to figure out, but the little accessories—such as counter sinkers and center punches—are often forgotten. You also need tools such as files, whetstones, scrapers, and grinders to maintain the other tools.

When our vintage boats were built, hourly wages were relatively low compared to the cost of materials and tools, but at the shipyards there was an opportunity for carpenters to manufacture many of their own hand tools. Swedish tool steel had a good reputation, and at auctions, people still look for blades and chisels marked with a shark (maker's mark of Erik Anton Berg, Eskilstuna). In order to survive as a carpenter, you had to be able to keep your cutting tools sharp; that also applied to various saws. If a carpenter had accidentally hit a screw so that the blade got dull on the plane, he had to use his spare time to sharpen a new edge.

Cutting down a lot of wood was more time-consuming in the past; lumber was sometimes cut by hand with a handsaw. The first machines were stationary; it was the band saws, planers, and jointers that were belt-driven by a centrally located steam engine or diesel engine. The electrification of the shipyards came relatively late; electrical hand tools came during the 1930s and 1940s to the larger shipyards.

Something that I have a hard time understanding is how boat builders managed to keep their boats fairly clean without a vacuum cleaner; many yards also used linseed oil throughout the construction process. Workers had their own sets of brushes and different shaped feathers from birds' wings to keep the nooks and crannies clean.

TOOLS FOR MAINTENANCE

For the construction of a boat cover stand you will need a hammer and saw. In order for the timber to not deteriorate, it is a good idea to use deck screws on the structure so that you can unscrew the stand in the spring. For this, you need screwdriver bits and a drill with variable speeds. Sanders, scrapers, files, and card scrapers for scraping the wood are discussed in the chapter on scraping the wood bare. Heat guns, vacuum cleaners, and masks are also needed.

The seams of the deck may need to be looked over so that the boat is kept sealed from the top. A simple seam scraper can be made out of an old, worn out file (see Figure 39). For the seam sealants, you need a cartridge gun.

When you scrape the wood bare, you may need to recess the plugs. Forstner drill bits are the best for this. Center punches are used for making a center mark for the drill bit; drifts to knock out rivets and bolts are also high on the list.

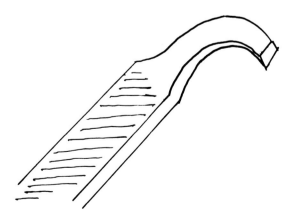

FIGURE 39 } A good seam-scraping hook can be manufactured from an obsolete file. The shaft is bent into a hook, and the tip is sharpened to an edge; the edge is then maintained by filing.

FIGURE 40 }

1 Forstner drill bit, invaluable in renovation and the only appropriate drill bit when old plugholes need to be enlarged. The long peripheral insert gives a nice cut. There are similar branch drills on the market with short peripheral cutting, but they tear old holes and fit better in vertical drilling machines.

2 Plug drill bits for manufacturing plugs. The most common dimensions are: 3/8", 1/2", 5/8", 3/4", 1", 1¼" (10, 12, 15, 18, 20, 25, and 30 mm).

3 The Yacht Association's conical drill bit with a screw enforcer and plug bit. Similar bits exist today, but they won't fit into the standard plugs.

4 Plug sinker for wood, available for 3/8-inch and 1/2-inch (10 and 12 mm) plugs, and for different screw diameters. It is a given variation during new construction or when a screw is used throughout. They produce some plugholes, but I've broken off many points while working with old wood that had hidden holes and broken bolts. Spiral drills can also break, but they are only a fraction of the price.

5 Stanley drill bit, convenient all-in-one bit, along with Stanley's plug bits in different sizes. Is only suitable in soft wood; the holes are too weak for the screw in hard wood such as Brazilian mahogany and oak. If the center bit breaks it can be replaced with a conventional drill bit. This plug bit does not make neat plugs.

TOOLS FOR DISMANTLING

When renovating, you first need demolition tools. A brace with a screwdriver is a must to get stubborn old screws out (see Figure 42). A crowbar is also convenient, as well as a cold chisel and a few rugged screwdrivers. A lump hammer provides more power than a carpenter's hammer. During demolition you can, if you are unlucky, dull several chisels just in one day, and that would require a small bench grinder and a whetstone to save the day.

MEASURING TOOLS

When doing carpentry you need a pencil and measuring tools to be able to measure and transfer the measurements. I have spent a lot of time searching for pencils and rulers at boat clubs when I've lost my own—it's frustrating. A folding ruler and a caliper (for internal use) are basic tools. Calipers are needed to measure screw diameters when drilling dimensions are to be selected. A combination square is great to have for the interior, but on the hull you have more use for a sliding T bevel and maybe a protractor. A level is needed when the boat is set up for the winter. A divider is used to set the dimensions when replacing planks and to take out circles. A compass is used for drawing the amount of wood to remove when fitting. When boatbuilding we use a lot of tools that cannot be bought over the counter, but rather need to be custom-made; for example, a pair of compasses: when fitting planks, you could use a "parallel-plated compass" and when fitting frames and floor boards you might find that a "level compass" could come in handy (see Figure 43).

Some form of straight-edge ruler or straight edge is required in order to draw reference lines. Feeler gauges are good for measuring gaps when you fit planking. A measuring device that I have had a lot of good use for in my work is a digital level; it allows you to measure with lightning speed. If the boat is inclined it allows you to note the incline angle rather than having to straighten the boat. If the boat is leaning 1.4° to port, then all measurements are made with that degree.

CARPENTER TOOLS

Carpenter's tools are largely edge tools—such as axes, chisels, planes, and knives. The axe has pretty much been replaced by the band saw, circular saw, and electric hand planer. The rasp is a nice tool for detailed pieces. You can make your own files with the right kind of shape by gluing on sandpaper on shaped wooden blocks. Hand tools with cord and plug are as much hand tools as those without; the only difference is that you can do more damage in less time with power tools. Electric planes, jigsaws, routers, and rasps facilitate a rough fit; for the more detailed fit, you need a hand plane and a chisel.

FIGURE 41 } Forstner bits: to the left is a Forstner bit with a long edge for cutting; it works to enlarge old plugholes. The one on the right with short edge cutting is hard to use in a hand drill; it fits better in a drill press.

FIGURE 42 } A brace drill with chisel is the best tool to loosen old screws and also to tighten screws during the last assembly of the planking.

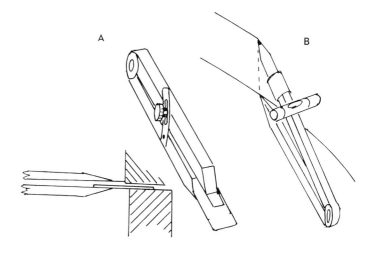

FIGURE 43 }

A A divider used for snug fits in the planking. The plank that is being finished is pushed down so that it is approximately 1/16" (a few millimeters) above the already assembled plank. The underside of the lower lip of the divider is laid flat against the lower edge of the table, and the divider is pressed in so that the upper lip leaves a mark on the upper plank. The procedure is repeated at regular intervals on both the inside and the outside of the plank, after which the edge is planed on the marks.

B A compass with a level is used when the floors are fitted. With the help of the level, all fit measurements are plumb.

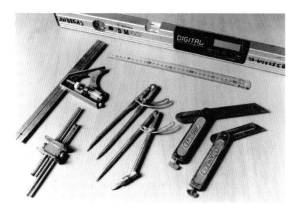

FIGURE 44 } Various measurement tools: digital level, adjustable square, steel ruler, marking gauge, divider and compass, and sliding T bevel—the right one is cut to be used in shallow rabbets.

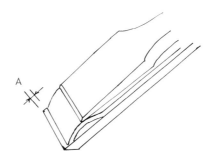

FIGURE 45 } Blade, chip breaker, or flap and wedge. Chip breaker close to the edge affects how easily the plane moves and how much it planes in more textured wood. The distance A may be varied between 1/64 and 1/16" (0.5 to 2 mm).

FIGURE 46 } With a slightly rounded blade you can choose how the edge of a plank is tilted by using one or the other edge of the blade. The corners of the blade won't make streaks in the wood either. The curvature is somewhat exaggerated in the picture.

Planes

The smoothing plane is made of iron. There is quite a difference in quality between inexpensive and expensive planes. With a better cast the material dimensions, and thus the weight, are reduced; a corrugated sole provides easier planing with less friction against the surface. The blade and the chip breaker are held in place with the wedge. The distance between the chip breaker and the cutter steel blades can be varied (see Figure 45). If the wood is straight-grained and readily planed, the distance is increased, resulting in lower power requirements. If the wood is more textured, the distance will shrink so that the chips will break and won't pull more fibers from the surface of the wood; planing then becomes heavier.

One trick when using a plane is to grind the steel so that it gets a little rounded and therefore cuts slightly deeper in the middle of the plane. This reduces the risk of the corners of the steel cutting into the wood and scratching it. When a piece of wood needs to change angles then the position of the plane will determine which edge is planed the most. This method is used, for example, when planing the plank edges of caravel planking (see Figure 46). This kind of shaving is also used to get glue joints tight at the edges. The plane will shave a few extra chips in the middle of the seam so that it has a tendency to become concave.

The shoulder plane is plane number two on the list. A shoulder plane blade goes all the way to the side and is used for folding and planing in corners. A shoulder plane is also used to clean up old plank edges when replacing planks. It is tight next to the frames, and thus the shoulder plane has a bad reputation among boatbuilders and is correctly called the knuckle killer.

When smoothing out the sheer of the covering board and the railing, a long jointers plane is the best tool. With a short plane you can shave along a line, but with a properly-set long iron plane it will be much straighter. You can often tell if there is an amateur or an expert boatbuilder who has used the plane, depending on how far the blade is sticking out (under the sole). The amateur's steel sticks out further; it becomes a plane to dig holes or make ski slopes with. If you want to plane straight, the sole needs to rest firmly on the wood along almost its entire length.

A flat face spoke shave is used for the frame and other concave areas.

Wood planes have an advantage in which you can have different planes, shaped soles, and blades, for different purposes. Useful wood planes are bowl planes with different radii for smoothing the planking in the keel and for shaving the curves in the rudder bows. The opposite is the mast-shaping plane, which is concave; a mast plane with the right radius easily creates a round mast.

Planes that are convex in the longitudinal direction are used, for example, for the underside of the deck beams.

There is a special plane for boatbuilding that is convex on the sole as well as on the other side (see Figure 47).

There is an iron plane with a flexible sole called a circular plane, which is used in boatbuilding (see Figure 48).

The right tool for coarse planing is an electric planer; it shapes the pieces of wood quickly, but for the last bit I always use a hand plane. There are two main types of planers: the heavier planers with long soles and the shorter and lighter planers. If choosing a planer for something other than shipbuilding, then the shorter one would be the one to get. Make sure that you set it so that you do not get all the chips in your face.

If an electric motor is to last it needs to be set on the speed at which it is the strongest; a planer should thus be revved up to full speed before you begin using it.

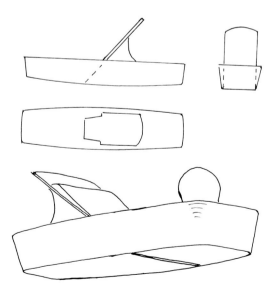

FIGURE 47 } A special boatbuilding plane that is convex in both the sole and the side. Its sloping edges of steel work as a regular shoulder blade. It is used with ordinary shoulder planes for shaping rabbets. If the shape of the hole is very skewed then a sharp hardwood floor scraper will come in handy.

FIGURE 48 } An electrical hand planer with unlimited cutting depth. The cutter head is stored only on one edge, so there is nothing sticking out on the other side. It makes it a good planer for rabbets. The finishing planer is a good all-around planer. The iron shoulder plane is used for corners. The wood shoulder plane is good for rabbets. The adjustable circular plane is a boatbuilding tool. The bowl plane and the mast-cutting plane provide concave and convex surfaces. A spoke shave is great for frames.

Chisels

Sharpening of chisels is described in the chapter *Plugging and Filling in Smaller Damages*. It's hard to keep the blade sharp when working on renovations; old finish slows you down, and nails and screws cause notches. Japanese chisels have a good reputation; they are made out of a fine steel blade, and the handle is designed so that they can lie flat on the work piece. But it hurts the craftsman when he chips one. You need a few simple chisels: 1 ¼-, ¾-, and ⅜-inch (30-, 20-, and 10-mm) widths are useful.

Saws

I do most of the rough sawing with a jigsaw; a good jigsaw can cut through 2″ (50 mm) of thick wood.

The hand saw is mainly used for finer cuts; in recent years I have come to prefer the Japanese pull saws. A pull saw, as the name implies, is pulled toward you when you saw, while a traditional saw cuts when pressed away from you. A pull saw can be made thinner, as it stretches and straightens out as it cuts. Japanese saws are available with or without a back.

The circular saw I use mostly when cutting with a guide—such as a fence, rib, or ruler. The blade can be angled to the sole of the saw so that it can be used to roughly cut the rabbet. Larger timber is roughly shaped with an electric or gasoline-powered chainsaw.

Clamps

Clamps are a constant scarcity. Many procedures require a large number of clamps to work—for example, when gluing laminates for the frame. There are no decent shortcuts to use instead of clamps; however, there are ways of getting around them when they are missing. Different systems with wedges, props, and jacks can be developed. When working with plywood, you can use regular staples.

FIGURE 49 } Chisels and a Japanese pull saw, scraper, hardwood floor scraper, Sandvik's paint scraper with replaceable carbide blades, mill saw file.

OTHER ELECTRIC TOOLS

These days, drills are combined drills and screwdrivers. The ability to tighten screws with a machine saves a carpenter's wrists, injuries to which used to be a common problem. To tighten screws with the precision required, the drill needs to have variable speeds and lots of torque—it is strong at low speed. A machine with around 400 watts with full speed at 1000 RPM is strong enough for screwdriving and drilling steel at low revs, as well as for plug drilling when the revs need to be high to keep the hole edges nice. If you use a drill with a keyless chuck once, you will never want to use keyed chuck again.

Today, there are convenient and powerful cordless drills, but the batteries are expensive and tend to be uncharged when you need them. The effect wears off in the cold. Charging cannot take place outdoors in the cold, and then the battery may be damaged. The batteries should not go too long without being used.

A router can be used for a lot of things. But we have a saying: "It is just a cut," meaning that in reality, things are not as easy as you may think. There are a lot of adjustments with guide plates and allowances and different cutting lengths and diameters needed before you are ready to actually cut. Sometimes it's tempting to get the chisel and the plane instead, but the router is a versatile tool. With a ball-bearing ogee cutter, you can make anything, from breaking edges (rounding off a sharp corner) to cutting handrails. A ball-bearing template bit is used when more copies will be made after the same template. A straight router bit and a ruler are used when the bead and groove need to be routed, or when an edge needs to be aligned for gluing. We also use the router for cutting plugs and to cut excess of splines when splining.

The belt sander is a sander with a narrow band that rotates over a nose wheel—with the wheel you can make various curves, and with the flat side you can easily trim out a shape from a line. The Multi-Tool (Fein was first and has set the standard) is useful for many purposes. The saw blade may cut deck beams for beam stringers, where it works as a chisel. Another blade is great for sawing the edge between the cabin and deck sealing. The seam hook will remove old rubber splining when you need to replace it. The flat blade will cut the rubber under canvas and hardware.

FIXED MACHINES

The main difference between the amateur and the professional boatbuilder is probably that the builder is able to rapidly produce his material with good dimensional accuracy using saws and planers and jointers. A band saw quickly transforms a shapeless block of wood into a piece of deadwood if there are good templates. These are services that the amateur may need to pay for. Good measurements and good templates are everything for this to work.

TOOLS FOR WORKING WITH STEEL AND METAL

If the renovator tries to get along with only carpentry skills, he won't get very far. Rivets, screws, and bolts hold boats together. The body may contain steel frames, steel floors, and steel knees. The angle grinder is a tool that is effective in both cutting and grinding, but it is almost banned from construction sites due to fire hazards. Make sure it is clean of dust and debris and do not use it during the last hours before you leave the boat. Metal cutting drills are the same as chisels and need to be sharpened. A rod with welded heads and handmade threads creates the long bolts that are required when the backbone is to be assembled. Many mounts and clamps for accessories and the boat's steering should be welded together using steel. Steel floors are both welded and bolted when first made. Boats should have tracks, rubrails and bowrails replaced. A stand for the drill provides more power for drilling steel. A vise that is secure is essential to be able to bend and shape metal.

FIGURE 50 } If you are going to get anywhere with screws that are stuck, you have to have sharp edges on your screwdriver, preferably with a little hook.

Threading tools are good when you are working on stubborn nuts and bolts.

Today, most boats have motors and many other facilities, and in order to not be left bewildered on the water, you need mechanic tools. Fixed wrenches are also needed to pull nuts during renovations. The M6 nut should be drawn with the 10 key, M8 with 13, M10 with the 16 (17) and M12 with 18 (19). A socket wrench is useful for many purposes; it is used with an extension rod for bolt replacements. Screwdrivers are more specialized than many people know. Screws easily become impossible if you go at them with the wrong screwdriver. Phillips screwdrivers are easily ruined; it is difficult to sharpen a frayed Phillips screwdriver. Slotted screwdrivers should be maintained as carefully as chisels.

Tools Available at All Times

One toolbox is my carpenter's pants; there are some things that I always carry with me. In my pockets I have the following:

- a ballpoint pen, a marker, and a pencil
- a folding ruler
- a 6-inch (15-cm) long steel gauge
- a screwdriver with two slotted bits and two Phillips bits
- an adjustable wrench
- a card scraper
- sandpaper
- center punch
- countersink
- bits for drilling
- ⅛″ and 3⁄16″ (4 and 5 mm) twist drill bits, extra long
- 1⅜″ (35 mm) brad nails (nails with a small head)

SUMMARY

Tools that are specific to wooden boatbuilding may need to be specially manufactured. It is entirely according to tradition, as the old-time boatbuilders made many of their tools themselves. Renovations require robust tools; wood contains many surprises in the form of nails and screws. Sharp tools quickly become useless without a grinder, a mill saw file, and a whetstone.

Electrical hand tools facilitate coarse cutting and screw driving, but it is not less of a handicraft just because there is a cord at the end of the machine. If you do not master the craft, you can do more damage in less time with electric machines.

For major renovations, different gauges and measuring devices take up a lot of space in the toolbox.

FIGURE 51 } The belt sander (Makita's belt sander) is a practical tool for polishing wood and grinding in templates.

PLUGGING AND FILLING IN SMALLER DAMAGES

All damages are not major. Sometimes the damage is just a local discoloration, a little rot, a dent, or a scratch. To repair this kind of damage, it takes a little bit of carving, some intarsia, some inlay work, some patience, and sharp tools. But there is great satisfaction when restorations are well done.

PLUGGING

The smallest damages can be plugged. I usually use a plug on damages up to 1 or 1 ¼" (25–30 mm) in diameter. If you have purchased an old wooden boat that requires maintenance, you will need at least a ½" and a ⅝" (12 and

15-mm) plug drill bit. You can buy plugs or you can get together with some boating friends to purchase the more expensive plug cutter bits.

PROCEDURE FOR PLUGGING

Start by drilling a hole with the correct diameter through a piece of plywood or MDF. Then use the piece as a guide for the drill. You always need that control if the damage is so deep that the center point of the drill cannot go straight into the wood. Drill the hole at least ³⁄₁₆" (5 mm) deep. Glue a plug with epoxy; make sure the grain direction of the plug is the same as that of the wood around it.

52

53

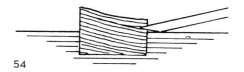

54

FIGURE 52 } Drilling the plughole. Plug-hole drilling with Forstner drill bits. Using a piece of MDF or a thin piece of wood with pre-drilled holes to provide good guidance for the Forstner bit when old holes are being enlarged. The uneven grid of the MDF also provides a good friction against the surface underneath. For more about the drills, see Chapter 10 on tools.

FIGURES 53 & 54 } Wood plugs. In order for the plug socket to work easily and not get hot, and for the chips not to stick, the plug is drilled out of a strip of wood rather than from a larger piece of wood. About ¹⁄₃₂" (a millimeter) of wood is left on the bottom so that the plug remains on the strip but can easily be broken off. In the break-off section, you can also see how

the fibers go in the plug and in what direction to cut it off; see Figure 54. Softer woods, such as pine, have to be drilled out of wood with vertical growth rings, otherwise the plug gets spongy and will swell out of the hole when it gets moist, or it will break off as it's plugged in.

Many people prefer to put the plug in the varnish, but it requires a deeper plughole for the plug to stay in, and when you stain it, the stain can discolor the edges of the plug.

Plugging Screw Holes

Plugging screw holes when replacing planks and similar tasks are quite time-consuming procedures. If you use glue when you screw, then you need to put the plug in before the glue has hardened, as the edges of the holes are easily filled with hardened glue. For a nice looking plug, you should plug before smoothing the wood; it is an advantage to have a ⅟₃₂″ (a millimeter) of wood to smooth off if there's some residue from the drill that sticks to the edge. Choosing a good wood for the plugs is important and will take longer than drilling them. The straightness of the grain will determine how easy it will be to cut the plug off nicely. The plugs must be drilled with the plug drill bit mounted in a drill press because the plug drill bit has no center control. When the plugs are cut, break them off from the remaining wooden strip. Put plugs on a paper plate with a thin layer of thickened glue so they get wet. Then you just pick up one plug at a time and tap it in into the holes.

Old plugholes are enlarged so they get neat edges; a piece of MDF to control it is necessary for this.

The most common drill bit sizes are ⅜″, ½″, ⅝″, ¾″, 1″, and 1¼″ (10, 12, 15, 18, 20, 25, and 30 mm). The depth of the plughole should be ⅓ of the plank's thickness but doesn't need to be more than ⅕″ (5 mm).

BUNGS

An inset of new wood is usually called a bung. The bung can be made in the shape of a rhombus or a diamond.

A cross wood end is more visible and will not glue as well as one that's on the diagonal. A strong adhesive joint requires an inclination in relation to the grain direction of at least 1 to 5 mm. If the fill is only partially made through the planking, the bung will get a larger adhesive surface on the flat bottom of the hole and thus become

FIGURE 56 } Router with a copying ring and router templates of plywood. The hole in this case will be ⅟₁₆″ (2 mm) smaller than the template and will end with a rounding of the router steel's diameter.

stronger and the angle relative to the direction of the fibers can be made steeper.

If the boat has many damages and you have access to a router, then you can make a router template of plywood, and the bungs can be cut out using a copying ring.

If the bung is done with hand tools, you will need a chisel, a saw, a plane, a ruler, and a whetstone. A sharp edge tool requires a good sharpener. I sharpen my edge tools on a bench grinder without water. It is easier to burn the edge with this method than with a wet grinding stone, so you have to use a light hand. Honing is done on the fine side of an oilstone; the oil can be purchased as honing oil or as a mixture of lubricating oil and kerosene.

When sharpening, the chisel is moved over the stone in a uniform circular motion with the sharp edge shaving toward the stone. During the grinding and sharpening, a raw edge gets folded over toward the flat side. You hone that off gently with the flat side lying flat on the whetstone. It is important that the flat side does not get rounded, as it will ruin the chisel.

PROCEDURE FOR FILLING IN WITH NEW WOOD

1 Draw a rhombus or diamond so that the contour covers the damage.

FIGURE 55 } Diamond (hexagon) and rhombus. Draw the outline so that the bung will be as low as possible and cut off a minimum of grains.

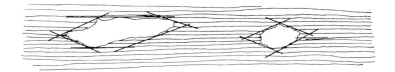

FIGURE 57 } Sharpening on an oilstone. The chisel is moved with the sharp side flat against the stone with an even rotating motion.

2   Measure the shape of the rhombus and cut it out of paper. Take the paper and fit it around the damage; attach the piece of paper with a pair of thumbtacks and mark out the grain direction and structure on the paper.

3   Remove the piece of paper and place it on the wood used for the bung in such a way that the grain and texture resembles it as closely as possible. Notes on timber choice: a piece of mahogany that is relatively fresh and has not been exposed to the sun will retain its dark red color much longer than the timber in the boat. Especially bung timber of Brazilian mahogany should be chosen much lighter than you might think. The bung timber should have a thickness of about one and a half to two times the depth of the hole.

4   Cut out the bung with a jigsaw or a good handsaw; Japanese saws make nice cuts. Shave the edges with a little clearance angle—1/64″ (half a millimeter) per 3/″ (a centimeter) thickness.

5   Hold the bung over the hole in the plank and mark around the bung's edges with a chisel. The streak mark of a chisel is more precise than a pen or pencil. Thus it is your finished bung that determines the final shape of the hole.

6   Chisel out from the center of the hole and out toward your marks; flatten the bottom out before the outer edges are finished. Sharpen the chisel when needed. Tap on the chisel with a hammer or preferably a wooden mallet when doing the rough work. Fine chiseling is done by hand. The depth of the hole should be at least 3/16″ (5 mm).

7   Try the bung out; it should fit but not fall into the hole because of the clearance angle. If the edges of the hole are straight and nice, then shave the bung gently with the plane instead. You get more chances; if the bung is a little slack when it reaches the bottom, it can be planed underneath. The clearance angle allows it to get wider again.

8   Glue the bung in. Make sure that the wood is warm enough so that the epoxy wets it and penetrates the wood thoroughly. Keep the temperature between 59 and 68°F (15–20°C) when hardening.

9   Shave off the surplus off and scrape the surface. Let the surface of the bung adapt to the humidity of the new environment for a few weeks, or moisten the surface with water to get the grains to rise before the finishing smoothing. The surrounding varnish does not need to get scraped off; it is sufficient if it is matted down.

SUMMARY

When choosing timber for plugs and bungs, you need to use very high quality timber. Straight-grained timber increases performance and shortens the labor time significantly.

I always glue the plug, and I like to use glued plugs rather than wood putty when attaching to the bottom of boats. It is easier to evenly clean plugs than wood putty.

Remember to weaken the structure as little as possible by cutting as few fibers with the grain as possible when putting in plugs and bungs.

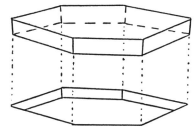

FIGURE 59 } Bung with clearance angles ready to be tried out in the hole. The bung has a thickness of twice the depth of the hole.

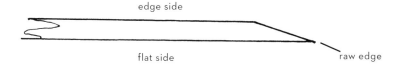

edge side

flat side

raw edge

FIGURE 58 } Raw edge. When sharpening, a raw edge folds over the flat side. It is gently removed with the flat side resting on the stone. For the chisel to work well, it is important that the flat side actually remains flat.

JOINTS

When two pieces of wood are spliced together in the longitudinal direction, this is called a joint. Joints can be formed in various ways. The most common are:

- Butt joints, when end grain faces end grain. The pieces are spliced with a backing block.
- Scarf joint, when the pieces are spliced together in the direction of its length. The joint can be either riveted or glued.
- Spliced joint, when the pieces are attached on the edge. The joint is glued.
- Key locked scarf joint with nibs, used for bows and garboards. The joint is bolted together.

This chapter is about plank joints. The key locked scarf joint with nibs is covered in the chapter on keels.

FIGURE 60 }

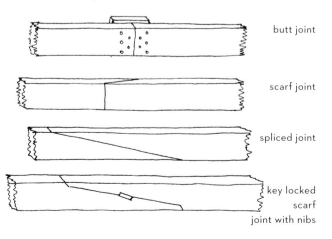

butt joint

scarf joint

spliced joint

key locked
scarf
joint with nibs

JOINTS OFTEN TAKE A BEATING FIRST

On our boats, it is often the joints that first show signs of age deterioration. Thus planking can be completely intact except near the joints. Typical examples are:

A butt joint where moisture has penetrated into the plank joint and condensation has formed between the backing block of galvanized steel and the planks. The galvanization has been sacrificed, the steel has rusted, the wood has frozen apart, and the plugs have released. This is very common on older boats; the backing block of galvanized steel was probably the most common block on carvel-built boats in Sweden up till the 1940s.

A scarf joint where the gluing has released; the varnish will also release here every year, and the wood will become discolored. Sometimes, the gap is so large that it is possible to stick a hacksaw blade through the joint and straight into the boat. This kind of damage is common in Folkboats.

A spliced joint on a varnished topside that sun has dried apart and that has been discolored by moisture penetration. The spliced joint is visible as a darker streak diagonally across the planking. Common on varnished Laurin Kosters.

END GRAIN SUCKS UP MOISTURE

In a butt joint, the wood's grain is cut so that the end wood is exposed. End grain absorbs moisture through the cells that once transported nutrition and water in the living tree. The channels then work like a straw for moisture. Good fittings and tight joints minimize moisture penetration through the end wood. Oiling or

SPACING OF BUTTS

There are rules for the spacing of butts. The most common (such as Lloyd's and the Square Meter Rule) indicates 47″ (1200 mm) in between joints in adjoining planks, 31″ (800 mm) if there's a planking in between. Three planks need to be in between for butts in the same frame section. In the bow and stern, you may make some smaller modifications.

The thickness of the wood backing block should be the same as the thickness of the planking.

The thickness of the metal backing block should be a ⅙ of the planking.

When gluing wood joints, the splice should be five times as long (along the grain) as it is wide (across the grain).

gluing also prevents moisture from entering, and long timber lengths reduce the number of joints.

WEAR AND TEAR

Caring for wooden boats is something of a ritual: we deny destruction that time wreaks on matter. If a boat is maintained carefully, it is expected to keep forever. That's not the case. How much time it will take before old age takes its toll depends on the boat's quality and the owner's skill and interest. This is also what determines the size of repairs. A diligent owner will notice that the paint is flaking from the joints and that some plugs are coming undone. He changes the backing block and rivets and seals between the planking and the backing block before the planking is destroyed. Another owner might be standing with a rusty backing block in one hand one day and two fractured planks in the other hand with water seeping through the next day. How do you fix it then?

If you want the boat to live on with as many original parts as possible, you may not need to replace the whole planking, but just fixing the joints might be more appropriate.

The methods of mending vary with knowledge, finances, and ambition, anywhere from a lead sheet on the outside, via epoxy and glass cloth, to routing bad wood and gluing in a spliced joint.

VARIOUS JOINTS

Butt joint with wooden backing block. (Figure 61) The backing block should have the same thickness as the planking. The grain direction of the backing block should be the same as the planking. The backing block should not lie against the ribs and suck moisture, but you should be able to surface treat in between the ribs and the backing block (see A).

The backing block should overlap the adjoining planks (see B); in the long run, backing blocks that are riveted onto the plank will perform better.

The backing block should preferably be riveted with copper rivets, but wood screws or machine-threaded screws and nuts are also common.

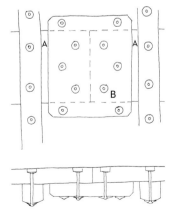

FIGURE 61 } Butt joint with a wooden backing block.

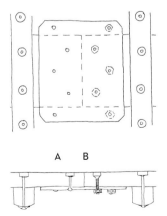

FIGURE 62 } Butt joint with a metal backing block.

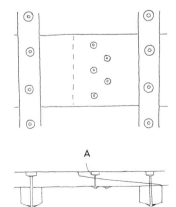

FIGURE 63 } Riveted scarf joint.

Butt joint with a metal backing block. (Figure 62) On older backing blocks, the metal of the block is made of galvanized steel or brass; today they also use stainless steel. The joint is shown with rivets as in A, and with screws and nuts as in B. For brass blocks you use copper rivets, and for stainless steel blocks you use stainless steel screws and bolts. The thickness of the backing block should be a ⅙ of the thickness of the planking.

Riveted scarf joint. (Figure 63) Common on older boats and clinker-built boats. Most of the time it was sealed with putty made of linseed oil and chalk, which dries over the years. The wood under the rivet head is often so thin that the plank has burst here, see A.

JOINT REPAIR
Repairing a Butt Joint
Replacing the backing block and replugging it can save a joint where the wood of the planks is in good condition. A stainless steel block can be used. It has to be hammered or bent so that it is flush against the planking without any space in between. Drill it into the old holes and fasten with a sealant of some kind, like a gum paste such as Sikaflex. Silicone is not used for repairing wooden boats. Adhesives are not used for the metal blocks, as it is difficult to obtain a permanent adhesion between the metal and the adhesive.

If you use a wooden block instead, it may be made of solid wood or plywood (see Figure 64A). You may want to glue it in order to strengthen the planking by the joint (if the planking is made of oak, the block should also be made of oak in the same grain direction and mounted with an elastic sealant). The backing block should be shaped to fit inside the planking and glued in place. The rivet holes should be plugged with larger plugs to get some good wood in the holes. See Chapter 15 on steel frames for a more detailed description. When you glue, hold the block in place with a pair of screws from the inside. When the adhesive has hardened, rivet the block and plug it (see Figure 64B). Note that end wood on the edges of the plywood block must be sealed with glue.

Repairing a Bad Butt Joint with Epoxy
This repair is to be regarded more as a temporary repair pending a future replacement of the planks rather than as a renovation (see Figure 65).

A A rusty backing block of steel with rusty rivets. The steel begins to corrode on the side facing the planking. This forms clumps of rust; the rust takes up more space, so the block can increase in thickness as much as $3/32''$ to $3/8''$ (3 mm to 10 mm); this allows the rivet heads to draw further into the wood and the plank ends to split. Then water can move freely in, and the wood will freeze apart.

B Remove the block, wood chips, and the most damaged wood and wipe out the soda.

C Soak it in unthickened epoxy; using heat if necessary, fill with epoxy putty and filler.

D Even with a sanding disc and glue and an epoxy-soaked backing block of plywood on the inside, make sure it is properly filled with glue. Hold the block in place with screws while hardening. If the wood is really bad, you can put a piece of fiberglass in the epoxy on the outside and fill evenly.

Repairing a Glued Scarf Joint
If the scarf joint has started to release, you need to cut it along it with a hacksaw blade. Wash the joint with acetone. Fill it with glue, either with a syringe or a trowel. Put a piece of plywood coated with plastic wrap on each side of the planking to keep the seam tight during the hardening process; choose a piece so thin that it will

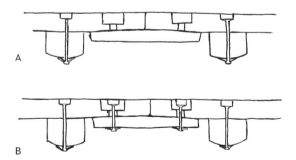

FIGURE 64 } Replacement of a wooden backing block.

A The replugging is done, and the block is glued.

B The block is riveted when the adhesives have hardened.

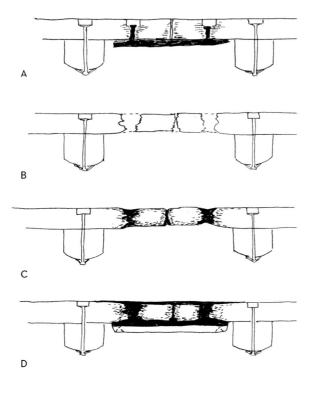

A

B

C

D

FIGURE 65 } Repairing a bad butt joint with epoxy.

shape itself to the planking, or use narrower strips. Screw the plywood with screws and bolts during gluing, then remove the nut and bolts and the plywood and plug the holes afterward (see Figure 66).

Repairing a Glued Spliced Joint

A spliced joint where the glue has released could be splined. However, it is difficult to make an invisible repair

FIGURE 66 } Repair of a glued scarf joint.

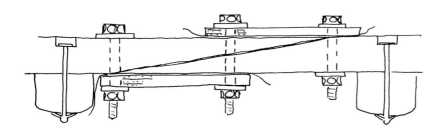

on a varnished topsides. One way to make a discreet repair is to cut the spline out on the diagonal from a piece of wood so that the direction of the grain corresponds with the grain of the planks. Be attentive to concealed screws (see Figure 67). These screws or nails were used to fix the tips during the planking process.

REPAIRING BY REPLACING WOOD

A nicer way to fix bad wood in joints is to cut away the butt joints and replace it with new wood. I think you have better control of glued joints with spliced joints. If the glued joint is to keep, it has to be at least a minimum of five times as long as it is wide (see Figures 67 to 69).

PATCHWORK

A disadvantage with spliced joints is that if the planks are wide—for example 8″ (20 cm)—the joint will be $(8″ \times 5) + 8″ + (8″ \times 5) = 88″$ ([20 cm $\times$ 5] + 20 cm + [20 cm $\times$ 5] = 220 cm). If you have a lot of joints that need replacing, the hull will look completely chopped up by joints, and it will make it harder in the future to replace planks with regular joint spacing.

SUMMARY

I prefer spliced joints if the plank ends need to be replaced; you have good control of the fitting, and the joint can be inspected both from the exterior and the interior.

Sometimes you can see examples of poor repairs with spliced joints. The reason is usually that the joints are too short (fewer than one out of three) and that the joints are sealed with an elastic sealant instead of glue. The rubber seams move with time, and the wood moves in relation to itself.

Another variation you see sometimes, but that I do not usually use, is the method with a new short piece of plank with two butt joints with blocks on each side of the place where the old the block was. The short plank piece weakens the planking and creates a cluttered look with multiple pieces so close together on the inside. Scarf joints are sometimes used, but it is difficult to control the fit of the scarf joint and difficult to screw scarf joints well.

With new construction of a boat today, I would use glued planking with spliced joints.

FIGURE 71 } The backing block is cut out, the butt joint is moved to the right of the frame, the plank has a spliced joint to the left.

FIGURE 72 } Nailing of the guide bar for the router.

FIGURE 73 } Routing of the plank edge with a router; in this case, the hole has first been roughly cut with a circular saw. The edges can then be cut with a router blade with a large radius that provides smoother cutting surfaces. If you cut the hole directly with the router, use a blade with a smaller radius, which does not require the same amount of force for cutting, but the surfaces will be more uneven.

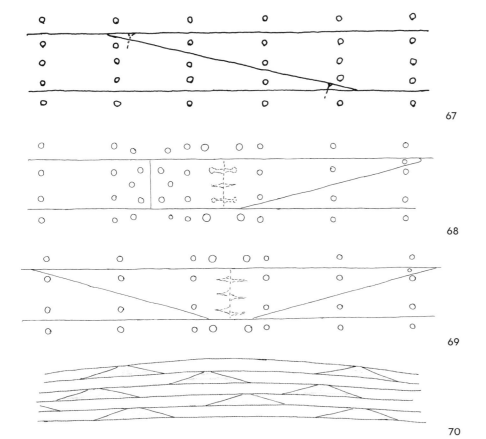

67

68

69

70

FIGURE 67 } Glued spliced joint.

FIGURE 68 } Replacing a joint with a spliced joint in one direction and an offset butt joint in the other. Here, the butt joint is moved to the next section on the left of the frame and the spliced joint is on the right. This joint approach preserves the boat's original structure with backing blocks. The tip of the spliced joint can either be kept as a tip or rounded off.

FIGURE 69 } Replacing joints with spliced joints in both directions. The advantage of this method is that there is no need for backing blocks. This can be a time-efficient way to renovate if combined with splining. In that case, you can concentrate on the fit of spliced joints. Plank edges are sealed by splining.

FIGURE 70 } Patchwork.

SPLINING

Splining is still a somewhat controversial method for giving old boats their original strength back. The procedure can't be undone; a failed splining is a serious deterioration and depreciation. This chapter is divided into two parts; in the first, I try to provide answers to common questions about splining; the second consists of a gradual description of the process.

METHODS FOR PLANKING ON CARVEL-BUILT BOATS

Until World War II, most boats were built without glue in between the planks. Working boats and some pleasure boats were built with a gap between the planks on the outside; this gap was then caulked with Oakum or yarn so the boat would be tight, but also so that it would get stiff and so that the planks would not rub against each other. As the hull opened up, the caulking was driven in further; this

could be repeated several times if necessary. The caulking used was tar Oakum of flax or cotton yarn.

Pleasure boats were built with a cotton yarn sandwiched between the planks before they were put together. Sometimes the yarn was set into a small incision in the board; sometimes it was tacked with small iron tacks, then linseed oil putty was applied to the planks, and thus the yarn and the planks were put together.

Planking on steel frames was done with only linseed oil in between—wedged tightly with the help of wedges and steel brackets that were moved up along the steel frame.

After World War II, boats were glued; thus hulls became denser and stronger and could be built lighter.

THE PRINCIPLE OF SPLINING

Unglued planking makes the planks shift in relation to each other when subject to bending, while glued planking behaves as a homogeneous panel and therefore is much sturdier.

If the boats were long and thin, the hull would eventually deform by planks sliding in relation to each other, either on dry land when the planks had dried apart and the boat had been set up incorrectly on a stand, or under heavy load while sailing. The boats then demanded more maintenance as the paint cracked along the seams every year. Slender motor yachts and Skerry cruisers had their paint crack along the seams when they where lifted into the water in the spring.

When the interest in old wooden boats rose in the 1960s, there were attempts to get old, tired hulls in shape by splining. Lars Bergström's and Sven Ridder's articles in the magazine *Till Rors* (At the Helm) on the splining of the 95 m² *Britt Marie* became an inspiration for many.

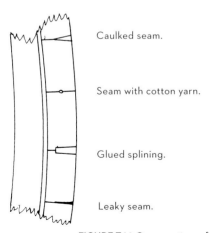

Caulked seam.

Seam with cotton yarn.

Glued splining.

Leaky seam.

FIGURE 74 } Cross sections of various seams.

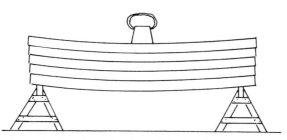

On unglued planking, the planks shift when bent.

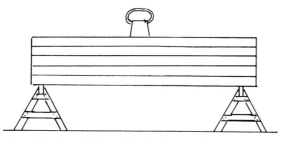

Glued planking will absorb the bending as a homogeneous plate.

FIGURE 75}

FIGURE 76 } Cutting grooves with a circular saw equipped with a conic scored blade. Sawing is controlled by using a guide attached with nails. The seam above is already sawn up. Once you have strips that fit, you can cut several tracks at once, but if the strips are too hard, the planks will be displaced when the strips are driven in and the last traces will become too thin.

The splining is done by sawing the joint in between the planks with a saw blade or circular saw or by routing it to a depth of ¾ of the thickness of the planking. The groove is cut with the help of a guide strip. The incision should be so wide that no old joint surfaces remain. The groove is preferably tapered and a strip shaped as the cut is glued in to the seam.

WHICH BOATS CAN BE SPLINED?

Mahogany boats with steel frames or laminate-glued wood frames are most suitable for splining. It is also possible to spline mahogany boats with bent frames and pine boats with steel frames. Pine boats with only bent frames and oak boats are not suitable for splining.

The boats that were built after the war were glued with carbamide glues, and now after forty or fifty years the glue is beginning to give up; it looks like dust in the seams. Well-maintained boats survive the longest. When glue seam cracks, the seam should be seam-glued. First of all, the entire structure depends on the hull being glued, and also on the wood in the seam not being surface-treated to resist moisture and rot.

UNDER WHAT CIRCUMSTANCES CAN SEAMS BE SPLINED?

The planking should have a moisture percentage between 13 and 15% for glue to work and so that movements of the wood during drying and swelling aren't too great.

The hull and the space where the gluing takes place must be at least 53°F (12°C) during bonding and hardening. For boats that are usually placed outside under a tarp in the winter, the best time for splining is from May to June, as it is often dry and warm then. Sometimes you may want to launch and let the topsides dry in the sun and then take the boat up and spline seams on land when the air temperature is high enough for successful bonding. If the boat is indoors in a heated room, the splining can be done when the hull becomes moderately dry. The hull needs to be so dry after the splining that it can stand on land during the winter without experiencing tensile stress in the planking. Wood is much less able to withstand tensile stress than pressure across the grain. A mahogany hull, which is dimensionally more stable than a pine hull, could probably be left on land over the summer as well, but a seam-splined pine hull can crack hard if left on shore for the summer.

A splining is preferably done the year before you plan to scrape the boat clean. After the splining, do a rough smoothing and surface treatment of the strips. Then launch the boat and use it as you normally would. For the seam strips, use dry wood, and the result is best if it can reach the same moisture level as the hull during the summer. Otherwise, the result of a consecutive clean scrape, splining, and smoothing can be that the strips swell afterward and that you sand into the strips the next year; then you will be caught in a vicious cycle in which the partially scraped strips swell further and the same story repeats itself again the following year.

CAN THE FRAMES BE TORN APART WHEN THE PLANKS SWELL?

Yes, there is a risk of that, and there is also the risk that the planks are pushed out from the frames at the bilge. An inspection of bolted and riveted joints and a mending of broken frames should precede splining. On round-bottomed boats, it is common for the planking to already have released from the steel frame from amidships and the aft in the area where the radius is small (see Figure 78). Sometimes the gaps are so large that rivet heads are drawn in through the planking and are visible on the inside; in that case, the plugs are the only things that prevent the boat from leaking. In this case, a splining can cause the over-bent wooden frames to break as well, which will weaken the planking completely. The easiest way to repair such damage is to remove the rivets and mend the planking by gluing in double plugs, fill the gap between the steel frame and the planking with epoxy filler, and finally refasten the frames and planks with longer screws. You cannot pull the planking to the steel frame as the wood frame will be so deformed that the hull will then be embossed. If the hull is to regain its original shape, you need to replace the wood frame as well.

Mahogany boats on steel frames or laminate-glued frames can usually stand one splining of both the topside and the bottom at the same time. A pine boat with steel frames can withstand a gluing of the topsides. If the bottom is to be splined, it should be done gradually over several years. If the boat is painted, I usually use mahogany strips, even on pine boats; mahogany moves less during swelling and is harder when tapped in. The risk that a leaky pine boat dries up and cracks if left on land after splining is huge. A lot of times, I have considered just applying glue to one side so that the hull

FIGURE 77 } Splined topsides. If the old varnish is left on the hull while splining, it will make it easier to remove splining residue. The strips are cut by the bow with the same shape as the circular saw blade.

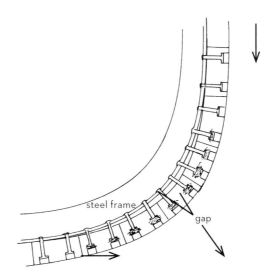

FIGURE 78 } A common injury in round-bottom boats is when the planking separates from the steel frame as it swells. The rivets are pulled into the planking and create gaps between the rivet and plugs.

steel frame

gap

can open up in the seam and to avoid the risk of planking ruptures as it dries further, but I've never tried it. Carvel-built boats with only bent frames have not been permitted in new construction since the standards for Nordic boatbuilding were set (1990). It's a weak construction, in such a way that if several ribs are overloaded and break, the hull may open up in a catastrophic way. Mahogany boats on bent frames can, from a splining standpoint, be treated like pine boats with steel frames. Pine boats with only bent frames should only be caulked where necessary and above the waterline.

Splining of oak cannot be recommended since oak is a strong wood with high moisture movement, and when it moves nothing can withstand it; moreover, it is difficult to glue.

A bare scraping, oiling until saturated, and proper coating, as well as regular surface treatments, allow the hull to move less. So that the strips aren't exposed to unnecessarily strong climate changes, you might want to varnish the interior with oil varnish or some kind of alkyd varnish.

To describe the effect of splining, imagine a slightly leaky hull has dried so that there is a little more than a ¹⁄₃₂-inch (1.5-mm) seam between the planks; if you have fifteen planks from keel to deck, then the total planking after splining will be ⁷⁄₈″ (22.5 mm) higher. When the planks have swollen, there is ¾″ (2 cm) more that needs to fit on the ribs than before the splining. If the hull isn't properly oiled and the surface treated, the ribs will break or the planking will be pushed out of the ribs.

WON'T THE BOAT BE TOO RIGID DUE TO SPLINING?

A thin planking of wood can hardly be so rigid that it does not keep up with the movements that the ocean and the rigging loads expose the boat to. In addition, with this reasoning, boats that were built with glued planking in the second half of the 1900s should not have been able to withstand their stiffness.

CAN YOU JUST SPLINE PARTS OF THE PLANKING?

I sometimes glue boats only in the topsides, and the strips will end just below the waterline in the end of the boat; I have never experienced any problems with this.

HOW LONG DOES EPOXY LAST?

I have splined with epoxy for the past thirty years. Previously, I used Aerolite, which is a carbamide resin glue; the glues seem to have a life span of about forty years. Nobody knows how long the epoxy will last, except that it won't last forever. The theoretical strength of the adhesive probably has little practical significance compared to how the gluing is done. The best ways to fail with splining are: to leave the boat unprotected on land over the summer, to have poor surface treatment of the hull that provides the elements an opportunity to put stress on the wood and glue joints, too much moisture in the hull when splining (more than 16%), cold and damp when splining with temperatures in the wood and in the air below 53°F (12°C), and shallow splining (less than ⅔ of the planking's thickness).

ALIGNING THE HULL

Splining should be preceded by an alignment of the hull, or the deformations will become permanent.

The perception a boat gives depends a lot on its sheerline, and the perception of a fair sheerline is harmony. You may not notice it immediately, but you will notice it if there is a lack of harmony, like with a deformed hull. The most common deformation of both powerboats and sailboats is a hanging stern and bow, known as hogging; the boat is shaped like a cat arching its back. This comes from a combination of poor storage on land and the lift of the water, especially amidships of the hull where the greatest buoyancy is. The latter effect is most clearly seen on old wooden ships that are at the dock for longer periods without sufficient ballast.

Boats that have been left for long periods (several years) on land tend to also be warped.

When a hull is aligned, it is not done by quickly bending it back; then the ribs can break and the bolts can loosen. Instead, you need to set up straps, wedges, and jacks and put the load on gradually and wait for results to appear. It will take weeks, maybe a month or so. The outline is checked by eyesight and according to the drawing, if it's available.

The lopsidedness is checked by means of a wire stretched amidships, a sinker down to the keel and stem, and with straight wooden slats put up across the boat

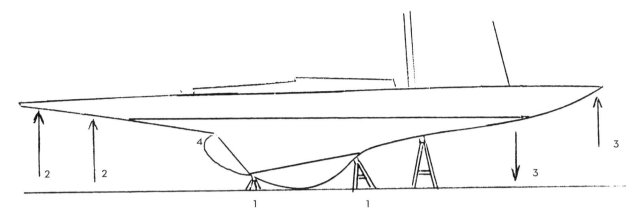

FIGURE 79

1 Support the keel firmly in the stern and bow so that the boat doesn't tip forward and the whole load ends up on the bow trestle. This can deform the hull by the mast.

2 Distribute the lift between several points on the stern. The deformation that is most difficult to straighten out is that of the aft edge of the cockpit. Also note that the rudderstock might need to be moved as the distance between the deck and rudderstock changes with the alignment.

3 On smaller Skerry cruisers, the area by the forestay is often lifted; here, you might have to ballast the hull or strap it down to the ground, while the bow up ahead is held up with a support.

4 Pay attention to the rudder stem's attachment to the stern, as too quick of a lift can cause a crack.

on the covering boards. On Skerry cruisers, usually the stern sags more; if you then lift the boat in the stern, it is mainly the trestle in the front of the bow that will resist, and the boat will have to much sheer by the mast forward of the keel. Instead, a strong support in the front of the ballast keel should lift the stern.

You should also keep in mind that it is the vertical part of the planking that primarily helps to maintain the sheerline of the boat.

How much of over curve or extra sheer is right? It depends on the circumstances; if the side deck is gone, no over curve is needed, but if is still there it will give some resistance, and you will need a bit of an over curve. If there are only a few standing plankstrakes, then the boat will lose its outline faster (see Figure 79).

PROCEDURE FOR SPLINING

This is a review of the procedures for those who are about to start splining. I hope that it can answer questions that arise during the process. Use a circular saw with a tapered blade. That's probably the most common method among boatbuilders. It is also possible to mill it with an end mill, but it is more time-consuming.

Many Different Steps

Splining consists of several different steps that take equal amounts of time, so when you calculate the amount of time, you cannot forget any steps. It takes just as long to apply glue in the groove as it does to cut it.

1 Choose the right time.
2 Make the strips.
3 Build the stand.
4 Nail the guide bar.
5 Saw the seam.
6 Move the guide bar.
7 Fit the strip.
8 Mix the glue and apply it to the strip and in the groove.
9 Mount the strip.
10 Wipe off excess glue and clean up any glue on the inside.
11 Tap pegs into the nail holes.
12 Plane off the excess.
13 Sand or scrape the hull.

FIGURE 80 } A saw blade with tapered teeth. The teeth are ³/₁₆″ (5 mm) in front and ¼″ (6 mm) 1″ (25 mm) from the front. The blade has only six teeth in order to eject the chips properly. In this case, the blade is in a circular saw with a lowering function. That is, the saw blade is lowered by the plate after it's started.

1   *Choose the right time.* This has been described earlier in this chapter.

2   *Make the trim.* The seam strip should be sawn or planed; it is easiest to order it from a carpenter. The strips are slightly more tapered than the kerf to provide the best possible fit on the outer edge and still give room for glue down through the joint surfaces (see Figure 81).

　　If you cut the strips yourself, a panel saw with feeder would be the best way. A conical insert in a planer would be another way to get the strips precise. An adaptable function to produce strips leads to other options. The time required for the fit and the results are significantly influenced by the quality of the strips.

　　The strip should be so hard that you can knock it into the last ¹/₁₆–³/₃₂″ (2–3 mm).

FIGURE 81 } The tapered strip allows the glue to remain on the strip and not rub off when the strip is tapped in. If the strip is slightly more tapered than the kerf, there will be room for the glue in the joint surfaces, but the glue joint will still be tight on the surface.

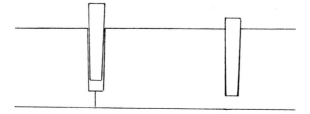

Mahogany strips are dimensionally stable during swelling and is therefore great for moisture; sometimes I spline painted pine boats with mahogany strips.

Do not choose too dark a mahogany for trim on varnished mahogany boats; be aware that the new mahogany strip darkens for the first years while the cleanly scraped mahogany hull starts to lighten at once after the scraping.

The strip should be ³/₈–³/₁₆″ (3–5 mm) higher than the groove depth so that there is an excess to tap on when the strip is assembled.

A guide bar is needed to operate the circular saw. As a guide bar, I usually use ⁹/₁₆–1³/₁₆″ (15–20 mm) of pine.

3   *Build the stand.* The stand should be easy to modify. The body's balance is the key for all carpentry work; the correct positioning of the feet and the body's center of gravity means that you can press the tool against the hull. Walking planks must be raised or lowered depending on the splining. It takes planks and clamps. It takes longer to get the planks at the proper height for cutting with precision than to cut the seam itself.

4   *Nail the guide bar.* The guide bar is nailed by means of a distance gauge that is made as follows: Measure the distance between the side of the sole of the circular saw and the center of the saw blade. Tap a nail through a block of wood at this length from the block end. The nail tip should stick out ¹/₃₂–¹/₁₆″ (1–2 mm) from the block. When using the gauge, press the nail into the seam and the guide bar will be pressed against the end of the block.

　　The strip is nailed underneath the seam that is to be cut. Thin nails, 1½″ (35 mm) long, may be just right. Do not drive the nail right down without leaving enough of it out to make it easy to pull out the nail with the back of the hammer. On varnished topsides, it may be better to nail opposite the frames where the plugs mask the nail holes.

5   *Saw the seam.* Sawing the seam is a two-man job—one saws and the other keeps track of the power cord. It is impossible to move up along the hull for 30–50 feet (10–15 meters) without the power cord getting stuck somewhere along the way, and if it does, you will easily get an uneven kerf.

FIGURE 82 } Nailing the guide bar using the distance gauge.

In order for the saw to glide more easily along the guide bar, you may want to wax the planking with paraffin or candle wax. The easiest way is to rub it with a candle.

When the blade is pressed into the planking, it may be hard to resist the pressure that a sunken saw creates; it may be necessary to clamp the end stop onto the guide bar. You can cut a groove of approximately ⁹⁄₁₆ inch (14 mm) with a sharp saw blade and a circular saw with a 1000-watt. The splining should be ¾ of the thickness of the planking, so if the planking is thick, it may be necessary to cut in stages. The conical shape of the blade makes the track wider when the seam is cut deeper, and therefore there will be great precision along the edges, even if the groove is cut in stages.

Finally, clear the track of sawdust and control the depth.

6 *Move the guide bar.* Since splining consists of several elements, it may be good to have several people helping

out. Four people, divided into two teams, make the work easier and faster. Two will nail the guide bar and saw, and two will fit the strip and glue it. If you set it up this way, it is a good idea to cut the seam on one side of the hull, then go to the other side and saw a seam there, while the other team glues the first seam and then continue to switch sides. If there are only two of you, then you can cut several seams next to each other in the morning and then glue in the afternoon. If the boat is leaky and strips are hard, there is a risk that the planking will be pushed away as you go and that last seam may be too narrow. Also, remember that wood is a living material and a groove that is cut on one day can change width the next day if the weather changes.

7 *Fit the strips* longitudinally and possibly for thickness as well. The beginning and end of the groove are formed as part of a circle with the same diameter as the blade—make a template with the correct diameter using a piece of plywood or MDF. Draw the circle and form the trim, and taper it a little sideways on the end to correspond with coning of the blade (see Figure 83). Test the fit of the strip. If it needs to be joined, this can be done with a butt splice; the planking will work well as a backing block. If the strip is loose, you should shave in the inner edge of the strip; the coning of the trim will make the width increase;

FIGURE 83 } Rounding off the seam trim ends using a template.

if the strip is too hard, you will need to shave on the side of the trim. You should be able to push in all but ¹⁄₁₆ inch (2 mm) of the strip by hand before it bottoms out.

8 *Mix the glue and apply it to the seam strip and in the groove.* Apply thinned glue to the strip and in the groove. Apply another coat of thickened adhesive. If the groove is open straight through, you may fill it in by applying thickened glue in the groove. The strip will then press the adhesive further into the seam.

9 *Mount the strip.* The adhesive lubricates the trim so that it goes in more easily. If the boat is round, the trims may have to be secured with nails at the ends so that they don't pop out after a while. Use a hammer and a block to tap in the strip. Sometimes on caulked boats you see that the trim has been tapped in so tightly that the planking has cracked on the inside. Take it easy and tap just in front of the frames (see Figure 84).

10 *Wipe off excess glue.* Wipe off the surplus glue from the planking, leaving only a small amount next to the strips. Make sure there's no surplus on the inside; if the boat has been leaky, then the cracks on the inside may be filled in with the surplus glue. A leaky plank that is just filled from the outside year after year will compress and detach from the ribs, but if the whole joint is filled with the strip and glue, then the plank will swell more evenly (see Figure 85).

11 *Tap pegs into the nail holes.* Tap pegs (small wooden sticks), or "toothpicks," with glue into the nail holes. It's hard to get glue into a small hole. The easiest way is by means of a small wooden stick.

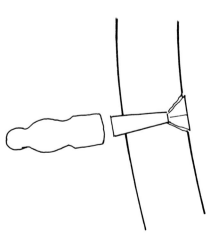
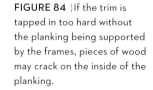

FIGURE 84 } If the trim is tapped in too hard without the planking being supported by the frames, pieces of wood may crack on the inside of the planking.

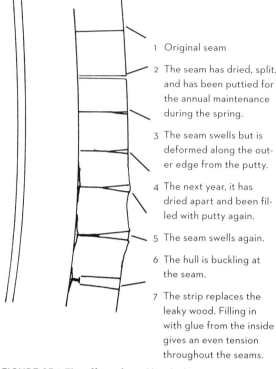

1 Original seam

2 The seam has dried, split, and has been puttied for the annual maintenance during the spring.

3 The seam swells but is deformed along the outer edge from the putty.

4 The next year, it has dried apart and been filled with putty again.

5 The seam swells again.

6 The hull is buckling at the seam.

7 The strip replaces the leaky wood. Filling in with glue from the inside gives an even tension throughout the seams.

FIGURE 85 } The effect of spackling leaky seams.

12 *Shave off the excess.* The quickest way is to cut off the excess seam trim with a planer described in the chapter on steel frames (see Figure 86). If you use a plane, you can tape the edges of the sole of the plane so that the blade does not cut into the planking.

13 *Sand or scrape the hull.* Scrape off the excess glue the day after gluing at the latest, before it becomes too hard. The moisture between the strip and the planking will even out better if the strip is left untreated for a while, and it will produce a smoother result. The hull can also be moistened with a cloth so that the strips rise up a bit before the final trimming.

When the splining is complete, the hull must be prevented from drying out any further, as wood can withstand pulling across its grain less than it can pressure across its grain. One way is to water under the boat during dry periods.

Always wear safety goggles and a dust mask. Sanding of half-hardened epoxy can cause allergic reactions.

FIGURE 86 } Trimming of surplus strips.

SUMMARY

Splining is somewhat controversial. If it fails, it means a severe deterioration of the boat, and it can't be undone. Boats with gaps can be made rigid due to splining in the same manner that ships and traditional boats are made rigid by caulking. A prerequisite for splining (and caulking) to be successful is that the planking be firmly attached to the frame. Align the boat before splining it; you won't get a second chance. Spline a moderately dry hull at the right temperature. Pine boats are more difficult to spline than mahogany boats. On boats with only bent frames, all frames may snap off as the hull swells if it (the hull) has been too dry while splining. Boats that have been glued when first built should be splined when the original joints release, partly because the boat is designed to have a homogeneous planking panel, and partly because the seams are not protected against water penetration and rot.

WOOD FRAMES

All parts of the hull of a boat work together and are needed for the boat to function. The boat should be as light as possible for the propulsive force to be minimized. Building heavy and strong is not that hard. But what our designers and builders had to fight for was to build light and strong. When you see all the old boats that still sail, you have to admit that they succeeded.

The frames are the ribs of the boat. Bruised ribs are usually the cause of leakage more than broken planks are. The frame should hold the shape of the hull and keep the planks next to each other.

In some boat construction, the planks are laid on the ribs, which are then used as templates for the hull shape. This applies to ships built on steel frames and boats built on laminated wood frames. That kind of frame is called a construction frame. On Swedish boats, there is often about 1⅔ feet (50 cm) between these form-holding frames; in Anglo-Saxon countries, there is 2 feet (about 60 cm); those are the frames that are on the blueprint, on the frame part of the construction plan.

In Sweden, the frames are usually steamed and bent into the hull when the planking is complete; during construction, temporary moulds/forms templates will shape the hull. Abroad, it is common for wood frames to be steamed and bent against ribands that is attached

TYPES OF FRAMES

The main types of frames are bent, laminated, and sawn.

Steam-bent frames have ribs that have been steamed soft and shaped along the hull while they were still warm.

Laminated frames are made out of slats that are bent and glued together, preferably on a template.

Sawn frames are made out of naturally bent wood, or the ribs have been cut or sawed out. The grain of the wood needs to follow the shape of the frame for the frame to be strong. These frames often need to be spliced either with scarf joints or by making them double sawn and fastened with scarf joints.

MATERIALS FOR THE FRAME

The materials for frames are usually oak or ash, but elm, pine, or mahogany are also used. Oak, ash, and elm are easy to steam and are used for steam-bent frames. Ash and elm are less rot-resistant than oak. Oak also has thick branches and roots that work well for sawn frames. Nowadays, pine and mahogany are used for laminated frames as they are easier to glue and are moderately rot-resistant.

ATTACHMENT OF THE FRAME

Most steam-bent and laminated frames in Sweden are attached with copper rivets. Sawn frames on old work boats are often nailed with hot-dipped galvanized nails; on pleasure boats, they are usually attached with wood screws. In old work boats, the sawn frames are sometimes attached to the planking with juniper plugs.

to the outside of the template before the planking process. Sawn frames are used as templates for the planking when carvel planking, but on clinker-built boats it is usually cut out afterward. Boats with hard chines are often built with sawn frames; the hull shape on either side of the chine is relatively flat so there is no problem with the grain of the ribs. These frames are often sawn from standing pieces—¾" (2 cm) wide and 3⅛" (8 cm) high is a common proportion. Sometimes different ribs are combined, such as having every third rib be a shape-retaining construction frame—either a sawn frame, a steel frame, or a laminated frame with two steam-bent frames in between them.

BROKEN FRAMES—A CLASSIC PROBLEM

With clinker planking the planks are riveted together, and that way you can accept more broken ribs without the risk of leakage. Carvel-built boats are in accordance with current regulations in Nordic boating to not be built solely with the steam-bent frame, because if multiple ribs break on the same plank at once, the planking won't hold together and it may result in huge leaks. Older boats are often built this way; some have done well while others have broken frames and deformations of the hull.

When you steam-bend, the ribs are subject to tension when bent; the tensions may lead to small cracks, and if the planking swells too much or deforms, the ribs may break. The radius of the ribs affects their tension—the smaller the radius, the greater the tension.

Repairing the Frame

Laminated frames. Laminated frames came into use after World War II with the help of the adhesives developed in the war industry. Today, there are frames from the 1950s that are coming unglued, especially those in which the rib ends have been exposed to bilge water. If the ribs are riveted or bolted, they will keep together despite the adhesive releasing. The design will have lost in stiffness, but the strength will still be good. Problems can arise in the most overloaded parts, such as the mast sections and in the ribs that are subject to the forces from the ballast keel. If you treat your boat with the respect that a fifty-year-old boat deserves, you won't have any problems.

TO STEAM-BEND OR LAMINATE?

Whether the frame should be steam-bent or laminated is something you can try out for yourself: if the steam-bent frame breaks, you can glue instead next time.

There are also different rules of thumb for what can be bent:

The radius of the bend = r
The height or thickness of the frame = h

If r/h is larger than 20, then the frame can hold the loads; if r/h=14 to 20, then some of the frames while already break while being bent; and if r/h is less than 14, the frame should be laminated or be steam-bent out of thinner strips.

Example: if the frame is 1" (24 mm) thick and the radius is 21" (500 mm), r/h will be 21, and the frame should last for a long time.

If the frame is 1" (24mm) but the radius of the bend is 12.5" (300 mm), r/h will be 12.5, and the frame should be laminated or steam-bent out of ½-inch (12-mm) ribs.

Source: Ole-Jacob Broch, Trebåten, 1993.

Under the floors on sailboats it is often in tight spaces, and boatbuilders often couldn't get enough room to rivet the ribs, so they were screwed from the outside with wood screws instead. Then, when swelling and drying stress the glue joints of the ribs, the laminates release and break out in a fan shape. If the wood is in good condition, the laminate may dry and be re-glued back on using nuts and bolts for extra support.

If the wood is bad, the ribs are cut with a scarf joint in a suitable place and a new bottom is glued and fitted (see Figure 87).

Sawn frames. The strength of a sawn frame depends on if the builder can find materials in which the grain of the wood follow the shape of the ribs. The dimensions of the ribs are somewhat forgiving for the grain direction. The joints are the most common problems. Bolts through the joints come undone or grains on the ribs are so oblique that the wood cracks on the bolts. Sawn frames are simple to repair in that the frames are easy to remove where there are natural joints, and structures are rarely glued. Sometimes the ribs are nailed with

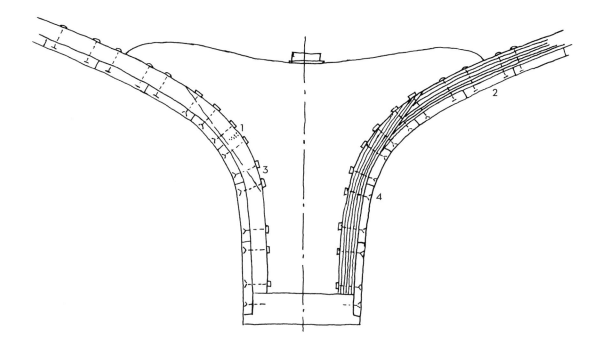

FIGURE 87 | Splicing the frame in the bilges.

1 Simplify the scarf joint by putting it in a place where it is easy to plane the joint surfaces, and therefore you will have good control over the fit.

2 For strength reasons, do not splice frames at the end point of the floors.

3 Old crack.

4 Laminated ribs that have come apart and are spliced with a new bottom, and as a precaution, have been fastened with nuts and bolts to avoid coming apart again.

galvanized boat nails that can be tricky to get out without damaging the planking. Drilling off the nail head and then tapping the nail further into the rib with a mandrel is one way. If the ribs are loose from the planking, you can saw off the nail with a hacksaw blade between the hull and frame. The damaged rib can then be copied from a piece of hook-grown oak, or a new rib can be laminated instead (see Figure 88).

Steam-bent frames. Steam-bent frames have tension in the surface from the bending; one side of the fibers is compressed, the second is pulled out. The steam bending gives the grains a possibility of adapting, but some of the tension is maintained. Thick ribs have more tension than flat; the flat ribs are more elastic and hold better, but are worse at keeping the shape of the boat. When the flat portions of the topsides and the bottom swell, the planking in the chines will be pushed out, and the radius of the frame will become smaller until it breaks. (See chapter on splining.)

An easy way to mend a broken rib is to laminate a new piece of frame and mount it next to the broken part. We call this type of repair "sistering a rib." The glued piece of the frame retains the shape and the doubled up part is stronger where it is mostly needed. The disadvantage is that it is difficult to adjust the deformation that led to the break, and it will be there permanently. Many people think it looks too patched up with those kinds of frames, but I feel that they are acceptable if the original structure of the boat is retained. (See Figure 89).

FIGURE 88 | Various joints on sawn frames.

1 The most common version with staggering joints be bolted in three places.

2 Hooked scarf joint.

3 Double-sawn frame where the difficulty of getting to comply with the bend is offset by making a dou with staggering joints. The maximum twist of the should be approved is the usual 1 to 3.

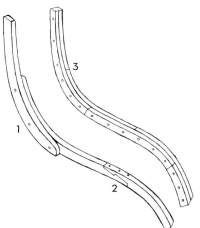

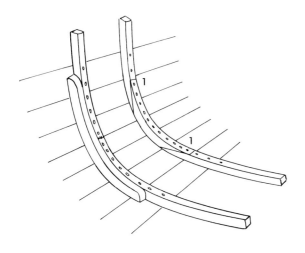

FIGURE 89 ⎮ Sistering frames and repairing them with a scarf joint.

1 It's hard to get scarf joints to fit in this section of the boat; it also creates long delicate tips where the tension releases and the laminates stretch out.

I prefer to use sistering rather than scarf joints in the chine, as they are weaker and it is more complicated and time-consuming to make scarf joints there. On the bilge keel, it's different, as it is easy to make scarf joints there (see Figures 87 and 89).

Generally speaking, broken ribs in the chine are more important to fix than frames that are broken in the keel bilge where the floors keep the shape.

As usual, it should be noted that a glued scarf joint should be five times as long in the grain direction than it is across the grain. Replacing the entire frame will be discussed later.

What makes me not want to touch on that while discussing the repair of broken ribs is the very complicated assembly of planking, beam shelves, covering boards and frames up and under the deck. To remove and install a new frame up here requires intervention and bending that may lead to consequential damage and subsidence, which in turn are complicated to fix. In a renovation in which the covering boards, and possibly the shear strake, are changed, it will be easier to replace the entire frame.

REPLACEMENT OF FRAME
Removing the Fasteners

There are various ways to remove the copper rivets. If you are alone and there are a limited number of rivets, you may punch them in from the outside. First, dismantle the wooden plug, then tap a punch mark in the center of the rivet head. Drill a hole in the head with a diameter slightly larger than the rivet; if you succeed, the rivet head will attach like a little plate on the drill, and the rivet will be easy to tap in with a punch. If it is the whole frame with lots of rivets that is being dismantled, then you can cut off the rove on the rivet from the inside of the frame. It can be done with an angle grinder or with a rubber pad with a coarse grinding wheel. The plugs are drilled off with a Forstner drill bit on the outside. After that, you can drive out the rivets from the inside with a punch. This is a two-man job; one person has to push

from the outside with a mallet or with a thick-walled pipe. Otherwise, the planking around the hole might split apart when the rivet heads are knocked out.

Gluing the Ribs

I use epoxy glue when laminating frames, mostly out of habit. Resorcinol glue is stronger but not as user-friendly, as it sold in large containers with limited shelf life. Resorcinol glue is used in the industry for laminated beams and waterproof plywood. Polyurethane foam glue is sometimes also used to glue frames, but it has limitations on its waterproofing ability. Epoxy adhesive also has limitations strength-wise if exposed to temperatures higher than 140°F (60°C), but that is unusual inside a boat.

The slats should be newly sawn at the gluing so that resins and oxide have not formed on the surface.

The slats should all be made of the same kind of wood and the same humidity—9–12% is about right.

The slats should be reversed and shifted so that defects in the material are evenly distributed.

The method I use is to glue the laminates over a mould. The mould can be sawn from a thick sheet of plywood or MDF. For larger projects, you may want to build an adjustable table (see Figure 90).

I think it's a good idea to make a template in the boat and then go indoors and glue the ribs, instead of stapling the slats inside the boat, which is sometimes done in connection to epoxy repairs.

A roughly curved template will make the first fitting of the rib easier. If you don't have access to one, you can make a template of the shape of the hull with a piece of MDF and a measuring stick, sometimes called a joggle or tick stick (see Figure 92).

The template is then made out of thin plywood or MDF and is carefully fitted. If the hull fits well together, then the frame shouldn't reshape it. Conversely, sometimes the template will be adjusted for the rib to straighten out a deformation of the hull.

It is important to keep track of whether the mould should be done as the exterior or interior of the frame. If you saw your mould out of wood, it is easier to use a convex inner mould (inside of the frame); then the thickness of the frame has to be deducted from the form template. If the frame is glued on a glueing table, it's more rational

FIGURE 90 } It takes a lot of clamps to glue frames. The template consists of a wood table with removable supports made of clamps. The clamps are fastened with a bolt and washer in the groove in the table.

FIGURE 91 } This template is a quick way to make a rough template of the frame.

HOW THICK SHOULD THE SLATS BE?

The thinner the slats, the stiffer the frame and the less the pressure on every joint surface. On the other hand, you will use more glue, wood, and time, and it can get too stiff compared to other surrounding areas.

Slats thicker than ⅜" (10 mm) are not advisable, and you need at least five glue joints in the frame to avoid the frame straightening as the clamps are taken off.

A rule of the thumb of mine is that the relation between the inner radius of the frame and the thickness of the slat is 100/1. 300 mm radius admits 3 mm slat.

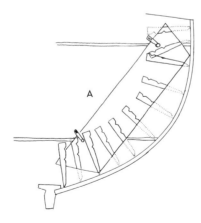

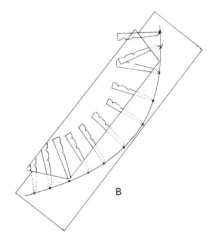

FIGURE 92 } Making a template for a frame with help from a measuring stick.

A The tip of the stick is held against the planking and the shape of the stick is drawn on a board that is temporarily attached across the boat in the middle of the rib.

B The board is then placed on a larger board, and the stick is fitted to the traced shape, after which the tip of the strip is drawn like a point on the larger board. The points then give the frame its shape. The template is then sawn out of the board.

FIGURE 93 }

1 With a limited number of clamps, it is easier to get good bonding when the slats are bent over a convex mould. In the chine, that means that the thickness of the frame must be measured of from the template of the inside of the hull when the glue mould is made.

2 In order to draw in a concave, you need more clamps so the curve won't be uneven.

and faster to use the template (the inside of the planking); see Figure 93.

It takes more glue than you may think when laminating: 0.5 lb per 10 square feet (0.25 kg per square meter) per glued joint. A roller is the most effective tool to apply the glue. Too much pressure and too thin of a glued joint is not good for gluing with epoxy; in addition, the volume of the adhesive decreases when the adhesive hardens, and to tighten the clamps after fifteen minutes is recommended. Allow the adhesive to cure thoroughly (at room temperature for 24 hours) before the frame is released, as the joints will be under a lot of pressure when the slats want to straighten out.

Then shave off the edges of the rib with a plane before the frame is mounted. The angle toward the planking must also be skewed, mostly at the end (see Figure 94). When making the frame, the 0-line is important (zero line). A zero line is a mark that is made between the piece that is fitted and the foundation so that the piece is tested in the same place each time. Without a zero line, it is hard to make a good fit. A small shift means that the boat might be reshaped. Start by putting a zero line on

the planking; transfer it to the template and then to the skewed frame.

Surface treat the laminated frames properly; coat them with varnish or epoxy. In my experience, there is no glue that can hold onto natural wood that gets wet and then dries, no matter what the adhesive producers claim.

STEAM-BENDING A FRAME

Either it works or it does not work. This is something that applies to most processes when restoring a wooden boat. You get to try all jobs that there are for boatbuilding, but just a little bit of everything and without the experience that the original boatbuilders got through their daily work. The jobs are complex; there are many parameters that need to be right. Steam-bending is a perfect example of this. You need to select the appropriate materials with proper moisture; the steaming apparatus needs to be designed so that it provides a suitable wet steam under moderate pressure. The ribs should be kept just long enough in the steambox.

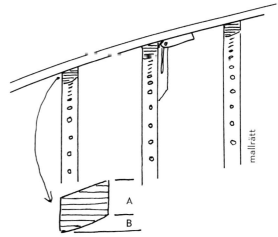

FIGURE 94 } The angle toward the planking can be determined with a sliding T-bevel, which is held against the hull and a surface perpendicular to the centerline of the hull. That surface is usually called the mould right. The angle is measured in three or four different places between the deck and the keel and fine-tuned when the rib is tested against the planking. The angle at the ends of the boat require that some slats be added such that the thickness will be sufficient. The thickness A is sufficient amidships, but at the ends, some slats need to be added for the angle B.

The radius of the frame cannot be too small. The frame needs to be put in place fairly quickly. It should be soft enough to be angled against the planking at the ends. If everything works as it should, then steaming is a quick and fun job in which several people work together, alternating quick effort with some quieter periods. The steam roars, and the heat spreads through the room. If it does not work, the hours will slip away, and the only result will be ruined ribs and grumpy carpenters.

Choice of Materials

Oak, ash, and elm are easy to steam. The growth rings should be parallel to the planking for the rib to be easy to steam and for less future tension. Wood with lower density and wider growth rings is usually easier to steam. Fresh wood is easier to steam than dried. Now, I mostly use American white oak for steam-bent frames; it is often straight-grained but imported hard dried to Sweden (6% moisture content). Dried timber should soak for a few days before steaming; otherwise the timber will become hard and brittle from the steaming. The time that the material is to stay in the steam is usually one hour per inch (2.5 cm), but it varies with the temperature and density of the vapor. Steaming is not so different from steam-drying; too long in the steam box—known as over-steaming—will produce hard and brittle materials.

The Steaming Apparatus

a simple steaming apparatus can be made from a metal boiler of approximately 5 gallons (20 liters) and a tripod. The heat can come from a gas burner or an oil burner. The steam box for frames can be a tube or plywood box.

In a steam box of this kind, the water is boiled in the boiler and steam directed into one end of the box; if it is cold outside, the box must be isolated to avoid the steam condensing too fast on the walls of the box. The steam pressure is not very high, so there should be a taphole for the steam at the other end of the box to make it pass along the ribs so fast that it does not have time to condense.

There are also steam generators for sale; they provide steam under pressure and quickly. But here, they work with pressure, and the unit works with pressure and must be set up to function with pressure gauges and relief valves.

Procedure for Steaming

1   Mark where the ribs go on the boat. The holes from the old rivets are a good guide. Plugholes must be drilled to proper dimensions for the new plugs to make riveting quick.

2   There are often square holes for the rib ends in the wood keel and the stems. They have two functions—they provide extra strength to the area where the planking meets the backbone and there is a quick way to lock the rib end when steaming. If you are using the holes, you need to check that the rib ends will fit. The holes were probably great at the beginning, but a lot of times moisture and rot spread from the water that has collected in them. With this method, it is also difficult to create good limber holes along the bows, and the planking tends to freeze apart here for that reason. If the holes won't be used, they should be plugged or filled with pitch or wax. If there are no holes to get rigging to position the ends, some other device must be set up for the rigging.

3   If there are holes in the hull from planking that has been taken out then you can clamp the ribs there. The clamps must be prepared and ready in the boat when the strips are removed from the steam box. If you can't use clamps, you need to cut up wood and wedges to hold the ribs in place while they cool off, push on the deck, and attach to the beam-stringer on the other side of the boat.

4   Then it's time to turn on the heat, and when the water starts to boil and there's steam from the box, it is time to put the ribs in. The ribs should have a little extra length if there is room for it on the boat. For it to be easy to pull out the right rib, you can label it with a note on a string attached to the rib end. The cord can also be used to pull the rib out. Use gloves with extra long cuffs as the vapor causes burns.

5   Once the ribs have been in the steamer long enough, they need to be fitted in the boat one by one; you need to be quick in order to get good mounting with little residual tension. It's good to have two or three people for this. One takes the ribs out of the vessel and passes it on, then he shuts the box and gets ready with clamps or a drill. The second person pre-bends the rib and passes it into the boat where the third person matches it against the hull. A lever

for over-bending will make it easier (see Figure 95). When the bottom of the frame is fixed and the rest of the frame is roughly shaped, the rib is pressed out at the turn of the chine by pressing or tapping down the rib end from above; if it is possible to set a clamp on the rib end, then you can screw the rib in. Then lock the rib with a few strategically placed rivets and move on to the next rib. Within half an hour, the ribs that are left in the steamer will start to become over-steamed, and it will be time to stop steaming and load a new round. Do not use the rib material over again as it becomes brittle from the steam-bending.

6   The final riveting can be done gradually during the steaming or when it is done.

Special Problems with Steam-Bending in Restorations

Steam-bending is a quick way to frame during new construction when the hull has no deck or beam shelf. During restoration, it becomes more complicated. On motorboats and at the ends of sailboats, you may bend the frame in advance with a lever and thread the end between beam shelf and planking. Then the bottom end is tacked on past the bow, and the rib is wedged into place. Here, it is important to calculate the length correctly. If the covering board is dismantled then the rib is placed between beam shelf and the planking with a little extra length to the rib. Then lock the lower end of the rib to the stem with a distance for the limber hole; a piece of wood with a U-shaped cut out will be good to fix it in place. The rib is then pressed down against the planking with a clamp set between the rib end and the beam stringer.

The s-shaped frames in boats with sunken keels are harder to get to, especially if the covering board is not dismantled. If the bilge is broad and shallow and the ribs are soft, then steaming could work well, but if the bilge is deep and fitted with high floors, you can get stuck. I have seen people steam the frame in two stages, but I have not tried it myself. A wrap-around splicing of the ribs in the straight section between the turn of the bilge and the turn of the chine could be another solution. You can of course also steam the ribs over a template, but you still need room to have them fitted in the boat. This is a problem that also can arise when installing laminated frames and steel frames.

Alternative Steam-Bending Methods

Instead of steam, sometimes people use a method to bend the ribs by placing them in a tube with boiling water. I have not tried it, but when it works, it's a good shortcut. It should make for less risk of over-steaming.

In the old days, they used to bend using the heat of an open fire; the wood was so heated up on the surface that it almost charred during the bending; it was used mostly for planking.

Bending the rib with linseed oil and a gas burner is another method that provides a waterproofing at the same time, but the fire hazard is great.

If a trim needs to be bent, you can put the strip in water for a few days and then heat it with a hot air gun while it's shaped into place.

TOOLS FOR RIBMAKING

Materials for frames or laminating are best cut with a table saw; if you don't have one, or a jointer, it may be convenient to buy the pieces already cut. A planer with carbide tipped blade is a good tool for removing the glue from the sides of laminated frames. A band saw works best for cutting out a sawn frame. If you don't have access to such tools, you are free to improvise and let your imagination flow. A good jigsaw with a rip saw blade is capable of cutting 2-inch (50-mm) thick oak. In order to fit the rib to the planking I use a plane and a spoke shave, but hardwood dulls the tools. Perhaps this is a good opportunity to use a belt sander (as I'm not recommending using it on the hull, see the chapter about scraping the wood bare). The joint surface on the existing frame is hard go over with a plane; an elegant solution is to make a fixture for the router, which is clamped onto the rib, and with the help of it router out a straight joint surface, the design varies from case to case. If you have patience and the time, you can cut the joint with a chisel as long you have marked out where to stop cutting.

SUMMARY

Leakage occurs more often from broken ribs than because of poor planking. If the boat has a shape-holding frames or is clinker-built, you can live with a pair of broken bent frames. If several ribs are broken one after another in the same plank strake in the turn of the chine, the hull will deform. The deformation of the planking can be stopped with sistered frames, but it is difficult to reshape the hull without replacing the frame. It is more important to fix broken ribs in the turn of the chine than in the bilge, where the floors often keep the shape. Laminating new pieces of the frame is often an easier method than steam-bending if there are only a limited number of repairs.

FIGURE 95 } Lever for pre-bending and over-bending the rib. If the rib has been over-bent while warm and not broken, it will have fewer residual tensions in the cold.

FIGURE 96 } Replacement of parts of the ribs. The picture also shows the old frame pieces, MDF templates, the belt sander and a spoke shave.

FIGURE 97 } Repairing frames in the turn of the bilge. The pieces are easy to make, but necessity is the mother of invention in terms of fixation while gluing.

FIGURE 98 } Sistered ribs provide strength where the original ribs are overloaded.

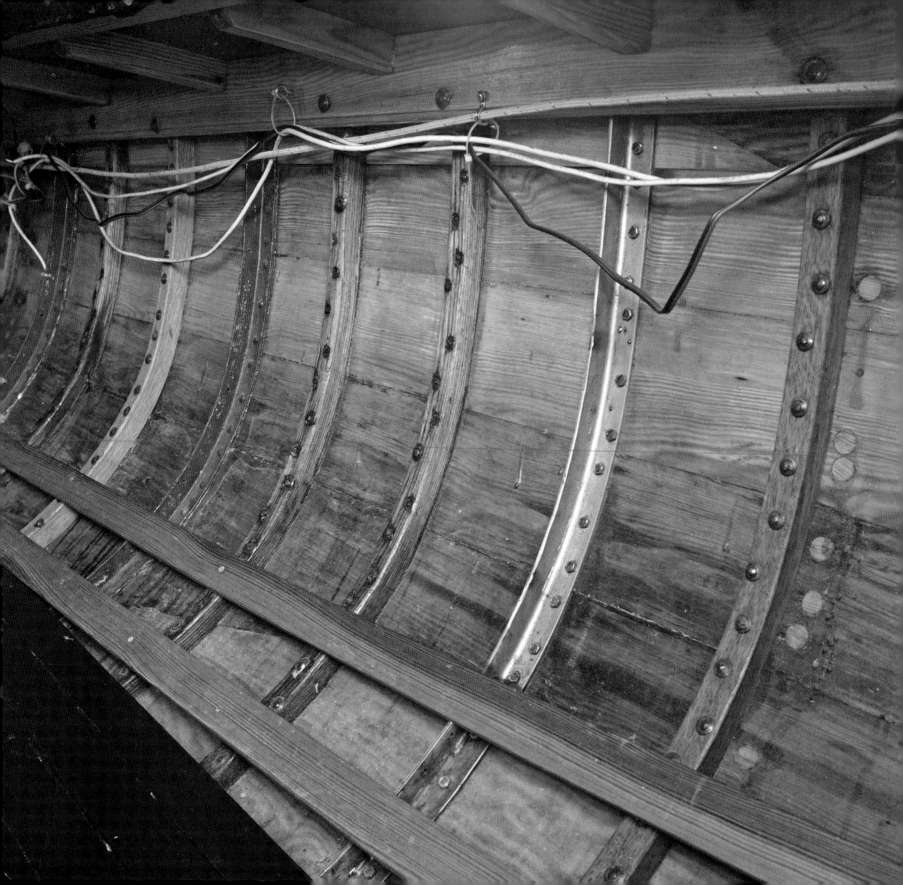

STEEL FRAMES

The Scandinavian method of building boats without caulking between the planks was based on dry wood planking and tight fits. Steel frames were a prerequisite to be able to push the planking together tightly, and also for the hull to keep together when the planking swelled.

Unfortunately, the frames will get rusty in the long run, and this is probably the most common reason for thorough renovations. The rust destroys the wood of the hull, especially if it is made of mahogany; pine will withstand corrosion better.

STEEL FRAME MATERIALS

The classic steel frame is made out of angle iron that has been bent and drilled and then sent to be hot-dip galvanized. Sometimes when the frames came back to the yard after being galvanized, the blacksmiths had to adjust the frames again because they had changed their shape during the heating in the galvanization process. The frames and the steel floors were then attached to the stems and the keel plank and were aligned with ribband as temporary "planking." Then the boat was planked from the bottom up. The ribs were riveted to the planking with soft, galvanized iron rivets.

For a rust-resistant steel for frames, they recommended angle iron as used for large vessels, but last time I asked about it, the size I was looking for was not available in Sweden. Hot-dip galvanized rivets are not available either today, so when renovating, you may use stainless steel AISI 316 Marine Grade machine screws.

When galvanized frames are mixed with stainless steel screws, it creates a galvanic element. This is something you have to put up with when old galvanized frames are screwed on with stainless steel screws. Glued, dense plugs and nylon washers under the nuts improve the situation considerably (see the chapter about screws and nails and the chapter about corrosion and nail sickness).

FIGURE 99 } The 2 SK 95-sq.-m. *Marga III* (18.30 × 2.80 m) under construction at the Stockholm Motorboat yard in 1918. The backbone is now finished, and the steel frame has been set into it. The frames are secured both lengthwise and widthwise. When the steel floors are riveted, the planking begins. Photo of the boat's designer Erik Salander. From the collection of SSHM.

For the last twenty-five years, I have used marine grade stainless steel when replacing steel frames to avoid compromising with different materials. This stainless steel is also user-friendly, as it doesn't need to be sent out to be galvanized but can be welded and finished throughout the renovation. Unfortunately, the domestic production of stainless angle steel has ended, and imported steel has been uneven in quality. Usually, the steel has been too hard and

FIGURE 100 } Rolling welded frames in a roller. The different radii of the curves are obtained by adjusting the distances between the three rollers hydraulically. In pairs, rolling makes equal halves. Making a template of the hull is important; an error here is transferred to the newly rolled frames.

brittle, possibly due to incomplete annealing after manufacturing.

Laminated frames of ash are an alternative to steel frames. Lloyds states that a 1¼ × 1¼ × ⅛″ (30×30×3 mm) steel frame is equal to a 1.33-inch-high and 1.22-inch-wide (34-mm-high and 31-mm-wide) laminated wood frame.

PROCEDURE FOR REPLACING AN OLD STEEL FRAME

When renovating, it is the number of steps that determine the time required. Here is a review of the steps involved in replacing a frame.

1   *Remove the obstructing interiors.*

2   *Scrape the exterior of the boat clean opposite the frame to find the plugs.*

3   *Cut, grind, or drill out the rivets on the inside.* Hammer and chisel easily cause mild bruises on your hands and work best at temperatures below zero when the steel is brittle. With some practice, you can work up some good speed cutting out rivets. Grinding with an angle grinder is fast but a fire hazard and also results in a lot of dust and gas. Drilling takes time and requires sharp drills at low revolutions of the drill and a lot of pressure. The choice of method may depend on the quality of the frame; a chisel, for example, won't work on badly rusted frames.

If only a few rivets need to be replaced, for example, when plugs are too thin as they are scraped clean, it is usually better to drill off the head from the outside. Start by tapping a punch mark in the center of the rivet head, then drill a center hole with a ⅛-inch (4-mm) drill bit; drill the hole ⅛–³⁄₁₆″ (4–5 mm) deep. Then drill a hole with a drill bit that has a diameter that is ¹⁄₃₂″ (1 mm) larger than the rivet diameter. If you succeed, the remains of the rivet head will sit like a ring on the drill bit. The rest of the rivet is then pushed through the planking and frames.

4   *Take out the rivets.* This is definitely a two-man job. One man with a mallet and punch on the inside, and another man on the outside with a tubular anvil and a heavier mallet. For any dismantling, the greatest weight should be on the anvil side to make the hits count. With the right tools, you don't need to take the plugs out in advance. A good anvil might be a thick-walled pipe with a hole diameter a little bit larger than the plug and long enough that it can be firmly held in your hand. Make sure the anvil is heavier than the mallet.

5   *Remove the frame.* The difficulty here is that the frame was recessed and screwed into the wood keel and the stems before the planking. Cut the frames end as close to the stem as possible. When the rib is gone, you can tidy up the end, protect it from rust, and leave it. You might be able to dig the frame end out from the recess if the screws are corroded, and then you can fill the recess with wax or epoxy. The beam shelf could also cause a problem; when major frame replacement is done, it is best to also replace the sheer strake to get better access. If the frames are in good condition higher up, it may be sufficient to only change the part that is underwater. The frames must then be spliced properly and overlapping. Two planking rows is the minimum length for a joint. Do not weld stainless steel frames in galvanized frames; it creates a galvanic element. Screw the spliced joint together instead and insulate it with a polyurethane compound (Sikaflex).

6 *Check the hull shape.* Check on the outside of the hull that the shape is smooth at the frames; use your eyes and a flexible batten. Also check that the frame has not changed its form during disassembly. Adjust as needed. If the frame is in a bad state, you need to make a template of MDF or plywood instead.

7 *Roll a new frame from the old or from a template.* The angle steel is welded together back to back in pairs and rolled in the roller or pressed in a straightening bench. Weaker (less than 1 ¼-inch, or 30-mm) frames might be bent over a support, such as a sturdy U-beam.

8 Adjust the frame to the right angle. Then angle the horizontal flange on the frame so that it will be tight against the planking. The angles are measured with the sliding T-bevel from the detached frame or template made from the boat. At amidships, the angle is relatively straight (90°), but at the tapering of the boat, the angle is significant. Almost all shipyards except for Holm's Yacht Yard turned the standing flange against the ends (Knut Holm often did the opposite). The angle is done best by clamping the standing flange of the frame onto a solid steel plank and angling the horizontal flange skis with a large wrench or a slotted steel bar. Angling is often a heavier and more time-consuming job than rolling.

9 *Plug from the inside.* The holes in the planking are often damaged by rust, so drill ⁵⁄₁₆- to ½-inch (8-12-mm)

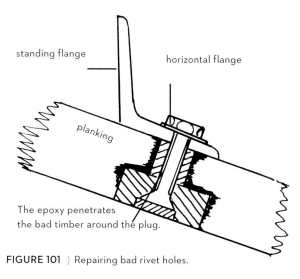

standing flange

horizontal flange

planking

The epoxy penetrates the bad timber around the plug.

FIGURE 101 } Repairing bad rivet holes.

holes from the inside; glue in plugs with epoxy adhesive. Be generous with the adhesive. Above the waterline, the holes may not need to be fixed. In that case, this segment and the next may be skipped.

10 *Plug from the outside.* Plug through half the planking thickness; use larger plugs, ¾–1 ¼" (18–30mm), as needed. Avoid drilling big plugs in the plank as it will weaken the plank. Epoxy-glue the plugs. For the gluing to be successful, heat is required during bonding and hardening. Use this method only where the planking is damaged by rust; a basic rule for renovation is to cut as few longitudinal grains as possible.

11 *Tidy up the planking on the inside, by the middle of the rib.* Cut the plugs. Adjust the planks so that there are no gaps between them. Scrape and sand.

12 *Apply rot protection and oil the inside of the planking.*

13 *Align the frame in the boat.* Drill a few holes for the fastening screws or clamp the frame into the openings from any removed planks.

14 *Drill.* If the old rivet holes are plugged, or if the planks are new, then mark out the location of the drill holes on the horizontal flange inside with a marker; remove the frame and drill it with a drill press. Reinstall the frame and drill the holes from the inside out through the steel frame and the planking. Or drill new holes from the outside through the mended part and into the frame so they create a mark in the steel; then remove the frame and drill it with a drill press. The latter method is also used when the rivet holes are in good shape.

15 *Countersink the plugs and heads of the screws from the outside.* Only countersink about ³⁄₃₂–³⁄₁₆" (3–5 mm) so that there is a newly glued plug left under the head of the screw.

16 *Mount the frame.* Attach the frame with a few fastening screws. If all of the planking is to be oiled afterward, the frame should be installed without any sealant, as the oil will seep in underneath the frame. I used to prefer applying a thick mixture of red lead below the waterline on the planking as an insulator where the frame goes, but now that red lead is prohibited, you need to try getting some other sealant or paint to insulate between the steel and planking; however, do not use silicone.

FIGURE 102 } Router with spacers. The blocks are screwed to the plate and the router cutter set out so that they are a little bit under the tops of the blocks. The blocks then slide along the planking while the cutter routers of the exes of the plugs.

17 *Attach the frame.* This is done either with a screw and nut or by threading the bolt into the frame, which can be done if the thickness of the frame is ³⁄₃₂″ (3 mm) or larger. The holes are drilled thinner for the used thread size, and the frame is threaded from the outside through the planking with a tap threading tap. The thread obtained in ³⁄₃₂-inch (3-mm) material is strong enough to pull the screw right through the planking. Both ways of doing this require two people. Threading is only recommended for stainless steel frames.

18 *Clean up the inside.* Scrape and wipe off red lead or residue; cut the screws that stick out too far.

19 *Plug the outside.* Keep the heat in mind, so that the glue hardens well.

20 *Cut the plugs.* This is done either with a chisel or with a router fitted with spacers.

21 *Sand the hull from the outside.* Use the long block and thin the paint edges to avoid using too much putty.

22 *Surface treat the outside.*

23 *Install the interiors.*

SUMMARY

You can't just "change a frame." When replacing a frame, there are a bunch of different steps—in this case, twenty-three. The cost of replacing a frame depends largely on how many steps the boat owner is able to perform on his own. To roll an angle frame at a workshop is perhaps 20–30% of the whole job, and this is not counting the removal and installation of the interiors.

The difference in cost between letting a boatbuilder replace the frame and having the boat owner just get help with the parts he can't do himself is far greater than most people think. The variety of steps and the many different possible solutions also explain why a boatbuilder has a difficult time to providing a cost analysis by telephone. This complexity is also true for most other parts of wooden boat restoration. I hope that this chapter does not persuade you to give up on such a difficult job, but that it creates a little understanding of how much is hidden behind a simple expression such as "to change a frame."

FIGURE 103 } Planking prepared for framing. The planks are scraped, plugged, and oiled and ready for the new frames.

FIGURE 104 } New frames and floors ready for installation.

FIGURE 105 } The frames have been replaced, the boat is launched, and the mast is on.

FLOORS

The floors connect the heels of the frames to the keel and are a major joint, much as the spine is essential to the ribs. During construction of a boat, the floors can be installed at various times. If the boat is built with iron frames or laminated wooden frames, the floors and the frames are mounted directly on the stems and keel. If the boat is built on moulds, the frames and floors are added when the planking is complete. The most common floors are wooden floors, at least in the types of boats that originate from old working boats and the boats that were mass-produced during the second half the 1900s. The pleasure boats that were built without splining used steel frames and steel floors for tight planking. This also applied to boats with heavy machinery, in which it was lighter and easier to create a stable truss with steel floors and an engine bed. The forged floors were used with wood frames.

FIGURE 106 ⟩ Forged floors.

WOODEN FLOORS

In Swedish boatbuilding, wooden floors are almost exclusively made out of oak. They are attached to the planking with screws or nails. In the upper corners of the floors—where it is low—copper rivets are used. Sometimes the floors centered between two pairs of ribs, but more often they sit next to the frames. If the frame is a construction frame (i.e., a frame on which the planking is laid), floors will be riveted to the frame. The attachment of the stem and keel is done with bolts; the bolt diameter should be no more than ⅓ the thickness of the floors.

A special construction method is used on fast motorboats with chine hulls. They have sawn frames and floors made out of relatively thin wood, and the frames are high (see Figure 117, E and F, in the following chapter). The floors are screwed onto the wood frame along its entire height. A lot of times, the keel bolt is drilled in the joint between the frames to avoid the thin floor to be weakened by the bolt.

When constructing old-style working boats, there are various kinds of sawn frames and floors used depending on what kind of timber is available; sometimes the floors are spliced near mid-ship; sometimes they are intact till the upper part of the frame takes over.

When a hull starts to leak, it may be the screws in the wooden floors that are bad; this is common if they are made of brass. Another reason may be that end grain wood in the floors that lay against the planking have absorbed moisture, have gotten freeze damage, and are cracked or rotted. The damage, occurs more quickly if the floors are standing in bilge water. If the rabbet line or the seam between the garboard strake and the next plank

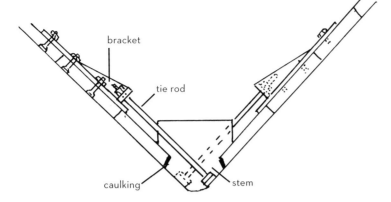

FIGURE 107 } One method to pull back and secure a rabbet that has been driven apart by caulking. The bracket with the nut for the tie rod is mounted through the planking with screws and nuts. This unit can be mounted permanent under a mast step.

on a motorboat, or the planks below the mast step of a sailboat opens up it is time to remove a few screws in the adjacent floors. Unplug the screw holes in the planking and remove the screws; if they loosen without resistance or just spin around in the hole, or if they have broken off and spin around, try to remove them with pliers or a pair of thin screwdrivers. Try if it is possible to get longer and thicker screws to grip in the old holes. Otherwise you need to drill new holes in between the old ones. If the new screws grip good in the wood of the floor you can settle with that. If the screws won't grip and the floor timber sound hollow when you tap on it, it is time for replacement.

If you try to drive the rabbet line with caulking when the floors are bad, it will just lead to a greater gap (See figure 107).

PROCEDURE FOR REPLACING WOODEN FLOORS
Remove the fasteners that go through the planking. If it is corroded steel screws with bad slots or iron nails the head can be drilled out and the fastener is driven deeper into the floor timber until it is clear on the inside of the planking. The next item is the bolts through stems or wood keel. Sometimes it is possible to loosen the nut and beat the bolt out (with a sledge and a bar). This is a job for two people, otherwise you will easily create more work as the bolt may go in the wrong direction and crack the outer stem or the wood keel if no one is (watching and) holding an anvil on the outside.

On some boats built after World War II, the floor timber bolt was drilled in a right angel (90°) towards the stem. The bolt was mounted through the stem and then

bent so it was standing vertical, and then the finished floor timber with a pre-drilled hole was mounted on the bolt. A bolt like that can't be beaten out from the inside, if you are lucky the bolt head can be drilled off and the bolt with its floor timber could be driven into the boat. Otherwise the floor timber has to be cut vertically in the grain direction along the bolt with a pair of chisels and dismounted in halves. After that the bolt can be bent back and removed. Another problematic bolting is when the floor timber is bolted only through the wood keel. The bolts heads are not accessible because they are hidden by the later attached ballast keel. If the floor bolts are in good condition it is possible to cut away the old floor timber and reuse the bolts for the new floor without removing them. Sometimes it is possible to drill the new bolts down through the ballast keel and use them as keel bolt as well (see figure 108). It is possible to drill in the ballast keel if it is made of lead or pure cast iron – on the contrary cast iron with a lot of slag dulls the drills at once. The recess (pocket) in the ballast keel for the nut can be drilled out with a coarser drill – large enough for the nut. Or drill two adjacent holes and cut the lead out between them to make a wider hole. If the wood keel is high enough, the recess can be cut out in the side of it just above the ballast keel without weaken it to much.

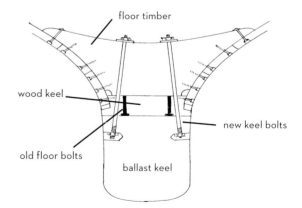

FIGURE 108 } A method of fastening a new floor timber when the floor bolts are not accessible. The old bolts are cut and left in the wood keel beneath the new floors. If no bolts are installed through the floor timber the keel will just hang on the garboard strake. This can make the garboard strake crack along the screws in the rabbet line when the boat is heeling heavy going to windward, or running aground when heeling.

FIGURE 109 } You can't be sure that the floors are equilateral in an old boat, so you have to keep track of which is starboard and which is port.

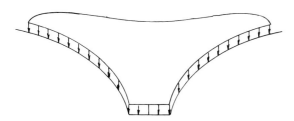

FIGURE 110 } In this sketch, floors are copied to fit in the bilge. The floors should be lowered straight down, so the measurement is taken plumb (all arrows on the diagram are plumb and the same length). The tool that transfers the measurement should have a plumb line or a level to transfer properly. A compass with a level—so that it can be kept completely vertical—is one way to do it (see Figure 43 in the chapter on tools). If the compass is held at a right angle to the planking, the floor timber will be too narrow at the bottom.

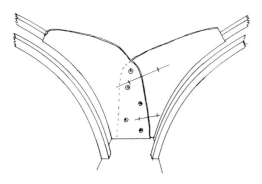

FIGURE 111 } An alternative is to make the template of the new floor timber in two halves. The halves are fitted separately and are glued and bolted together. Mark it with some lines just in case the glue detaches.

Making a Template of the Floors

The old floors can be used as a rough template. It can be difficult to copy them straight off as the important attachment area against the keel plank is often damp and cracked and needs adjustment. When using them as a direct template, it's also easy to make errors by turning it the wrong way (see Figure 109). If you place the largest side of the floors against the new piece of wood for the floor, you will have copied the contour of the backside. It will work if the beveling is made after the contour is sawn, but if the floors are cut right away with a bevel, they will be inverted or too large. A template for floors is made of MDF; make the template a bit too high from the beginning and don't draw the final upper edge until the template fits the planking.

When making a template for a floor timber or another curved shape, such as a bulkhead, it is important that the measurements are taken at the right level (see Figure 110). If you just adjust a compass and draw the same measure as the planking, the drawn plot will have a different radius, with slots at the ends or the middle depending on whether the shape is convex or concave. In order to make it easier to lay out the template in the best way on the new material, the side of the floors facing the middle of the boat should be made into a template—that side being the greater. Then, the bevels should be measured with a sliding T-bevel and sawn, planed, or sanded out. A shortcut for making a template in the boat is to fit a template one half at a time and then glue the halves in place with quick-drying glue (see Figure 111).

The oak timbers at the bottom should keep at 12–17% humidity. This corresponds to timber that is stored under cover in an unheated space. The grain direction in the floors should follow the planking shape as much as possible, and the pith should not be in the floors.

When I make a floor timber, I start with a rough cut-out of an oak plank, which should be around ⅜″ (10 mm) thicker than the finished floors. Then the new material is machine planed to the correct thickness. The more detailed work is done with a band saw with an adjustable table for cutting out the bevel directly. When I fit the floors in place, I use a plane—a smoothing plane for convex surfaces and a spokeshave for concave; a circular plane is also good to use. Other tools used are a good jigsaw to cut out the shape, a planer or belt sander with coarse paper to bevel, and a belt sander for adjusting it.

Don't finish the upper surface of the floors until the other sides fit against the planking; if the upper edge is level, it can be used as a support for the floorboards.

Don't forget to make limber holes; they should be large enough for a folding rule to go through ¾″ (17 mm).

Assembly

The hole in the floors for the bolt can be drilled in various ways. If there is a hole in the keel (with the right angle), then you can drill through the hole and up through the floor timber. If you are unsure of the angle, you can drill through the hole from the outside to get a mark in the floor timber and then remove the floors and drill with the help of a guide (see Figure 112). If the bolt is still there and is going to be used again, you have to measure its position and then drill from the bottom up with the same guide. There are fine wood bits for this purpose, but we mostly splice up common drills for metal work (see Figure 113A). Drill bits can be spliced by welding them to a rod. In order for the drill to not be too tight, the rod should be a ⅛″ or so (a few millimeters) thinner than the drill. Splicing can be done end to end by welding all the way through. A good way to get straight splices is to place the drill and rod in the corner of an angular profile of aluminum; the rod will be supported so that its center is level with the center of the drill, and the weld does not stick to aluminum.

Fastening or floor bolts often have rectangular heads—partly so that they don't spin around during

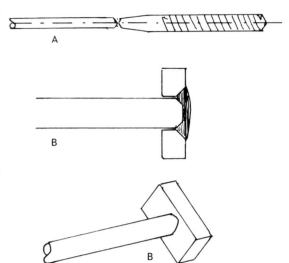

FIGURE 113 }

A A drill bit can be spliced by welding it to a rod.

B The head of a welded fastening bolt.

assembly, partly because you want as narrow holes in the bow as possible. The head is made of a piece of sheet metal, ¼–⅜″ (6–10 mm) thick, which is drilled and then countersunk at the top. File the bolt and insert almost all of it in the hole. Then weld the head from the end (see Figure 113 B).

When using conventional assembly without glue, the bolts are made out of Marine grade stainless rods that are threaded at one end and fitted with a welded head on the other. The skull is threaded with light wick yarn and mounted traditionally with red lead; today, you have to settle for something else, such as linseed oil, tar, or sealant. If you use glue in the design, the bolt can be made of a stainless acid-free threaded rod that is coated with filler-mixed epoxy during assembly.

The best finish for the edges between floor timber and planking was red lead. Today, it is oiled and mounted in a sealant that will have to do—unless the construction is glued and the floors are glued in place. The most important thing is that the wood in the joint not be left untreated, as it will rot in the long run.

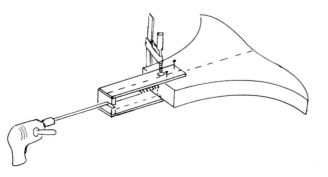

FIGURE 112 } A guide for drilling the fastening bolts.

STEEL FLOORS

On boats with steel frames, the floor has a galvanized sheet of steel—usually of the same thickness as the material in the angle steel frame. The plate is angled at the bottom and provided with a gusset for the fastening bolt. The upper edge is sometimes provided with a flange—made of angle iron—which also serves as a bottom for the floor boards. Frames, plates, and angles are riveted. The dimension of the rivets should be at least twice the thickness of the plate and the distance between the rivets around nine times the rivet diameter. When renovating, usually screws and nuts are used as fasteners. The floors should be outfitted with limber holes and ventilation holes wherever possible. The ventilation holes facilitate ventilation under the floorboards—something that diminishes moisture and subsequent corrosion. The ventilation holes also make it possible to mount hoses under the floorboards in a more comfortable manner. In the ends of the boat, the floor is sometimes made out of angle iron, and is mounted at the opposite angle to the angle steel frame and riveted to it.

The big yachts that were built with glued wooden frames in the fifties and sixties often had welded steel floors with flanges to the planking, and they were also bolted to the wood frames.

Steel floors rust. If they are in bilge water, and especially if it's salty, they will rust more quickly. The quality of the steel of steel frames and steel floors varies greatly.

FIGURE 114 } Rusty floors. This renovation has to begin with a broom and a shovel.

I have changed planking reusing the old steel frames of boats that were ninety-five years old, but I've also changed frames and floors that were fully rusted apart on forty- to fifty-year-old boats. If you are going to be able to rust-treat old frames in the bottom of boats, then the planking needs to be disassembled so that the steel can be blasted all over and then epoxy-coated; the remaining galvanization does not need to be taken off. If you think it's enough to treat the visible steel on the inside of the boat, then you need to scrape and sand with subsequent warming of raw linseed into the steel; in the old days, it was red lead that was the obvious choice for the coating. Now that red lead is prohibited, you can try a zinc-rich coat if the frame and the floors have any galvanization left or are clean to the steel, but not on rusty surfaces—they can be maintained with hot linseed oil.

REPLACING STEEL FLOORS

It is common for rust on floors to cause them to be the first to need renovation on a well-maintained wooden boat. If it's a sailboat with a deep bilge, then it is most often the lowermost parts of the floors and the angle of the fastening bolt that go bad. If the floors have rusted apart, then the only part that can hold the loads from the ballast keel is the garboard strake, with the risk of leakage as a result.

On motorboats, it is difficult to get the last bilge water out; it sloshes around over the keel throughout the bottom. You need the limber holes to be open, yet it is common to have rust on the lower parts of the frames and floors while they might be in good condition a few inches up. The floors on motorboats are often mounted to the keel with lag bolts of galvanized steel; they are usually so rusty that they look more like nails and release fairly easily from the keel. There is often a gap between the angel of the floor and the keel. This happens when the decrepit ends of the steel frames and the lag bolts can't withstand the swelling of the planking that presses the keel down away from the floors.

The floors are best changed in conjunction with changing the garboard strake. Then you can change the lower rusted ends of the steel frames simultaneously. If the steel frames are in good condition on the upper half of the floors, you can cut them off and the new ends of the frames

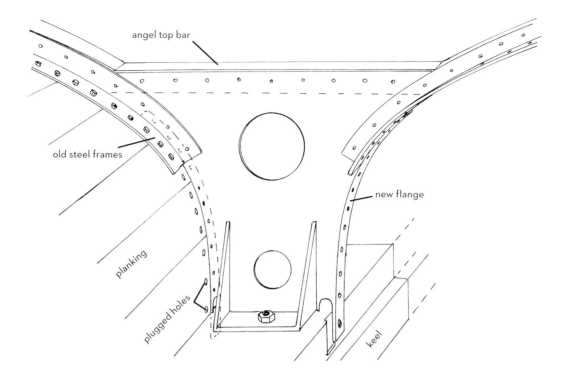

angel top bar

old steel frames

new flange

planking

plugged holes

keel

FIGURE 115 } New steel floors with welded flanges instead of the old cut-out steel frames. The flanges overlap the frames that are in good condition where they haven't been exposed to bilge water. Four rivets connect the old frames and the floors, and at least 8″ (20 cm) or two planks overlap, which is the minimum for a good joint. The flange for the keel bolt is pre-reinforced with two welded vertical flanges to better carry the forces up into the floor. The limber holes are at the lowest point, and the two ventilation holes are higher up in the floors. You can pull hoses and other installations through them. The floorboards are placed directly on the angel top bar. The design benefits from the garboard strakes being gone, so that the floors flanges can be screwed into the keel.

can be made of flat steel bars, that can be welded right onto the side of the new floor. Attach the flat steel bars on the opposite side of the floor so that they can be pulled up past the new ends of the old frames and thereby create a strong transition. In addition, the planking is often in better shape on the side of the old rivet holes so the screws attach better.

PROCEDURE FOR REPLACING STEEL FLOORS

1   Remove the floors by chopping off the rivets that go through the frames and then knocking them out.

2   Loosen the lag bolt or the nut of the floor bolt. If you can access the floor bolt, then replace it with another made of Marine grade stainless steel.

3   Cut out the rust-damaged bottoms of the steel frame. If the planking has not been dismounted, you either have to try to coax out the rest of the frame between the keel and the planking, or cut and let it sit. In that case, it is especially important that the floors are bolted through keel so that no structure is weakened.

4   Make new floors and frame ends out of stainless steel or steel plate of good quality and hot-galvanize it when holes are drilled. Don't just use any kind of iron, as it won't last. I tend to reinforce the angle of the keel bolt with a pair of flanges. Do not forget to make limber and ventilation holes.

5   The floors are fastened with screws and bolts both through the planking and through the old frames. If you use stainless steel in the floors, you have to isolate them from the end of the old frames with gum paste or a plastic liner.

FORGED FLOORS

Especially in Norwegian and Finnish boatbuilding, floors were often forged of galvanized steel. Forged floors have no stiffening metal sheets but provide a more resilient structure and are mostly used when the boats are built with bent or sawn frames and with caulked seams. Since the steel in floor is forged it is rust-resistant, and the floor have so much material from the beginning that we sometimes reuse them and re-galvanize them when we renovate. The forged floors are mounted on the inside of the frames and are bolted through the frame and the planking. To get an idea of the dimensions you can imagine a motorboat of 5 metric tons with sawn wood frames could have been built with floors of an arm length of 14.5″ (370 mm) and the cross section $^7/_{16} \times 1^1/_4$″ (11 × 31 mm) at the keel and $^1/_4 \times ^7/_8$″ (6 × 22 mm) at the tip of the arm.

HANGER STRAPS

Sometimes when you replace planking you need to cut out rusty steel frame ends where they are bolted to the stem and keel. To reinforce the attachment between keel and planking, we use hanger straps. It is simply a stainless steel strip, which is affixed at regular intervals to the rabbet. They are screwed with wood screws into the rabbet and screwed into at least two planks with nuts and bolts. 1 × $^1/_8$-inch (25 × 3 mm) material may be a suitable dimension for a 3-tonne boat.

A lot of times when renovating, we find that some planks are not well-fitted to the stem; the angles are such that one plank is just screwed into the stem while another one is attached to the frames; sometimes it may be like that for 27.5–31.5″ (70–80 cm). If the boat is stressed a lot in the water, the planks may open up. This also can be corrected with hanger straps in conjunction with a planking replacement.

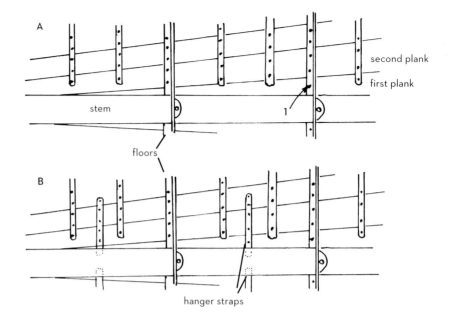

FIGURE 116

A Sometimes the first and second plank at the stem are not attached well. The rivet by arrow 1 is the first connector between the lowermost strake and the remainder of the planking. If this is what it looks like underneath the mast foot, you are certain to have a leak there.

B A couple of hanger straps would do the trick when replacing planking. The hanger straps are fastened to the rabbet when the planking is replaced, or on the side of the stem when you repair without replacing the planking.

SUMMARY

Floors hold the backbone and the sides of the hull together. Bad floors are a common reason for leakage.

The most sensitive parts of sailboats are under the mast foot and over the ballast keel. On motorboats, the floors are often weakened as they have been cut to replace engines and exhaust systems. The lag bolts through the keel plank have sometimes released too; this leads to the rabbet opening up.

The floors must be securely attached to the backbone in order to transfer loads.

PLANKING

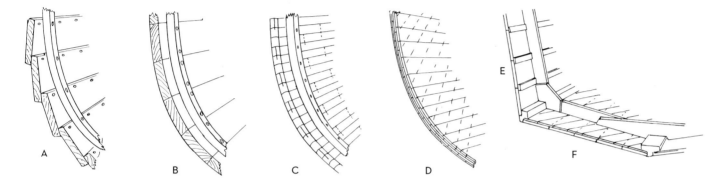

FIGURE 117 } Types of planking:

A Clinker-built or lapstrake, the overlapping joint is called a lap.
B Carvel-built, the planks are mounted against the ribs.
C Strip planking, the strips are gently rounded and are nailed to the strip underneath.

D Cold-molded planking.
E Rib carvel, the ribs are installed before the planks.
F Double planking, the planks are often riveted to each other between the ribs.

PLANKING METHODS

The main different types of planking are clinker, carvel, and laminated.

Clinker-built or lapstrake is characterized by the planks overlapping on top of one another. It creates planking that is strong and tough longitudinally.

Carvel-built can be done in various ways—the most common is that the planks are edge-to-edge, adjacent to each other, and are held together by the ribs. In recent years, the planks have also been glued to each other.

Rib carvel: On thinner planking, a rib is sometimes screwed in the middle of the plank seams on the inside of the planking; it is both a stringer (longitudinal stiffening)

and a sealant. This construction method is common on high-speed motorboats.

Strip planking is a different construction method that was especially common along the northern coast of Sweden. Here, the planks are made of thinner, machine-planed strips, which are nailed or screwed to the frames and are nailed to the underlying strips. The strips are often cupped and glued to each other. This is a fast construction method, but it is difficult to repair because of the bowled shape and the hidden nails in the strips.

Double planking, in which the inner planking is often placed on the diagonal and the outer is carvel-built; this is common on the bottom of speedboats. Sometimes there is a sealing canvas between the planking layers. This type of planking is tough and elastic. It is used more abroad, as it is not as suited for a climate with freezing temperatures. Trapped water freezes between planking and pushes them apart so that the screws may come out. This method is common in the USA for motor boats that are not kept in the water but are trailered.

Cold-molded planking is glued with veneer in several layers with varying grain directions. Cold molding has been used since the mid 1900s—partly for construction of single boats, partly for construction of smaller boats built in greater quantities. The older boats are often glued with carbamide glue, and those built in the past twenty-five years are glued with epoxy. The planking becomes self-supporting, so the frames can be replaced by reinforcements in the form of bulkheads and stringers.

Another version of cold-molded planking is where the planking is performed by strip planking, which is coated with fiberglass and epoxy on the inside and veneered on the outside. Repairing a cold-molded hull is more like repairing damage to a fiberglass hull than conventional wooden boat restoration.

Plywood planking was used in the time between conventional wooden boat construction and when plastic took over—during the 1950s and 1960s. Domestic plywood manufacturers could supply plywood that was sufficient for the entire length of the boat. Plywood restricted designers to structures with simple curved surfaces and hard chines. This, and the problem with moisture penetration in the joints of the end grain, made this construction method less interesting. Plywood is still a good method for amateur boatbuilding. However, it is difficult to get a hold of marine plywood in Sweden, but it is readily available in North America and the UK in a wide variety of grades and face and back veneers. The plywood that is available here is of such low quality that it risks making boats with short life spans.

CLINKER-BUILT PLANKING

Clinker planking or lapstrake is a Scandinavian construction method with ancient traditions. (Clinker is a European word for this type of planking and is nearly identical to Lapstrake planking here in the United States.) It is the conventional method that is best suited for construction of small boats with thin planking. The planks seal by

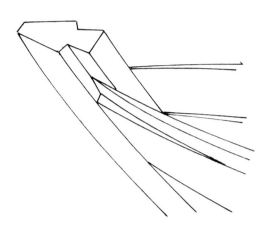

FIGURE 118 } The planks are of uniform thickness except at the bows, where the laps are cut out with a plane so that the planking connects smoothly to the inside the rabbet.

overlapping one another, and the double planking in the laps increases longitudinal strength.

The ribs can be placed further apart than a carvel-built ship. The boats are usually built on moulds, and frames are added later. They are either bent frames or sawn frames that are cut to fit the clinker, or combinations of both methods. The ribs are only attached at the laps, except for when attached with juniper Trunnel or Tree-nail. As the lap would nearly be cut of by the big hole for the trunnel. With this method, the Trunnels or Tree nails are mounted in the middle of the planking, and the frames are sawn so that they are right on the planks.

The planks are of equal thickness, except at the bows where the lap are cut out with a plane so that the planking connects smoothly at the rabbet (see Figure 118). The lap were sealed in different ways, ranging from the surfaces just being streaked with linseed oil or tar, to a strip of tarred cattle hair that was laid in the lap and riveted.

The width of the lap should be 1.5 times the thickness of the planking.

The joints should either be butt joints with butt blocks or scarf joints.

Repair of Clinker-Built Planking

It's harder to fix clinker planking than carvel planking. For carvel-built planking, a repair is supported by the dense ribs; for clinker-planking, the joint surface gets more stress.

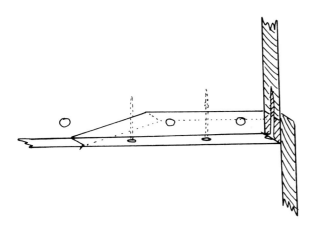

FIGURE 119 } Do not repair clinker planks unless the adhesive bond can be secured with screws through the joint. The repair is glued only to its own plank, not to the lap.

For example, we don't spline the clinker planks, even though weather cracks are relatively common in the middle of these planks. They swell, and the traditional repair method was to fill the crack with a soft tallow- or wax-based seal or to nail a sheet of lead on top of the crack. You can't seal the crack with glass cloth and epoxy from one side of the plank, as it will bulge and become convex when it swells. If you fill the crack with hard putty, it will act as a wedge when the plank swells and make the crack even longer.

Water can collect in the lap, especially if they have been sealed from the outside with a sealing compound. The water can't drain out when the boat is taken out of the water in the fall, so the lap is at risk of freezing apart when the cold weather comes. To avoid this, you can turn small boats upside down over the winter, or scrape out the sealant from the edge of the lap amidships on larger boats.

In laps where the rivets become loose, you can use the same tools to tighten them as were used to first rivet them. The rove is driven in a bit farther with the set, and the rivets are cut again if necessary, then riveted like before.

If the plank edges are frozen so there have been cracks in the row of rivets, you can remove the rivets and cut out the edge. A new planking edge is made out of a trim that is glued to the plank and secured by edge-screwing with stainless steel decking screws (do not forget to pre-drill), and then riveted to the second plank (see Figure 119).

We have a rule about not gluing with the clinker planks unless the adhesive bond can be secured by edge-screwing, so in cases of a crash or severe weather cracks, the planks need to be replaced.

PROCEDURE FOR REPLACING CLINKER-BUILT PLANKING

1   *Begin by deciding where the joints should be.* Think about trying to get a good joint staggering, which will also permit future plank replacement. The planks that are most difficult to change are those with cut-out laps by the bows, especially if the planks are nailed on the stem. If it's a weather crack or damage from a crash in the middle of a plank, the quality of the repair would be better if the plank is butt-jointed at both ends so that no more planks need to be loosened from the stem, risking fractures and deformities. This procedure will describe the replacement of such a plank.

2   *Drill a series of small-diameter holes in the plank at the location of the new butt joint and saw off the plank with a handsaw.* You can also cut the plank using a router and a guide bar, cutting as far as you can and then cuting the joint further upwards. Cut the joint so that the plank that is to be replaced will be longer at the bottom—meaning that it will get a open bevel so it can be released by being tapped downward (see Figure 120).

3   *Cut off the rivets on the inside of the planking and knock them out.* If the planks are attached to the sawn frames with wood screws, then they need to be removed; if the planks are nailed with galvanized boat nails, you can carve out the wood of the lap on the plank to be replaced and pull out the nail with a pair of pliers. Galvanized nails may need to be "awakened," which means striking a hard blow to the nail head and

FIGURE 120 } Open bevels in the joints make it possible to knock the old planks out. The joints can also be fitted more precisely as the new plank is pressed into its spot.

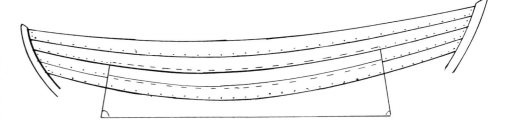

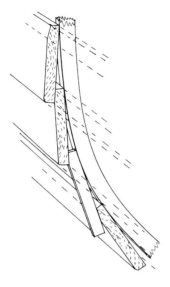

FIGURE 121 } The bevel at the edge of the seam can be taken from the old plank, but it may be useful to determine whether they comply by using a stick of the same thickness as the planking that is beveled to fit between the plank above and the frame.

hopefully shaking the nail in the frame will release it. The nail in the plank above it might be harder to get out. To remove the plank, you can cut off the plank edge on the inside, right in front of the frame down to the nail; the plank can then be removed and the nail can then be coaxed out or cut off at the rib.

4 *If possible, the plank is dismantled entirely and used as a template for the new plank.* If the plank is jointed or if you suspect that it will change shape because it is weakened, a strip of plywood can be screwed onto the outside of the plank for support before it is dismantled. The open bevel of the joints makes it possible to take out the plank when the rivets are gone. The thickness of the disassembled plank and the adjacent planks are measured to determine the planking thickness. The bevels at the edge of the laps can also be taken from the plank, but you may want to check if they comply with a stick that is beveled to fit the lap (see Figure 121).

5 *Select the timber for the planking.* For more on the choice of timber, see Chapter 7 on boatbuilding timber. For pine and oak, you want to place the core outward.

6 *The new material for the planks is preferably machine-planed to the desired thickness.* The old plank is clamped flat on top of the material (it is important that the plank is flat and parallel without any tension or the plank curve may be wrong), and plank edges and lengths are sketched out. Then cut the plank out with some extra length. If you need a little margin for the fitting, cut the plank slightly wider.

7 *Copy the width of the top lap;* if the lap needs to be beveled, you need to transfer the bevels from the old plank. In the bilge, the bevel will end up in the lower lap; measure it in the same way.

8 *The new material may need to be steam bent before it is fitted* if the dismantled plank is very bent or warped. In that case, set up studs and wedges as a mould with following the disassembled plank form; exaggerate the bend at the ends. It is easiest if you can attach the mould to a wooden floor; otherwise you can improvise any which way. Bending is described in the chapter on wooden frames. After bending, the plank needs to be clamped into shape and needs to get used to its new shape for a few days.

9 *The plank is then cut to length,* with the slightest overhang at the ends, and fitted into place. The open bevels of the joints means that the plank can be pushed upward and the ends can be fitted one by one. Tap the plank up so the marks for the top lap's width are in at the old plank's bottom edge. It is important that the plank is not too long, as the butt joints will be tight and you won't be able to pull the laps together. If the plank has a wrong curve, it will fit in the lap on one side but there will be a gap on the other. If the plank is pushed in so that it seals in both laps, it will get a wrong curve instead. If there is an excess of plank width, it can be used to adjust the curve. When several

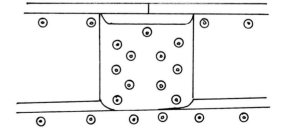

FIGURE 122 } Backing block with rivets.

planks next to each other are replaced, the plank can be held in place with clamps.

10 *When you are satisfied with the fit, it's time to make the butt blocks*; they should be as thick as the planks and have a width that allows double rows of rivets at each plank end. The butt block goes up to the plank top, and a rivet is drilled down through butt block in the center of the joint and out through the plank above as a sealing of the joint (see Figure 122).

11 *Now it's time to assemble the plank.* The sealing of the laps can take many forms; one option is to do the same as has been done before. An elastic adhesive can be another option. If you want to make sure that you don't get wood shavings that prevent attachment in the lap, you can drill the holes before the plank is taken down the last time. The rivets in the lap are drilled through the old holes from the outside in the plank above, and from the inside out by the plank below. The butt blocks are mounted with elastic adhesive or some form of traditional mastic or tar—a basic mix for this kind of "goo" is a one part

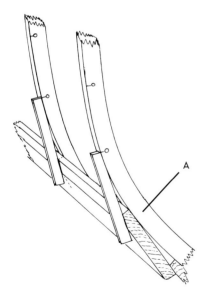

FIGURE 123 } The bevel of the inner lap edge can be planed in place and measured with the aid of the height of the next plank that was copied off onto the rib before the planks were dismantled.

A It is important that the plank is right against the rib when measuring.

raw linseed oil, one part pine tar, 5 parts of chalk and one part of sheeps tallow. Riveting has been explained previously in the chapter on screws and nails.

12 *When the plank is mounted, it is sanded or scraped.* The rivets are covered with putty or plugged depending on how it's done on the planking in general. A base for classic putty can be made out of oil-based window putty. Another possibility is one part oil varnish to four pieces of chalk.

Alternative

If an entire plank has to be replaced, the next two planks above must be taken out of the rabbet. The planks are wedged out with flat wooden wedges in the rabbet, so the planks that are being replaced can be knocked out without breaking. The ends of the plank is copied to the new plank, and one end is fitted with the other lying outside the rabbet. A base line is set amidships, and the other half fitted with the first one outside the rabbet. Then the whole plank is tested in its place and assembled.

If several planks next to each are replaced, then the edges of the planks are marked on the ribs before disassembly. The planks are formed like the old ones and set up with clamps. If the planks need to be steamed in place, this can be done in place with the ribs as a mould. The beveling of the upper land can also be done in place and is copied with help from the ribs. The steps will be like with a new construction (see Figure 123).

CARVEL PLANKING

Replacing planking is considered one of the major works on a boat; it means that part of the boat needs to be rejuvenated and given a longer life span. Fifty years is a reasonable perspective on planking, but the planking is just the shell; it is the planks along with the backbone that give the hull its strength.

Sometimes I get inquiries by telephone about replacing planks because the boat in question is leaking. During a visit, it often proves that the fault lies in the frame—such as in broken ribs or cracked floors. Or the fasteners are poor, often old, brass screws. An inspection of the fasteners and the structure of the frame was then sufficient to solve the problem.

Repairing the frame is more cost effective than replacing the planks; new planks that are fastened poorly won't hold tight. Sometimes there is a need for plank replacement, such as with accident damage, frost damage, and electrochemical damage of the wood caused by metal hardware—for example, by the frames.

An estimate of the cost of replacing planks is usually done by length. This varies depending on difficulty and size. If several strakes of plank are replaced, it will take less time per length of planking.

The planks in the bilge (the concave planks between the bottom and keel) are the hardest to replace. Here, it may be economical to continue and change the first flat plank above the bilge to get a simple plank to shut the planking.

The workflow described here uses a shutter plank, i.e., a plank that fits between two existing planks.

PROCEDURE FOR REPLACING CARVEL PLANKING

1 *Determine how much should be replaced.* Inspect and decide where the joints should go. It is important to stagger the joints so that the hull isn't weakened. Rules for staggering joints have been previously described in the chapter on joints. To maintain good joint staggering, it is easiest if the whole plank is replaced. Often the wood at the joints is so bad that the new joints may be moved further to the side.

If there is damage to a glued hull, it may be enough to router away the old wood and then cut in new wood in the planking closest to the damage.

2 *Remove the old planking.* Try saving the old planking as a template if it is very skewed—that is, if it rotates like a propeller. A good way to get an old plank out is to cut with a circular saw through almost the entire thickness of the plank next to the seams. The edges can then be carefully chiseled off so that the tension releases along the plank. The rivets are cut off on the inside and then tapped out through the frames and planking, and then the plank can be disassembled.

3 *Clean up the edges.* Router them or use a bull-nose rabbet plane to shave of the adjacent edges. Make sure they get a draft angle. This is an important step that many are careless with; the fit of the new plank will never be better than what the old plank edges around it allow. The bevels of the adjacent planks must be open so that the new plank has room to fit in (see Figure 124). A router is fine to use if the planking is convex. Nail a guide bar for the router just as when you spline. If the planking is concave, you need a bull-nose rabbet plane or fillister. It is a tool that many have cursed, with bloody knuckles from the ribs and the plane skipping. Here, it is important to have a sharp plane—the blade held short—and patience.

For the joints to be tight and easy to fit, it is important that the adjacent ends are flattened and that the planks are given an open bevel. If you have access to a router, it will be the fastest tool. Nail a guide bar and route the plank end straight. Fit a wedge to the router plate so that there is a bevel in the joint.

4 *Make a template of the plank.* When the hole for the plank has smooth, open edges, and the joints in the adjacent planks are ready, it's time to make a spiling board. The spiling board should have half the thickness of the planking and fit into the opening with a ½-inch (1-cm) gap all around. Put the splining board in the plank hole. Make sure it is not tight but flattens well against the ribs without touching the planks nearby. Nail or clamp it to the ribs. A spiling board that has half the plank thickness makes the compass move correctly and provides an accurate measure (see Figure 125). The spiling board can be made of fir or pine; plywood works well, too.

Spile (mark) the shape of the plank edge on the spiling board with a caliper. The distance between the tips should be about ⅔–¾ of the plank width. Make caliper marks at each rib, and maybe a spile in between the ribs. Make more frequent marks by the ends and where the shape of the adjacent plank is more questionable. Don't forget to mark the caliper width on the spiling board. Then number the frames and put the numbers on both the spiling board and on the surrounding planking. Make a note of the control measurement of the opening's width.

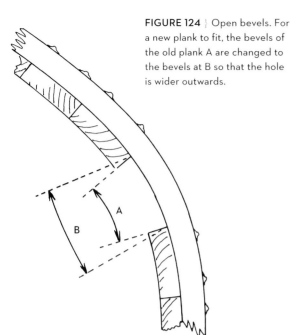

FIGURE 124 ¦ Open bevels. For a new plank to fit, the bevels of the old plank A are changed to the bevels at B so that the hole is wider outwards.

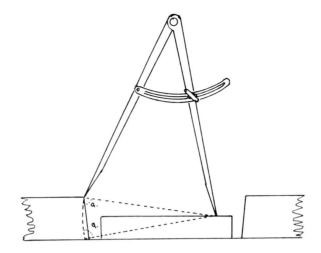

FIGURE 125 ¦ If the spiling board's thickness is half of that of the planking, the caliper will transfer the correct measurement to the new plank material when the spiling board is placed on the material. One tip is put right at the plank's outer edge, and the other tip is used to make a clear mark on the spiling board.

Also mark the joint locations with a compass. Then it's time to take down the spiling board and put it away for a while.

5 *Make a template of the corner angles and the rounding on a piece of MDF.* Cut a piece of MDF to make it as wide as the plank is at its widest point and tapering to about ½″ (1 cm) narrower than the plank's narrowest point. Insert the MDF at each frame and place the longest side against one edge of the plank; then draw the shape of the frame onto it. Repeat for each frame, and number it the same as the numbers that were previously listed on the planking in the middle of the ribs (see Figure 126). Repeat the process along the other edge of the plank. Note that the angle between the new plank's back side and edge is the angle that is obtained between the MDF's side and corners of the curve, not the angle between the MDF's side and the curve's nearest corner (see Figure 127).

Measure the thickness of the adjacent plank. Now you have enough information to go to the workshop and make the new plank.

FIGURE 126 ¦ The MDF board is placed into the plank opening adjacent to the frames. The template is placed as far in as possible to the plank width. The template rests on one edge of the plank, and the curve and angle is transferred to the MDF board.

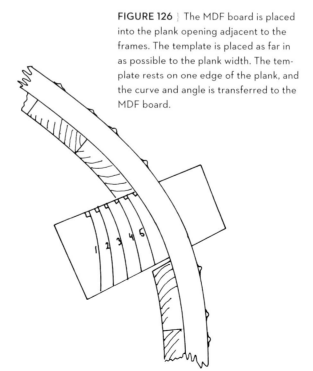

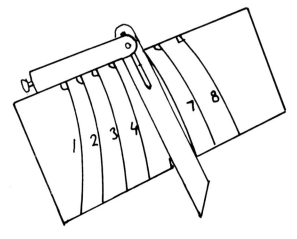

FIGURE 127 } The sliding T-bevel is used to transfer the bevels of the plank edge from the MDF template to the new plank material. In this case, the sliding T-bevel shows the bevel between the inside and the edge of the new plank at frame 6.

6 *Select timber for the plank.* (You can read more about selecting wood in the chapter on wood for boatbuilding.) If you replace a whole plank between two original joints (and a little more if the adjacent plank ends need to be cut and moved to the side), then it can be hard to get wood that is long enough and of good quality. The plank material can then be made out of two boards joined with a glued, spliced joint before the board is measured and marked.

With the knowledge of the adjacent plank's thickness and maximum curvature on the plank taken from the copies on the piece of MDF, it is possible to determine the necessary thickness of the new plank. I usually try to get a thickness that is $\frac{1}{16}$" (2 mm) extra, if the timber permits it. It makes it easier to clean off pressure and impact marks from clamps and hammers that may occur when the piece is fitted. Furthermore, you get a second chance if the plank is too narrow. The open bevels allow for the plank to become wider again if it is planed on the back.

7 *Transfer the spiling to the new plank.* Place the spiling board flat on the plank so that the wood is used most efficiently, and transfer the measurements with a compass. Transfer the rib numbers and their positions and the control measurements of the width as well.

Compare the caliper marks with the measurements. If the measurements are incorrect—for example, if the width of the caliper marks is consistently narrower than the control measurements—then the caliper marks can be increased somewhat. There is a pitfall here that is shown in Figure 129. Connect the caliper marks with a spline and draw a line; then cut just outside the line. Make the plank around 4" (10 cm) too long on both ends.

8 *Plane the plank edges at the right bevel.* Then plane the plank edges with the angles marked on the MDF board. The angles are transferred from the MDF board with a sliding T-bevel. If you have been careful with the rabbet plane on the old plank edges, then the plank edge will get a nice shape with a smooth open bevel all along the way. Shave down to the line so that half the holes from the stick marks remain.

9 *Cup the plank.* Cup the plank on the inside using the curves plotted on the MDF board. The cupping can be transferred with an aluminum strip that is bent into shape. A common misconception is that you can steam the cupping, but if you do then the plank will split along the fibers. Steaming is a rare phenomenon in carvel-built boats. From the start, a good boatbuilder could already lay the planks so that they twisted minimally and so that steaming would be unnecessary. The exception is the two or three bottom planks in the bow and the top planks in the bow on motorboats and in the stern of double-ended boats.

10 *Now it is time to fit the plank.* This calls for ingenuity in order to get the plank to stay in the opening. It takes studs, wedges, and jacks in large quantities. We use jacks with cranks of the type usually found on military vehicles. They can easily be extended with a piece of wood.

Hopefully the plank will fit so that it goes in between the old plank edges but not down to the bottom. Try to fit the plank in the most difficult end first.

11 *The 0-line (zero line).* It is important to determine the position of the plank in the longitudinal direction; when fitting, it is important to, as quickly as possible, get a reference line—a 0-line—so that the piece that you are working with is tested in exactly the same position throughout the work, otherwise the piece will abut at different places every time you try it. When the first half fits, you put a 0-line by the middle of the plank and the other half can

FIGURE 128 } Measuring the plank with a stick caliper and a spiling board.

fit without the first one needing to be installed again. A 0-line is a sharp mark made with a pen or chisel crosswise over the old planking and the new.

How long the fitting will take depends on how carefully the old plank edges are prepared, how well the spiling was made, and how well you managed to shave the new plank. Places where the plank is tight need to be marked with a pencil with an estimate of how much should be shaved off—it should be less than ¹⁄₃₂″ (1 mm). It is important to check both on the inside and outside; the angle may well be wrong. A feeler gauge gives a good sense of how big the gaps are between the points where the plank is tight.

12 *Tight fit or gaps?* You often hear that renovators are afraid to fit planks with a tight fit, fearing that the ribs will burst or that the old planks will be forced apart by the joints. This can be avoided if one can control the humidity in the planks. A 7% difference in the moisture may be an upper limit—for example, 17% in the old planks and 10% in the new.

I prefer a tight fit, but then you have to make sure that the old fastening in adjacent planks is checked again and is good. The rest of the hull is often a bit leaky and may need to be tightened up. The new

planks should be at around a 10–12% moisture level. If the wood is moister, it risks drying and cracking after the installation. The timber must be of good quality. In practical terms, it is also difficult to produce a plank with an even gap, and if the gaps are uneven, the planking will have a hard time swelling and sealing up.

13 *Drill for the fastenings.* When you are satisfied with the fit, it's time to drill for the fastenings. It is easiest to drill through the holes in the ribs and out through the new plank. If it's hard to access the inside, then the marks for the holes are transferred over to the neighboring planks by using distance lines. With the new board in place, the marks are transferred over to it, the hole locations are marked off, and the holes are

FIGURE 129 } When there is a surfeit of plank thickness and the plank bevels are more open, the width must be corrected and increased according to the sketch.

A If the caliper measurement is kept, the plank will become too narrow when the edge of the plank is re-angled.

B The increase in the plank thickness is compensated by measurement C having been added to the measurement made by the caliper.

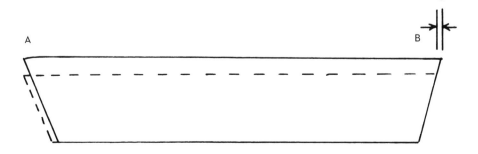

drilled through the plank and the rib. Countersink the plugs; approximately a ³⁄₁₆-inch (5-mm) thick plug when the planking is completed and faired is desirable if the planking thickness allows. Then the butt blocks are made and drilled.

14 *Installing the plank.* Paint behind the ribs and in other places that cannot be accessed after the installation.

Glue the plank if it was glued before or if the boat is made of mahogany. If the boat is made of pine and will be on land for a period of time, then just oil the plank. Different ways of fastening have been discussed in the previous chapter. When riveting with copper rivets and when screwing with nuts and bolts, you need to have two people.

15 *Fairing.* When the plank is replaced, you need to shave off the exterior and clean off the inside. If the plank is concave, you will need a special plane. Caulked holes slow the plane and cause it to bounce.

HOW MUCH WORK IS IT TO REPLACE A PLANK?

As with most jobs on boats, the whole work is the sum of a limited number of steps; the carpenter's professional effort is just a part of the whole work.

A relatively flat plank of about 4.5 yards (4 m) in length can take a boatbuilder about sixteen working hours:

- Removal and determining the placement of the joints—1 hour.
- Preparing the old plank edges and ribs for good attachment—4 hours.
- Template making—1 hour.
- Manufacturing the plank from the template—2 hours.
- Fitting into place with supports—2 hours.
- Joints—1 hour.
- Drilling and installing—4 hours.
- Fairing—1 hour.

REPLACING MULTIPLE PLANKS

If several planks next to each other need to be replaced, they have to be measured out like before, but on the edge of the open side just mark a few of the control widths. The plank may be a little too wide during the fit, and do not finish shaving off the edge of the open side till shortly before the installation.

You think you will remember how the planks were on the boat just yesterday, but when the planking is off, you will be left scratching your head. Therefore, mark all the planks on the ribs before they are removed.

I have mentioned earlier planking that was not caulked—"The Scandinavian Way." When boats were built, the planking was forced together with wedges that attached to the steel frame with clamps (see Figure 131). It is said that the boats had a tendency to be skewed if the planking on both sides was done right-handed and the wedges were hit in the same direction. On laminated wood frames, you can screw on brackets to hold against the wedges. If there is planking nearby, the planking can be forced together with car jacks that are stretched between an old plank edge and the new plank. The plank is held in place against the ribs with a clamp during the fitting.

SUMMARY

Clinker/Lapstrake built planking is the strongest planking for smaller boats. The lap—the portion where the planking is double—provides density and longitudinal strength, even for thin planking.

It is important that the laps fit well before the planks are riveted together; misalignments and gaps will lead to tension and cracks in the planks.

When building clinker planking, the old planks are used as templates, but when I build carvel planking, I start from scratch.

To make sure the new planking is well sealed and that the edges of the new plank are easy to work on with the plane, I carefully adjust the plank edges of the adjacent planks so that they are smooth and have open bevels.

It is important for the strength of the boat to make sure that the staggered joints, or butt spacing, are as long as possible.

FIGURE 130 } Two planks (in Swedish called crying planks) aft by the top of the rudder post. The planks are ³⁄₄" (20 mm) thick in finished condition and cut out of 3¹⁄₆-inch- (80-mm-) thick timber. At the front of the photograph are a caliper, a bull-nosed rabbet plane, and curved wooden planes.

FIGURE 131 } Planks wedged with clamps of the type that are used by plyms at the Neglinge shipyard. Here you can also see the numbering of the ribs.

THE BACKBONE

When constructing a new boat the boat builder starts with the lofting. The drawings and the offset table are interpreted and transferred to actual size and the lines are faired-checked to see if they match. Thereafter, the boatbuilder makes templates of the backbone in the boat's center line with all joint areas. The templates are used to cut out the stems, keel, and knees. They are formed laterally by means of measurements from the frame drawing. When the wood pieces are formed they are laid out horizontally on the lofting floor, and the bolts of the joints are drilled. Then it is all raised up and set plumb and level. The number of parts required will depend on the size of the boat and the availability of suitable timber. To prevent the joints from sliding, they should be equipped with different types of dowels, wedges, and stopwaters (see Figure 132).

FIGURE 132 } The stem joint of *Beatrice Aurore*. A well-bolted hook joint between old and new. The joint is drawn together by the wedge, which is visible in the middle of the joint. It may be a double wedge that is tapped in from both sides or, in this case, a wedge-shaped recess that the wedge is tapped into.

Then the floors and frames or frame moulds are installed. Sometimes yachts are built with the ballast keel mounted, which will make the boat very stable. Sometimes it's installed afterward.

THE BACKBONE ON MOTORBOATS

The keel on motorboats is often T-shaped. Sometimes it is made in two halves—an outer keel and an inner keel, or hog—that are bolted together. The width of the rabbet should be at least 1.5 to 2 times the plank thickness. If the hull is pointier and more V-shaped, you can give the keel a more rectangular shape and still have room for the rabbet (see Figure 134).

The best way is to make the stem in one piece, but sometimes there is not enough wood so it is made with a loose outer stem bolted to the inner stem. The stem knee should be able to take a turn that can be as wide as 90°, and it requires hook-grown timber. By the stern, the outer keel is often made higher for the sake of stability and is drilled out for the propeller shaft. It is hard to put a bolt through the keel when it has a hole for the shaft log; in that case, you can attach it with metal strips (see Figure 135).

The weak spot of the motorboat's keel is where the outer keel ends and only the inner keel continues aft; boats are often dented inward here from winter storage trestles. If the design is such that the engine bed continues past this point, the boat will retain its shape better. This also applies if the garboards are built deep so that they add strength. The keel ends with a knee in which the transom center post is attached.

Deep-sea boats and motor sailors have a more evenly shaped keel that turns into the counter timber via a hook grown knee in which a hole for the propeller shaft is made.

FIGURE 133 } Various keels.

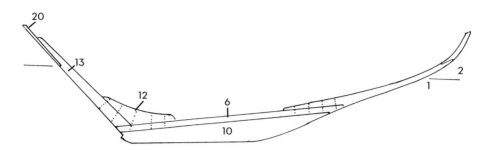

FOLKBOAT

The joint in the stem is placed according to timber supply; sometimes there is enough wood so that it is not needed at all. The transom is screwed to the rudderpost.

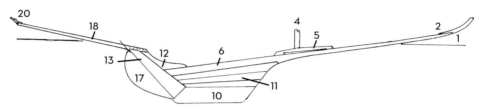

SKERRY CRUISER

The keel of the Skerry cruiser is so narrow that the bilge can't be built any deeper; you get a little too much weight with this kind of big deadwood. In this construction, the stem and keel are made out of one piece. The location of the mast where the mast and ballast keel are not positioned right opposite each other causes the problems that the Skerry cruiser has with strength and stiffness. Between the keel and the mast, there's a twist in the hull that can lead to leaks and even cracks in the forefront of the cabin.

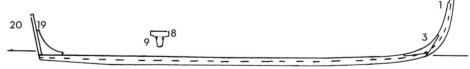

MOTORBOAT WITH OUTBOARD

The keel is usually made with a hog and outer keel. The design of the joint in the bow is controlled by the availability of crooked timber; when these boats were built in mass production, the stem was usually laminated.

MOTOR CRUISER

The number of joints on the keel depends on the boat's size. If the keel part with the shaft hole is to be made out of one piece, it will require large timber. You should avoid making a joint in the part where the shaft comes out of the plank.

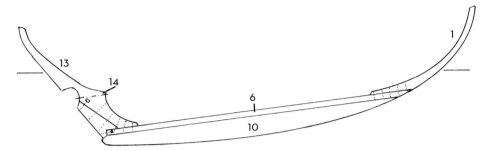

DOUBLE ENDER

Koster boat with inboard motor. The top bolt through the rudder post could not be drilled all the way because of the pipe but is in a pocket of the rudder post. With this construction, with the recess for the propeller, you must be careful such that the rudder post is not too weak above the recess. With a bow this short, you might find appropriate timber that the whole stem can be cut out of.

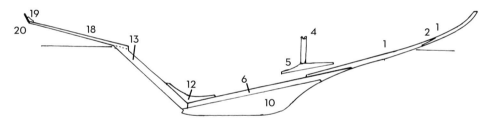

6MR YACHT

The 6mR yachts are extreme in the sense that of the total weight of 4 tonnes: 1 tonne is boat, rigging, and sails, and 3 tonnes is the lead keel. Material dimensions are at a minimum; the planking is $^{11}/_{16}$" (17 mm) thick. Yet, designers and builders have succeeded: many 6's are around seventy years old.

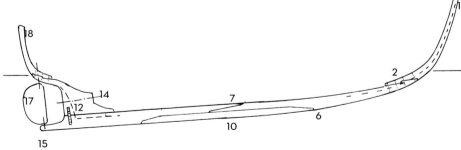

DOUBLE-ENDED HIGH SEA BOAT

The timber in the stern is interesting; it is difficult to obtain sufficiently long joints here, and it is not unusual for them to get gaps. An iron keel is an excellent butt block; splicing the keel above it won't weaken it at all.

1   stem
2   stem joint
3   knee
4   mast
5   mast step
6   wood keel
7   keel joint
8   hog
9   outer keel
10   ballast keel
11   deadwood
12   knee
13   rudder post
14   propeller shaft
15   skeg
16   shaft strut
17   rudder
18   counter timber
19   transom knee
20   transom

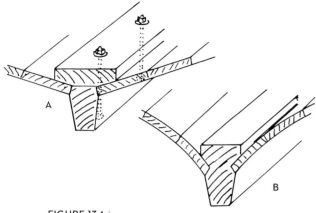

FIGURE 134 }

A Keel of a motorboat with a flat bottom. If the keel is made from one piece, it requires a big piece of wood. If it is made with a hog with a rabbet and outer keel, you will use the timber better; the keel should be bolted every 10″ (25 cm).

B On boats with more V-shaped lines or a sunken keel, it is easier to cut the keel out of one piece of wood because the rabbet becomes steeper and does not require as wide of a inner keel.

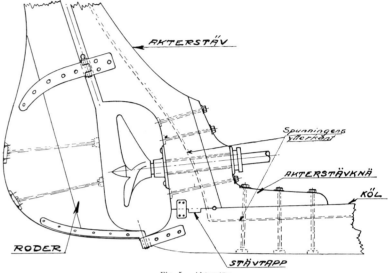

Fig. 5.   Akterstäv.

FIGURE 136 } Knee and stern/rudder post according to KMK's excellent handbook from 1929.

FIGURE 135 }

A It is difficult to have room to bolt through the keel on the side of the shaft hole. Sometimes the keel is already strapped when built before the planking is laid.

B If necessary, an old keel can be pulled together with ties as in the diagram. The bolt ends are welded to a steel strip, and the holes are drilled through the rabbet right next to the keel.

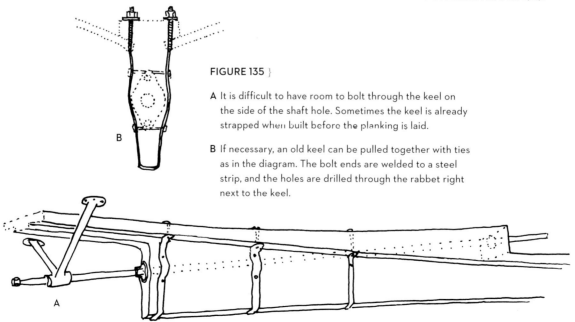

THE BACKBONE ON SAILBOATS

The wooden keel of a sailboat is usually wider than it is high; it is supposed to provide a nice transition to the wide ballast keel. In the forefront of the keel is the joint to the stem. The stem can then have another joint on the waterline before the stem curves up to the deck. At the stern above the keel, there is a knee that connects to the rudder post. If the boat has a flat transom the transom is bolted to the rudder post. On a boat with a longer stern the rudder post is jointed to a counter timber; that joint can be made in many different ways. The rudderstock passes through the counter timber adjacent to the joint, and this joint is often a source of problems. It tends to open up if the boat isn't supported right by trestles in the winter and if the boat stays on land for a long time. The counter timber ends with a knee that holds the transom. The underwater part of the backbone can become heavy, especially if it absorbs moisture. The oak has a density of about 750 kg/m³ at construction; an old water soaked keel's density increases and, for example, might have a density of more than 1000 kg/m³. (Wood that has soaked in the ocean for a long time may have doubled its weight.)

At the great leap in the development of sailboat construction in the early 1890s dimensions of the backbone were reduced, and then in order to maintain strength screw and bolt fastenings were increased. That is why so many of the old boats remain today. The oak timbers weren't large enough anymore to tear the hull apart when they dried and swelled, and the joints could keep tighter; moisture was not prominent, and the risk of rot was reduced. Meanwhile the demands on the joints increased in the thinner backbone so that they could transfer the loads of the hull. Therefore, it is very important that the joints and fastenings are not weakened during a renovation. Finding new places for joints with healthy wood is the biggest challenge for a renovation of the backbone; when you have solved that part half of the job is done, and half of the job is just carpentry.

GLUED KEEL

In the 1950s, they began to glue the hooked parts of the backbone. Stems and knees were glued oak laminates. This has led to a lot of work and many repairs when the gluing hasn't been able to resist the oak's moisture movements. Laminated stems have become unglued along the waterline, and moisture has migrated both upward and downward. If the stems were firmly bolted together, the design's strength won't have weakened, but the moisture in the laminates leads to rot in and above the waterline. Below the waterline, the oxygen has no access so there is no rotting there. Above all, it is the slats in the outer bows and the rabbet that have taken a beating; the laminates that are on the inside of the boat where it's airy and relatively dry have done much better. Sometimes the straight sections, such as the keel, were also glued, so that they could reduce the demand for quality timber in the individual parts, and the straight pieces were made of thicker laminates. If they are just firmly bolted, they will do better, but you have to remember that the once glued surfaces lack both mould protection and waterproofing (oil) against the water. If laminated constructions are to last, you have to use consistent gluing where the wood is surface treated so that the moisture movement is minimized (see the chapter on gluing).

REPAIRS

During repairs and renovations of the parts that are involved in backbone, the big problem is choosing the right limitations for the job.

Should damage from an accident be repaired then joints must be placed so that the boat's strength is retained. Often the parts around the damage has age deteriorations that it would be wise to fix at the same time. The Insurance does not cover this. The boat owner must decide what ambitions he has for the boat. Does he want to maintain an antique or does he only want his old tub to float for a few years? The carpenter must try to find a solution that maintains strength and that is financially feasible. What he should consider is:

- cutting off as little directional grains as possible (see Figure 137)
- trying to get healthy wood in the joint surfaces
- bolting and screwing the joints properly.

Often it may be economical to replace more wood in order to end up in a place where it is easier to plane a new joint. If you need to remove and replace a plank to provide access to make a new joint surface, you could consider the plank that is in poorest condition.

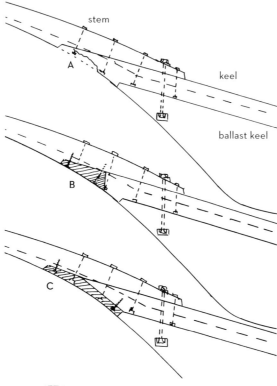

FIGURE 137 }

Example of a repair that impairs the joint more than the damage has done.

A A damage in the forefront of the wooden keel after a careless crane lifting sling cut into the wood.

B The repairman thought "It's just fresh wood; it will be fine," and sawed off a third of the contact surface of the joint; the piece is just screwed in with wood screws and the forward bolt of the joint has been cut off.

C A mend that takes into account the direction of the grain of the wood; the bolts have also been replaced.

RESTORATION

When boats get older, it gets to a point when it's time to replace the keel or put the boats in a museum. This goes specifically for sailboats with deep bilges and heavy ballast keels. None of the eight 95-sq-m Skerry cruisers that remain today in Sweden have their original wood keels left. The boats were built between 1909 and 1922; the first one to receive a new keel was only ten years old

when it was replaced, as the original keel was initially weak. The second one got her new keel when it was fifty-five years old (see Figure 138).

When it's time to renovate and open the planking, it is good, if possible, to renovate all that will need to be addressed in the foreseeable future. Ten years is too short of a perspective. Twenty-five years is also a short time span. On good, old boats, it may be reasonable to do renovations that will last as long as the original structure did. A renovation is a major procedure, both operationally and financially, and should be planned several years in advance. Meanwhile, maintain the boat, and if necessary, strengthen it provisionally with epoxy and fiberglass.

When renovating, there are mostly three parts that need attention: the planking, the keel with its bolts, and the floors with frame ends. It is not uncommon

FIGURE 138 } Changing the keel on the 95-sq-m Skerry cruiser, *Kerma*. The large knee (deadwood) aft has been added, as the bilge was so deep and narrow that it was impossible to keep it clean. The knee wasn't covered by the planking but got a rabbet in its leading edge so that moisture would not get trapped between the planking and the large knee.

for the cost to be the same for the three different parts. For the keel and floors to be accessible to change them, you need to remove the planking. When the planking needs to be replaced, you do not screw it into rusty frames and poor stems. Although the boat is opened wide, it may be difficult to set the limits for the work. Then you put on blinders and focus on the area that you're working with, and then just make sure that the new joint surfaces are placed so that later, it becomes as easy as possible to continue with the adjacent areas. Sometimes the boat is otherwise healthy, and the limits are obvious.

REPLACING THE KEEL

The procedure could change; there are many decisions made during the work. The wood keel of the sailboat and the propeller shaft connector of the motorboat are the most complex parts of the keels. Below, I have chosen to describe a replacement of a keel on a sailboat.

Procedure for Replacing the Wooden Keel

1   *Remove the rudder and rudder stock while the boat is hanging from the crane so that you don't have to dig a deep hole in the ground for the long rudder stock.*

2   *Set the boat higher than usual*; there should be at least 12″ (30 cm) between the bottom of the keel and the ground.

3   *Position the boat in level at least in the transverse direction.* What are the vertical and horizontal measurements in the transverse? There are several measurements that ought to remain fairly stable from the time the boat was built. The heights of the covering boards, the beam between the cockpit and cabin, and the berth and floorboards level are some such measurements. The engine bed on motorboats and the heavy deck beams to the mast of sailboats are others. The vertical measurements can be taken from the center of the beams down to the center of the keel. The measurements taken at the ends of the boats are more dubious; hulls often skew over the years.

4   *Build sturdy trestles for the ends*; remember that the center of gravity on a boat without a ballast keel will be high up in the hull. The supports must be rigid in the longitudinal direction as well; don't forget that the hull will lose ground contact when the keel is removed (see Figure 139). The stands made by Seaquip have made a lot much easier for the boatbuilder.

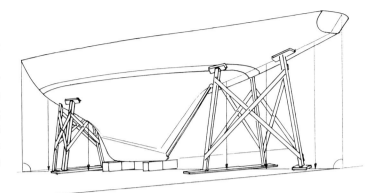

FIGURE 139 } Stands that are steady both latitudinally and longitudinally should be complemented by a pair of stanchions amidships. The important center line is set plumb. You need to make sure that the boat is correctly balanced throughout the replacement of the keel. For the boat to sail equally on both tacks, the center level of the keel must be consistent with the boat's center level.

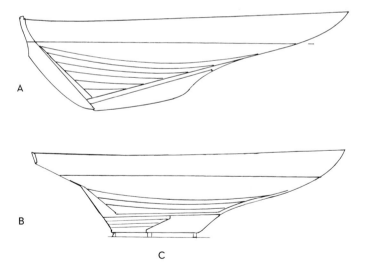

FIGURE 140 } The number of planks that must be removed for the keel to be exposed varies greatly between different types of boats. The double-ended boat in diagram A has five planks affected while the offshore cruiser B has only one plank. When the ballast keel is mounted only in the front part of keel (C), it is important that the ballast keel is also supported at its aft edge. Otherwise, the loads on the aft bolt of the ballast keel could cause a deformation in the wood keel.

FIGURE 141 } Rigging jacks on the 6-meter racer *Lillevi*. Two jacks are mounted on a beam through a keel pocket, and a hydraulic jack is under the keel's aft edge.

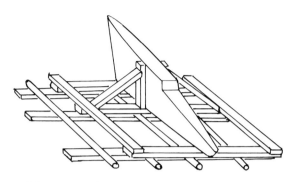

FIGURE 142 } The keel can be rolled to the side with the help of water pipes made of steel, which are placed between two levels of the planks. The keel is locked in sideways with braces.

5 *Remove the garboard strake at least on one side*; some boats only have one against the keel; others may have four to five. Here, you can make compromises; it always takes longer to change the keel with the planks in, but it takes time to change the planks as well, and this may be unnecessary if the planks are in good condition and the floors are good (see Figure 140).

6 *With a couple of planks dismantled*, it is easier to identify the keel bolts and easier to communicate with the person working from within. Loosen the nuts to the keel bolts (this is described in more detail later.

7 *When the bolts are removed*, a few bolts are retained in a couple of holes as guides when the balllast keel is lowered. The keel is lowered by the means of jacks; at least three are necessary (see Figure 141). Alternatively, the keel is lowered a bit and then slid sideways so that the bolts through the joints with stem and knee can be loosened (see Figure 142).

8 *When the joint bolts are gone*, the wood keel can be dismantled. Remember to check that the boat is vertical and where the center line runs on the old wood keel before it is dismantled.

9 *Here comes the next difficult decision*: are the knee and the rudder post in such good condition that they may remain so for another twenty-five years, or should they be replaced? We decide, for simplicity's sake, that they can remain in place.

10 *Order oak for the new wood keel*. It should have the right thickness and already be planed, unless you have access to a jointer and thickness planer yourself. Most wood keels are made this way. It is convenient for the builder to start from a parallel material of uniform thickness; all measurements are easy to carry out from top to bottom, and then if the ballast keel's upper edge is made horizontally, it will end up vertical under the boat. The width of the plank should have an extra inch or so (2–3 cm). For the wood keel and the other parts of the backbone to last and not crack, they should be cut from wood at the side of the heartwood. The pith rots and cracks easily. The sapwood cannot be involved. This means that large trees are needed as starting material. Timber of this size dries very slowly; it will be wet when sawn or cut, although the timber may have been at a material yard for years. That the plank is relatively wet with approximately 25–30% moisture content is not so bad, since the stem and the knee that it will be connected to will probably maintain the same humidity. If you work with a fresh oak plank, it is important to prevent it from drying out too quickly on the surface and cracking. I like to varnish it with old varnish when it's left for more than a few days. Linseed oil is not enough; it does not prevent moisture from escaping. If the oak is too dry, it can cause major problems.

A dry oak plank suitable for carpentry (12% moisture content) absorbs water and, after one season's use, will end up with a 20% moisture content. The swelling of oak in that moisture range is 1.5–2.5%. A 12-inch- (30-cm-) wide keel plank will increase its width by about ¼″ (6 mm). If the garboard strakes are partially mounted to steel floors and partly to the keel, they may crack in the middle of the bottom row of screws in the floors.

11 *Make templates.* Make a template of the keel-side view with the joint toward the stem and the joint surfaces of the knee and the rudder post. Make another template of the topside of the ballast keel with exact marks of the keel bolts, and one of the wood keel's topsides with the rabbet. It is important that the templates of the keel top and bottom have center lines that coincide with each other (see Figure 143).

12 *When the keel timber is delivered,* it is shaped using the templates and measurements from the old wooden keel. Make the keel with a little extra allowance if there's no old planking that it will fit behind; otherwise it has to be made to measure right away. The old holes in the stem and the knee provide control for drilling the stem bolts; if the floors are in good condition, they will also provide the location of the keel bolts there. If the keel bolts go up through the floors, the bolt holes are used as guides for drilling as well. If the keel bolts only go through the wooden keel, then the holes are drilled from the template made of the topside of the ballast keel; the angles of the bolts in relation to the keel topside are measured with a sliding T-bevel, and the wood keel is drilled from the bottom

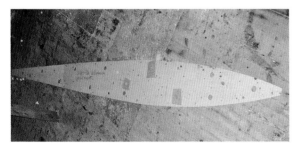

FIGURE 143 } Keel template. The holes in the keel template are made in excess. The template is placed on the ballast keel, and keel bolts are inserted into the holes. Then cut the small pieces with precise holes, place them down over the bolts, and glue them to the template.

of it before installation on the boat. A good control of the keel to be exactly positioned could be obtained by looking down the hole for the rudder stock. The centerline of the keel and the rudder bracket should be in the center of the hole.

13 *When the plank is drilled,* it is mounted with bedding compound in the joint surfaces. Drill stopwaters through the joints. I have almost always mounted the keel with red lead; today, as red lead is prohibited, wood tar might be an alternative. Elastic Adhesives can also be used, but not with wet, raw wood. The elastic adhesive forms a membrane between the pieces that prevent moisture migration; moisture migrates from inside the raw pieces of wood outwards. When it is stopped by the membrane the moisture is collected there, and when the wood is frozen the moisture freezes into ice crystals that break away the elastic adhesive from the oak. Then the adhesive will just remain as a moisture-retaining seal in the joint. If the keel is built of dryer timber, the rubber sealant may well hold for twenty-five years.

14 *Place the keel back under the boat,* fine-tune it with jacks, and insert the bolts.

In the surface between the ballast keel and the wood keel, I have used all kinds of sealants over the years: red lead, Thioflex, Sikaflex, bedding compound, and bitumen mastic. If the keel needs to be dismantled after a grounding, then a gluing rubber sealant, such as Sikaflex, will be difficult to take apart; the wood cannot be waterproofed by treatment with linsed oil as the sealant would not stick to oiled wood.

15 *When everything is fixed,* the rabbet is faired with a plane after the floors and the wood keel's dimensions are adjusted to the ballast keel and stems.

It sounds simple enough. The most important thing is to get the ballast keel center level to align it with the boat's center level.

Large motorboats have gotten new keels made of welded steel plates in recent years. That could be a good solution if you pay close attention to the transitions of the wooden hull and if you make sure to have corrosion protection of the steel construction.

REPLACEMENT OF STEMS

When it comes to damages from accidents, it is usually the outer stem that is damaged. If you have such damage, you can cut in a shorter new piece. Or you could replace

FIGURE 144 } Stem joint with knee. The bolts have T-heads so that they fit on the stem front.

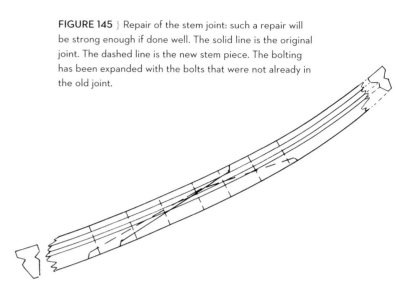

FIGURE 145 } Repair of the stem joint: such a repair will be strong enough if done well. The solid line is the original joint. The dashed line is the new stem piece. The bolting has been expanded with the bolts that were not already in the old joint.

the whole outer stem; then it should be bolted to the inner stem at least every 8″ (20 cm).

Usually the stem was made out of one piece from the beginning, but sometime it was divided from the beginning, particularly on mahogany boats where the outer stem also could be made of mahogany.

The stem usually gets bad at the joints first especially if the boat is left for a few seasons on land so the joint surfaces dry out and the bolts loosen. A weak joint can be reconditioned if the joint surface is cut in one direction and a new splice is cut in the other direction and then a triangular piece is bolted in place (see Figure 145).

If the entire stem needs to be changed, you have the choice of dismantling it outward or inward. If the planking is so bad that a lot of planks and plank ends, sometimes called nib ends, need to be changed they can be dismantled, and the rest of the planks can be dismantled from the stem. Thereafter, the stem is removed outward. If the planking is good, the floors and the keel bolts can be removed; then loosen the rabbet screws and lift the stem into the boat. To make it easier, you could even cut or chop off the outer stem. If the stem has held its shape, it can be used as a template; if it's old and patched from before, you need to make a plywood template at the center line. The angles of the rabbets are marked at lease at each floor timber.

The best starting material for a stem above the waterline is oak dried to 12–17%; fresh wood cannot be used here because it will dry and wrap. If the stem is to be laminate-glued, then Brazilian mahogany is a better option than oak. On a blue water boat made of oak, one alternative is to glue the inner stem but make the outer from a solid piece of oak to avoid visible cracks from the glue releasing.

A stem is formed from one piece; the right fiber direction is obtained by using laminated or hook-grown timber. The thickness is achieved with a thickness planer; subsequently the bow profile is cut out with a band saw from a plywood template, and the edges will then be perpendicular to the sides. With this piece, it is then easy to make bevels and symmetrical rabbet lines (see Figures 146 and 147). During a new construction, or when most of the planking is being replaced, the rabbets can be planed to size. When renovating, the edge between the remaining planking and the rabbet in the outer stem is fitted by testing the stem, then the rabbet and plank ends are fitted to each other.

The rabbet can be cut out in several ways. One way is to first cut out the rabbet from templates for each two feet (50–60 cm). They are cut in with a chisel and a mallet, then the rabbet is roughly sawn between cut-outs with a circular saw that has an angle and depth adjustments. You can also chop with an axe, or cut with the router, or use a planer with a large rebate depth. The finishing is done with a straight rebate plane and a bull-nosed rebate plane where it is more curved.

What is important is to keep track of is how much the measurements can vary (see Figure 147).

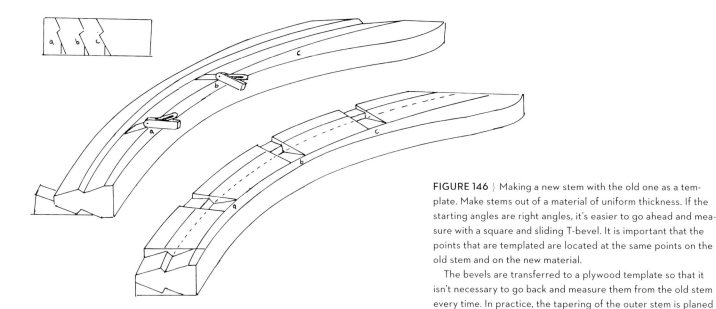

FIGURE 146 } Making a new stem with the old one as a template. Make stems out of a material of uniform thickness. If the starting angles are right angles, it's easier to go ahead and measure with a square and sliding T-bevel. It is important that the points that are templated are located at the same points on the old stem and on the new material.

The bevels are transferred to a plywood template so that it isn't necessary to go back and measure them from the old stem every time. In practice, the tapering of the outer stem is planed when the rabbet is complete, except for complex stems, in which case the rabbet will change the skew over in a short distance. There, you will need to be in control of several areas simultaneously during the manufacturing.

FIGURE 147 } Transfering measurement between the old stem and the new piece.

A Put the old stem in level so that it will be easier to measure the true bevels. Measure the rabbet outlines in relation to the vertical surfaces of the new blank that has been planed square. Note where the measurement (1) ends up in this case; this is because the blank is thicker than the original stem at this point, it is easy to make an error. Set the measurements on the blank

B Shave the rabbet to the right bevels, being careful with the rabbet toward the planking's inside. But leave excess on the leading edge of the rabbet that the plank ends lie against (2), in case the surface might need some fine-tuning against the existing planking.

C Make a measuring stick with the same width as the thickest planking that will be placed in the rabbet, and mark the planking thickness at the forefront of the rabbet. Then plane the corner of the outer stem; you can leave a bit of excess here for the final fit when the stem is in position (3).

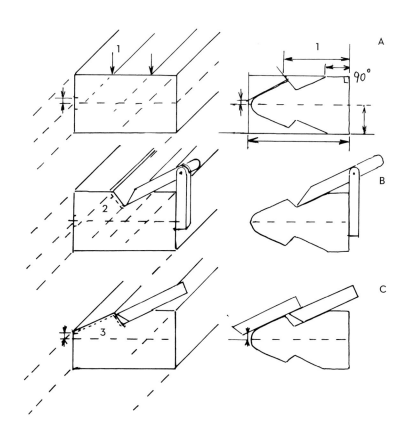

REPLACEMENT OF KNEES

The knees are made out of hooked oak to make them strong. The knee between the keel and the rudderpost on sailboats is often weak. It sits on the deepest parts of the wood keel and is lined by planking, so it never gets an opportunity to dry. There is also a row of bolts in a fan shape that goes through it. The difficulty with replacing the knee is accessibility for drilling. Drillings are long, and the floors, bottom of the cockpit, and engine are often in the way on the inside. The longest drilling we've done was around 6 feet (1.8 m), and the hole came out in the middle of a rudderpost, which was 2⅓" (6 cm) wide. If parts of the planking are dismantled, it is possible to rig up straight ribs to guide the drill lengthwise. If you can't do that, you need to mount blocks with pilot

FIGURE 149 } Knee with wooden wedges. The sternpost is tucked in between the old plank ends.

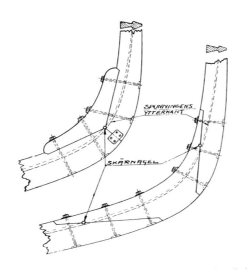

FIGURE 148 } Various stem joints according to KMK's handbook. This highlights the importance of drilling in stopwaters in the rabbet to prevent the penetration of water into the joint; the wood plugs are made of a softer type of wood so that they swell and seal the joint. The wedge is used to tighten the butt ends of the keel joint against each other.

holes on the inside of the planking before the old knee is dismantled. For this kind of knee, I would never choose a laminated construction in a conventional construction. However, I have used it with epoxy construction with glued planking, with the knee made of mahogany.

REPLACEMENT OF THE RUDDER POST

In order to change the rudder post on a sailboat, you need to dismantle a couple of planks in the transition to the counter timber. It's hard to keep track of the joint surfaces otherwise. These planks are in the rounded bilge, and are difficult to reassemble, as they are wider on the inside of the planking.

FIGURE 150 } The stem knee continues behind the old planking above the waterline. The good grain direction in the knee meant that the outer stem and the wood keel could have a shorter piece jointed between them.

FIGURE 151 } Drilling a shaft hole with a pipe drill.

In order to solve this problem, you may also want to change the first plank above the rounded bilge to get a simpler shutter plank. It will pay off time-wise.

The rudder post is not very complicated in general. It is best to start with a block of wood with the sides at right angles. The slot for the rudder on the sailboat is roughly cut with a circular saw and planed with a special plane. An alternative is to router the slot. The rudder post is partly planked, and the bottom part tends to bend sideways. That's why most rudder posts are tenoned into the wood keel or into the ballast keel. These wood tenons are good during building but often end up decaying and breaking from freezing. When renewing the rudder post the lower attachment for the rudder be made so as to hold the joint in place.

REPLACEMENT OF THE PROPELLER SHAFT CONNECTOR

On older boats, drilling in the keel for the propeller shaft can sometimes be several feet (meters) long. The thickness of the wood on the side of the hole can be as small as an inch (2–3 cm). There are often damages in this area. The wood can split from vibration and moisture that has frozen in to ice.

The cavity in the wood side of the pipe is usually filled with pitch. Both the pipe and the pitch are heated, and when the pitch is fluid it is poured down to the cavity through holes in the top of the wood keel spaced at 20–40″ (50–100 cm) intervals in the keel top. This is the best method today as well; the pitch may be exchanged for wax or paraffin. For the pitch to have room to flow out before it solidifies, the hole should have a radius at least ¼″ (5 mm) larger than the pipe. Nowadays, many owners of old motorboats talk about wanting to put in larger engines. These also bring with them heavier shafts. Today, the same axis dimension already has a wider pipe as a standard than the pipes that were used when the boats were built. Therefore, it is difficult to make such an engine replacement without replacing the keel in this area.

We drill shaft holes with homemade pipe drills, which centers very well (see Figure 151). An ordinary steel drill will go sideways if you try to use it to drill along the grain. At the shipyards, they used to drill a smaller center hole. Then they used special drilling rods with replaceable lathe steel to make the right dimension of the hole. On some boats the outer keel is made in two parts with the hole routed out as halves in each part. The joint was then held together by bolts, strips or a board on each side of the keel at the center of the parts.

REPLACEMENT OF DEADWOOD

Some designers used deadwood in order to place the ballast keel correctly over the boat's center of gravity. Olle Enderlin is a good example of a designer who used this solution. The ballast keel is toward the forward part of the wood keel; aft of the ballast keel there is a deadwood made of oak. This design requires that the boat be propped up on a trestle with two pallets under the ballast keel; if it is only propped with a trestle located forward and one back at the rudder, the keel may deform by the aft keel bolt (see Figure 140). This construction method is also sensitive to grounding. If the deadwood, which is high and narrow at its aft edge, bends, the lower rudder pin will be askew and will bend the rudder, as a result. This construction also requires large amounts of oak.

These deadwood areas will not last as long as the rest of the hull, even if the requirements on timber quality and density are not as great as for the rest of the boat's construction. When it is to be replaced, it is the bolts that are the hardest part; it is equally difficult to access this area in order to drill as with the knee.

It is often time-saving to dismantle and replace the garboard strakes to make it easier to find the bolts and in order to communicate with other people helping out.

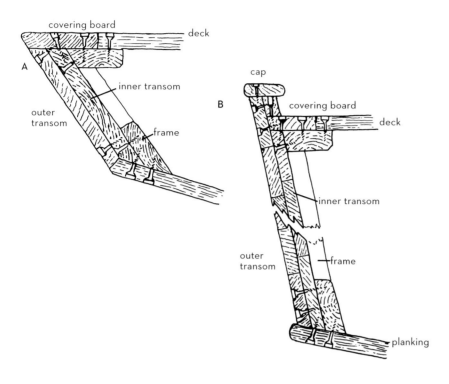

If the garboard strakes have been around as long as the deadwood has, it is probably time. There have been times when the garboard strakes we replaced were the second or third since the boat was built.

An appropriate thickness of deadwood pieces is 4–5″ (10–12.5 cm); it is quick to build without being too heavy. Straight and leveled planks make it easier to fit them. The deadwood is fitted first, piece-by-piece, against the ballast keel, with excess on the sides and stern. The center is marked on all pieces and they are shaped symmetrically of the center. The bolt holes are drilled from the inside out through the knee and the wood keel. Optionally, the holes could be drilled only through the first plank and then dismantled; then the rest of the deadwood is drilled off the boat with the first plank as a guide.

During assembly, red lead was formerly the given choice; today, tar may be an option.

REPLACEMENT OF THE STERN POST

The stern post or counter timber often made similar to the stem. The part that tends to get bad on sailboats is the transition to the rudder post.

REPLACEMENT OF THE TRANSOM

The transom is sometimes counted as part of the backbone. The design of the stern of the boat varies a lot from boat to boat. On a sailboat, the transom is sometimes just a small mahogany board. On a motorboat, it can be

FIGURE 152 } Various transoms.

A Sailboat. The hull has beveled plank ends on the outside transom so that less end grain is visible at the edges of the transom.

B Motorboat. In this case, the transom goes past the covering board. In this structure, it is not uncommon for moisture to collect and cause decay. Plank ends are not tapered but go past the transom, and it is easier to attach the screw closer to the outside of the transom. Of course, there are some sailboats with plank ends projecting past the transom and with a transom that extends past the covering board, and many boats have beveled plank ends. Otherwise, the personalities of wooden boats would not be so fascinating.

Note all the screws; in reality, they don't sit next to each other but are displaced laterally. The sketch shows how important the screws are. It is important for strength where the screws end up; one row of screws that ends up ¼″ (5 mm) off so that the screws that are in a joint can wedge apart the entire joint.

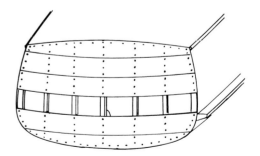

FIGURE 153 } For it to be easier to fit the planks in the transom, it is advisable to fit the longest piece last; the others can then be inserted where the transom is wide and then moved up, or down, into their correct, shorter position. Shown are the ribs that hold the transom planks in place. If the transom is domed, the boards should be bent or laminated so there is no tension in the corners of the transom.

built out of a frame, transom post, ribs and an inner and outer transom.

The transom puts great demands on the designer and boatbuilder; wide wood panels with different grain directions need to be fitted to ensure that they are tight when the hull dries and swells. Here, the wood pieces need to fit without tension; if you use force to get the pieces of wood in, this will lead to leakiness and deformations in the long run.

Many older boats have oak in the interior transom and an exterior transom of mahogany; mahogany moves only half as much as oak does, so when you are replacing, the oak should be wetter than the mahogany; otherwise the swelling oak will pull the mahogany transom apart. The moisture level in the mahogany should be consistent with that of the planking. If a transom with a 7–8% moisture level is placed into a boat with an 18% planking humidity, it can swell and lift the deck, with a leak in the deck in the corner between the transom and side as a result. The moisture is also transported between the halves, so I feel it is better to make just one transom when renovating. Today we glue the transom, but back in the day they usually made them with a swelling trim, in the same manner as the cabin roof and the board deck. The transom is often curved laterally. It must then be bent, or the boards can be laminated over the template; ¼-inch- (6- to 8-mm-) thick laminates are enough so the screws can get hold of the outer laminate and prevent tearing. It is not exactly fun to scrape a boat down to a glue layer for a transom glued to thin veneer. Diagonally glued transoms are great, but they must be very well made if they are going to have a life span of over thirty years. It may seem like a distant perspective, but from the point of view of the life of wooden boats we would hardly see any wooden boats afloat today. The average age of our wooden boats is probably more than fifty years.

When renovating, you should remember to make a template of the curvature and contour before the old transom is removed; if you miss that, it will be nothing but qualified guess work to try to make out the shape of a new transom. When choosing timber lengths, you have to remember that the boards in the transom are often longer on the inner side and that the curve needs more timber than if the transom were straight. Often, the frame around the transom needs to be replaced. In order to place the frame under the covering board, you

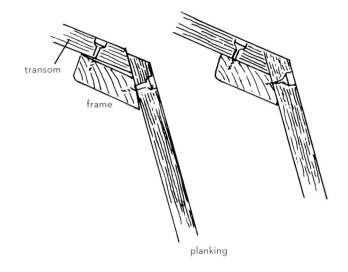

FIGURE 154 } A common damage to boats built in the 1950s and 1960s. The transom has been glued to the frame, and the boatbuilder did not put enough effort into screwing. When the glue released, the frame twists, and the transom shifted aft. This damage is not unusual on Folkboats.

sometimes need to replace the aft-most of the top planks. The transom that is easiest to change is the one on race boats. It is often mounted outside of the planking, and the corners are then shod with a nickel-plated trim.

The transoms of sailboats are smaller—often so small that they cannot be accessed from the inside—but the framework needs to be replaced from the outside through the hole for the transom.

BOLTS

In both sail and motorboats, bolts are used for joining the heavier wooden parts where rivets and screws are not enough. Here we separate two kinds of bolts, joint bolts that go through the joints in the backbone, and the keel bolts that go through the ballast keel.

Stems and keels are made according to the lofting (the name of the full-scale drawings made by the builder prior to construction of the vessel) and are often bolted together lying down. These bolts and the bolts that attach the floors are called joint bolts. In the stems, the bolts are often made with T-shape heads, i.e., with a square head a few millimeters wider than the bolt diameter and a length of two to three times the bolt diameter (see Figure 113 in the chapter on floors). The heads are so narrow that they can be folded into the stems behind the stem rail and can be withdrawn without the need to be held on the outside. This kind of bolt should be wrapped with light wick yarn dipped in linseed or tar as sealant.

The bolt is driven in with a cylindrical punch and a small sledgehammer, then the nut is tightened. Next the head is given a blow so that it goes in, and the nut is tightened one last time. The last blow is important for the bolt to sit well.

On sailboats, the floors were often bolted to the keel plank before the ballast keel of lead was mounted with separate keel bolts. This style of building with two separate bolts was used because it was easier to take down and seal between the ballast keel and the keel plank when grounding and in order to reduce the risk of galvanic corrosion of the steel floors. I have seen boats in which the lead keel has been bolted directly to the steel floors. These steel floors have rusted significantly while those fore and aft of the keel bolts were intact. On boats with an iron keel there are no galvanic problems with mounting keel bolts into the steel floor if the bolts are also made of galvanized steel.

For those who are mechanically inclined and used to working with steel, the dimensions may seem rough, but powerful dimensions are needed for the wood to resist side forces in the holes, for instance from running aground.

The keel bolts were mostly made of galvanized steel, but sometimes bronze bolts were also used. Today, we mostly use stainless steel. Marine grade stainless steel bolts are a good choice; bronze is certainly a better quality option, but the cost is quadrupled, and bronze

rods aren't sold in Sweden. Galvanized steel bolts start to rust after twenty to thirty years, and the rust destroys the oak around the holes. (You can read more about materials in Chapter 8.)

Sometimes a renovation or maintenance plan is included in a survey. On boats in good condition with an onset of corrosion in the bolts, I usually recommend replacing the bolts with stainless to stop the discoloration of the stem and extend its life.

Here I could mention that on some boats built after the war, the bolts on the floors can't be taken out as they are bent between the floor timber and the stem (see Chapter 18).

KEEL BOLTS

One of the most common questions during surveys is about the state of the keel bolts: how much is left of the bolts? This is determined by several factors, such as steel quality, quality of the galvanization, and if there has been a good seal between the wood keel and ballast keel. Here, it goes without saying that if a boat is left to dry out and crack on land one summer, it will be susceptible to water damage and rust along the bolts. The exterior of the bottom of the hull, and especially the joint between the wood keel and the ballast keel, usually give some indication of the condition of the bolts. If there are no cracks in the paint between the ballast and wood keel, and no signs of rust streaks after a summer in the water, you need not worry.

There is equipment to x-ray keel bolts, but it is costly.

The coarseness of joint and floor bolts is stated in the building regulations; the Square Meter Rule states:

M²-CLASS	15	22	30	40	55	75	95	120	150
DISPLACEMENT, IN TONNES (APPROX.)	1–1.5	1.2–2.2	2.2–3.4	3.5–4.5	4.5–6	6–9	9–12	12–15	16–20
AMIDSHIPS*, IN MM	8	10	12	12	12	16	16	20	20
ENDS, IN MM	6	8	10	10	12	12	12	16	16

*Within ⅔ of Lx = Ideal length that is approximately the sailed length or wave-building length

According to Lloyds, it's indicated as follows:

LENGTH OF BOAT, IN METERS	6–10	10–12	12–14	14–16	16–18	18–20	Over 20	12–15	16–20
BACKBONE, IN MM	10	12	14	14	16	18	20	20	20
KEEL JOINT, IN MM	8	8	10	12	12	12	14	16	16

If you are worried or thinking about embarking on a long voyage across the sea, it may be advisable to take out a pair of keel bolts to check the condition. Keel bolts are oversized from the beginning to withstand rust; three to five times is a common factor for safety, which allows the replacement of a pair of bolts to provide adequate security against the keel loosening. The safety factor is the difference between safe working load and breaking load.

It is not common for sailboats to lose their keels. When it happens, a wooden boat will lie on its side and flood, but it would not sink, and everything will float around the boat. I have been told about the surprise of those who suffer this and the dreamlike moment as charts, floorboards, cushions, and other loose equipment flow out of the boat and set off across the bay.

When replacing bolts, the new ones are usually dimensioned so that the holes can be re-drilled and the worst of the rust removed; if you replace the wood at the same time, you can keep the original dimensions of the bolts.

For those technically inclined, it may be mentioned that the Square Meter Rule's old formula for keel bolts is:

$$A = 2 \times \frac{V \times h}{b}$$

Where: A is the sum of the core area of the bolts in sq. cm

V is the weight in tonnes of the ballast keel

h is the height of the ballast keel

b is the ballast keel's greatest width by the wooden keel

The tensile strength of steel has been set to 3500–4000 kg/cm² in the requirements. Other materials of other strengths need to be accounted for proportionally. It should be mentioned that Marine grade stainless steel is less elastic and less able to recover its original shape, because of this stainless steel is measured only by its yield strength that is about 2000–2500 kg/cm². In practice, it is probably offset by the fact that stainless steel does not need a safety factor for rust removal. Many believe that stainless steel is stronger because it is harder to work with using cutting tools, but its tensile strength is lower. This is also noticeable for power-boats in which a propeller shaft may have greater dimensions when switching from a steel shaft to a stainless steel one. It is important that the keel bolts are made of Marine grade 316 stainless steel. Sure, it can be tempting to use the old stainless steel propeller shaft that has a slightly higher strength value, but it has lower resistance to corrosion.

Copper was used pure and in various alloys for bolts. Pure copper stretches more and requires an increase in the core area of about 50% when figuring out dimensions; a copper bolt may require tightening at regular intervals. Various bronze alloys exist; you often won't know which alloy has been used from the beginning. This calls for thorough cleaning and inspection for cracks that may be hard to find. However, we have recycled copper and bronze bolts that were up to ninety-five years old when replacing the keel.

Double rows of keel bolts are used the most when building boats today and on wooden boats with wide keels; they have been used for a long time, as it's easier to get a good seal between the wooden keel and the ballast keel this way. But that's just the bolt on the windward side, which may be included in the formula in the design. The leeward ones won't take the movement, but on this side the keel and the ballast keel are pressed against each other when the boat is heeled.

If the keel bolt is only in the keel, it is important to have large washers under the nuts on the inside, particularly when the wood in the keel is getting old. The washer is made square for the sake of simplicity and with a side of 3–4 times the bolt diameter; its thickness should be ⅓–¼ the bolt diameter.

PROCEDURE FOR REMOVAL OF KEEL BOLTS
Open the Keel Pocket

Shallow ballast keels often have keel bolts that go all the way through, and then there will be a nut or a head in a recess under the keel. Deeper keels have pockets on the side where the nuts are; on iron keels, the pockets sit quite high up, as the material of the keel is stiff. On lead keels, the pockets are located further down in order to avoid deformation of the soft lead. Some iron keels have bolts threaded directly into the cast iron.

It can be difficult to find the pockets on the side of the lead keels as they are often filled with lead. A narrow line in a square on the side may be all you can see when scraping the keel; on an iron keel, it is easier to find your pocket because there will be a different material filling the pocket. The pockets are filled with concrete, wood, or lead. The different materials in the pockets influence the keel weight; if the keel had been made heavy in the casting, you could fill your pocket with wood, and for a lighter keel, the pockets were filled with lead.

Different materials require different techniques for disassembly:

- Concrete fillings are cut out with a demolition hammer or by hand.
- Wood is drilled and wedged away.
- Lead is melted with a gas flame (a regular gas burner is not enough); lead is a very good conductor of heat, but the oxide in the keel pocket's edge doesn't conduct as well, so you can burn off just the lead used as a filling. Place a steel plate under the keel pocket to collect the lead, both for environmental reasons and to use it to cast new fillings. For health reasons, you should wear a mask with a gas filter, as the lead gas may cause lung edema when inhaled.

Loosen the Bolts

Bronze bolts and stainless steel bolts are usually not hard to remove. Steel bolts in lead keels are easy enough. Steel bolts in iron keels are often hard to loosen. Appropriate tools are sledge hammers, a rod to strike on, jack, chisels, steel wedges, pipe wrench, socket wrench, and drills.

First, try to loosen the nut in the keel pocket; it will have been warmed during the burnout of the lead and may have loosened then, as heat is the best way to loosen nuts. Unthread the nut with a chisel (see Figure 155) or drill a series of thinner holes through the nut to the bolt and wedge apart the nut a bit, then unthread it with the chisel.

Strike the bolt from the inside with the sledgehammer and rod so that it moves a bit. Try turning the nut on the inside—not primarily to loosen it, but to get the bolt to move. Wedge with steel wedges between the bottom of the pocket and the partially loosened nut; this tends to be effective (see Figure 156).

A jack with a yoke can be rigged in different ways. If you can, try to loosen the nut on the inside. Then the yoke is placed over the end of the bolt, and the nut is threaded back in. A combination of lifting the jack and wedging in the pocket usually does the trick (see Figure 157). If you have company you don't have to jump in and out of the boat all the time. Bolts that go right through the ballast keel or deadwood could be knocked out with a sledgehammer from inside the boat. This is also a job for two people: one holding a rod on the bolt end and the other hitting with a sledgehammer. The person holding the rod will feel in his hands if the force goes down in the bolt or just turns into vibrations of the rod. When the bolt is about to be loosened and the bolt end protrudes into the boat, you can use a thicker rod. When the bolt is well released and is down into the keel plank, use a rod that is ¼" (6 mm) thinner than the bolt. Turn the rod and make sure that it doesn't show signs of going to the side of the bolt and wedging itself. Rusted keel bolts can have a wasp waist within the wood; it is easy to knock down the tips so they overlap (see Figures 158 and 159).

FIGURE 155 } Loosen the nut in the keel pocket by means of a chisel; you'll have great force that way.

FIGURE 156 } A good way to get the keel bolt going is to thread the nut down ½" (1 cm) with the chisel and then wedge the bolt with the chisel and pallet washers made of steel.

FIGURE 157 } One way to arrange a yoke with a lever and jack; most boats are different in the bilge, and you can experiment with different solutions.

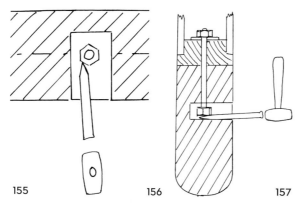

155   156   157

Alternative

If the keel is being removed, it may be advisable to loosen the nuts on the inside then lower the ballast keel straight down; often the bolts sit parallel and in a line and will loosen from weight and blows by a sledge-hammer to the bolts. Then the bolts can be removed from the keel without any work from inside the boat.

MOUNTING KEEL BOLTS

New keel bolts are made of stainless steel. M16, M20, M24, M27, M30, and M33 are the dimensions that you can get stainless steel nuts for. This allows old 1-inch (2.5-cm) holes to use 1-inch steel bars where the part to be threaded is turned to a (24 mm) before the thread is turned. The bolt end is turned down to the thread core dimension of approximately a ¼-inch (6-mm) length so that the thread isn't damaged when the bolt hammered in the hole, something you should still do with a block of end wood as a spacer.

This core dimension at the end also makes it easier to get the nut to thread in the bolt in the keel pocket. The holes are drilled either exactly, so a bolt dipped in linseed oil or tar must be driven in, or ¹⁄₁₆″ (2 mm) too big. Then cover the bolt with sealant before it's mounted or fill the hole afterward with liquid paraffin or wax.

When constructing with epoxy technology, use a threaded rod and fill the thread with thickened epoxy before mounting. The hole is drilled oversized and the thickened epoxy is placed in the hole before the soaked bolt is driven in.

SUMMARY

The boat doesn't get stronger just because you replace a (rotten) damaged piece of wood with new wood. The difficulty in replacing parts of the backbone is to find good locations for the new joints so that the loads are transmitted beyond the damage.

It is difficult to get glue joints in oak to hold, especially underwater. Use massive oak as much as possible. Glued constructions should also be bolted together so that they don't collapse if the glue releases.

Replacing much of the backbone is a complex job that few amateurs are able to perform without assistance. A significant amount of work is in measuring and controlling the outline of the boat, making sure that she retains her true shape.

To extend the life of stems and the keel, you may want to replace galvanized steel bolts that are beginning to rust with new, acid-free stainless steel bolts before the wood has taken too much damage.

Beating out bolts is not a one-man job. One man is needed to hold back against the hits so that the bolt heads are not breaking the wood on the outside.

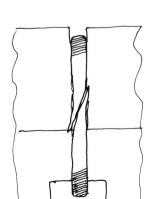

FIGURE 158 } Rusted keel bolts that have ended up overlapped and wedged. All I can say is that you need to avoid this situation.

FIGURE 159 } Rusted bolts. When this boat, a Baltic-6, came to the workshop, half of the bolts had rusted apart; as luck would have it, the crane truck driver put the sling around the keel during lifting.

DECK

When you come strolling along a pier, a deck is often the first thing you notice. A well-maintained wooden deck gives character to the whole boat. The condition and maintenance are significant, but it is the balance of the outline that is not so much visible as it is sensed that determines whether the viewer's eye finds harmony in the boat or loses focus to disharmonious partial solutions.

Caulked laid decks have always been both a satisfaction and a headache. In the old days, the headaches were mostly those of the hired help who had to wet and mop the deck to keep it tightly sealed. Long-distance sailors probably thought that caulked decks only belonged to the jetties in Sandhamn and Långedrag; for "real" waters, the canvas deck was the only option.

BEWARE OF LEAKS

The deck and superstructure are the parts of a boat that can deteriorate rapidly. For example, if the covering board leaks, then rainwater will find its way down through the beam shelf, deck beams and backing blocks.

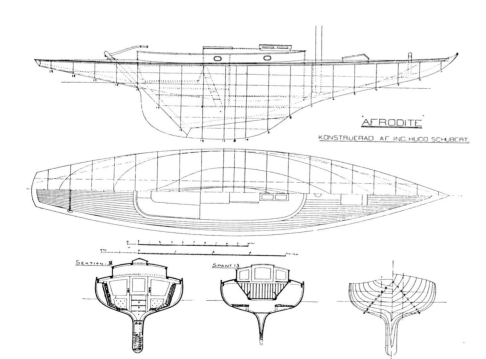

FIGURE 160 } Hugo Schubert's *Aphrodite* from 1897 with a tapered pine deck without a king plank. *Aphrodite* was a successful racer with the dimensions 12.8 × 2.6 yards (11.7 × 2.4 m)

From "Kryssare och Kappseglare" ("Cruisers and Racers"), Hans Wahrolen, 1979.

And when the sun heats up the deck, it creates the perfect breeding ground for rot in the stagnant, warm, and humid environment in pockets and nooks below deck.

Leaks in the deck reveal themselves in two ways: first, through the annoying drip in the berths in the rain, and by the varnish coming off after the first frost in the fall. The drips can often be located; even though the water may find its way far into the deck, it won't get moisture trapped. Varnish coming off is a sign of trapped moisture—moisture that has penetrated through the cracks but won't get any further through the lower layers of wood. The moisture will gather in the wood in the deck but will be hindered from evaporating by the varnish. In the fall, the moisture will then freeze into ice crystals, which lifts the varnish. Here, it doesn't help to scrape the bear wood, but leaks must be located and sealed to prevent the varnish or paint from coming off in the same place next year and rotting over time.

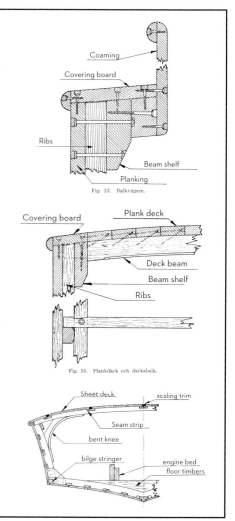

The deck is made of planks or sheets with or without canvas.

Plank deck, Figure 15, made of Oregon pine, mahogany, pine, or teak. The deck thickness is determined from Table III. With larger dimensions, it is easier to get the deck tighter. The deck is made of narrow planks, chosen so that the wood grains stand on end. The planks are attached at an angle to the beams with copper or galvanized nails and fastened to each other between the beams with two nails. The joints are staggered in the same manner as has been determined for the planking. All plank ends should be well supported. Where required, particular support is attached. The deck is caulked with cotton yarn where, as it is carefully observed, the seams are not damaged. After previously completed treatment with Xerotin, the seams are filled with deck putty. (A suitable putty is prepared from boiled linseed oil, oil, rubber solution, and chalk and carbon black for the black color, or just chalk for white putty. This is worked on by means of hammering for so long that the putty does not stick to the hammer any longer.)

A sheet deck is typically made out of mahogany and inserted into large widths, Figure 16, and is generally made thinner than plank deck. Sheets are attached to the beams and are lowered into these seam strips with brass screws, which are set so close together that any curve formation in the deck is prevented. The sheets are inserted in intervals, filled with a thick varnish or the like, whereupon a sealing trim of mahogany is pressed into the gap. This method enables the seal trim to be replaced if the deck dries up.

Canvassed decks. Canvassed decks are usually made of pine, but not of ribs with tounge and groove, as the groove easily cracks by swelling. Since the deck is laid in relatively narrow widths, it is oiled to saturation, and it is puttied carefully over all the screws. The deck is coated subsequently with thick oil paint, over which the deck fabric is stretched tightly. The cloth must not be too thin, that blistering will occur. If the cloth is folded over the deck edge, round it off so as not to damage the cloth. When the canvas is firmly affixed, oil and paint it. The canvas should not be puttied.

FIGURE 161 } In 1929, KMK gave out the "Bestämmelser sat Råd och Anvisningar för Motorbåtars Byggnad och Utrustning" ("Rules and Guidance and Instructions for the Building and Equipment of the Motorboat"). It has a lot of useful information for boat owners. This excerpt is from the chapter on decks, with drawings.

Consistent with this, the deck is sealed at the surface, definitely not down through the deck or from the bottom, but there have to be drainage possibilities. A coaming that is screwed on with a string of sealant, both at the top and bottom, becomes a moisture trap.

A RETROSPECTIVE

In the late 1800s and early 1900s, sailing yachts were often built with tapered Oregon pine or Scots pine heartwood decks. The deck planks were at their widest amidships, tapering off at the ends. A tapered deck was plotted using long battens on the deck beam. In short, they created a curve that used a smooth plank width amidships as a starting point. The line was then drawn out into a slight curve aft and stern of the deck. The distance between the curve and the center line was divided into an equal number of parts on each deck beam, and then tapered planks were fan-shaped so that no king plank was needed. The principle was that all planks had the same width on the same deck beams.

The covering boards were also tapered at the end of the ship and made of teak or mahogany. Common measurements on the covering board of a 12-m- long yacht could be 6″ (150 mm) amidships, 4⅓″ (110 mm) at the bow, and 5″ (130 mm) at the stern. The deck planks could perhaps be 2⅙″ (55 mm) amidships, 1″ (25 mm) in the bow, and 1⅓″ (35 mm) in the stern. The veins would always be upright in the planks (quarter sawn). The deck planks were nailed at an angle to the beams and nailed to each other between the beams so as to avoid movement. This complex way of laying the deck was probably primarily for aesthetic reasons, as a means to increase the harmony of the lines. Although the yacht looked imposing, the ends still looked slender.

On motorboats, there were often just covering boards of mahogany between the hull side and the side of the saloon and sitting room. Stern and aft deck were either laid with parallel planks from a tapered king plank, with tapered planks or with narrow deck planks that followed the covering board. The planks were made of Oregon pine, teak, or mahogany and were often varnished. Sheet decks of mahogany with seal trim were used on both types of boats but where more common on motorboats.

Towards the middle of the 1920s, the design of decks that is common today came into use, i.e., with equal-sized, curved planks laid along the covering board and with a king plank.

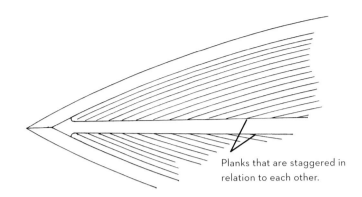

FIGURE 162 } Planks bent along the covering board. The covering board and the king plank are tapered forward. The deck planks should come against the king plank lined up on both sides. Any staggering can be adjusted during assembly by shaving down the width of the plank with a plane.

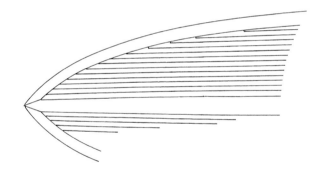

FIGURE 163 } On boats with a rounded bow, the planks cannot be bent along the covering board without snapping. To place the planks parallell with a tapered king plank instead is common on powerboats and double-enders.

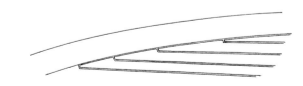

FIGURE 164 } When the plank ends are too pointy, they are unable to stand straight up during caulking without the tip breaking. It's a nightmare to have one of those planks break at the tip. To avoid this, the tip is nibbed, and the plank next to it is designed with a hook.

Even here, the covering boards are tapered toward the ends, and the king plank is tapered. A tapering of the king plank is essential for the eye not to perceive it as broader at the end. A normal tapering of the king plank is ³⁄₁₆–³⁄₈″ (0.5–1 cm) per 40″ (100 cm) of length. At this time, teak also became common, especially in racing yachts and the emerging offshore cruisers, while the Skerry cruisers had varnished Oregon pine decks.

Untreated wood decks could be made of teak or Oregon pine and bleached with oxalic acid or citric acid and scrubbed white with sand. Gray and dark gray, dirty teak decks are a recent invention that have never been considered "ship shape." In the rest of Europe, they still build boats with untreated pine decks, and they don't understand how we Scandinavians can hang onto our glossy, varnished decks.

When a deck was built for canvassing, they first laid planks of pine or spruce. Then they stretched the canvas, folded it around the deck edge, and fixed with tacks; next the covering board moldings, rails, hatches, and superstructure were fitted.

After World War II, they began using composite decks. It was all about planked decks on masonite and, later, plywood. The caulking and sealant were replaced with elastic rubber caulking. But the look of the decks did not change.

Today, epoxy-treated plywood can be used as an alternative to canvas and thin veneer strips that are glued to plywood for plank decks.

LIFE SPAN AND MAINTENANCE

A couple of hundred-year-old Plym boats still sail with their original varnished decks. In this, we find two of the factors of a sustainable deck, namely high-quality craftsmanship and good materials. The Schelin, Fröberg, and Plym boats will sail a long time with their original decks.

Maintenance is a third factor. A deck cannot withstand being run down and neglected for several seasons; it becomes difficult to manage and very demanding; recurring leakage and flaking varnish will occur after each season.

Renovating an old, run-down Oregon pine deck is probably the most hopeless task you can undertake. The angled nails in the hidden fastening are surrounded by black rusty spots that grow in size the deeper you scrape, and the deck is hopelessly thin, as movements between the planks will cause even the best caulking to come out.

Having few owners is also an important factor. New boat owners often think that they are renovating the deck just because they scrape off the varnish and a some thickness of wood. That may look nice when it's launched but it is mostly a nail into the coffin; moisture damage will come back in the fall again. When scraping down to bare wood, the new varnish should last more than ten years and should be combined with a more thorough facelift involving re-caulking poor caulk and replacing bad wood. New boat owners typically have insufficient knowledge about their boat's idiosyncrasies to make such an intervention.

On racing yachts and motorboats built for speed, the decks were too thin after only a few scrapings. They were often laid according to the minimum sizes according to the rules, and the rules were designed to make light boats.

A solid, caulked planked deck of the traditional type is probably the longest-lasting deck. In a driven deck, cotton yarn is driven in between the planks when the deck is laid to stiffen and seal the deck. Such a deck made of dry timber and "driven" by cotton yarn is tight even without the seam filler if it is used regularly. Make sure not to tear out the yarn when maintaining the deck. The problem with a driven deck or decks that are redone is that when the deck swells it risks pulling the beams out of the beam shelf. Boats with solid driven decks should have tie rods between the beam shelf and the cabin carlines to prevent this.

A driven planked deck is the traditional way to lay a deck—a method that has come out of use in the past fifty years since the Thioflex, one of the first elastic seam caulks, came into use. In the 1950s, growing prosperity with higher wages made it difficult for shipyards to live off on-demand builds. An increasing mass production of wooden boats made time-consuming and adhesive-destructive oiling go out of style. Caulking the deck with the oiling of plank edges and subsequent sealing with putty became too time-consuming compared to filling the joints with a rubber sealant that promised to result in a maintenance-free, sealed deck.

Since then, elastic sealants have totally dominated, new types of sealants have come and gone, the big manufacturers have regularly presented new and improved products that they say will eventually provide watertight decks, but leaks reappear. In a gum-caulked deck, the seal is in the sealant; if it breaks, the deck will leak.

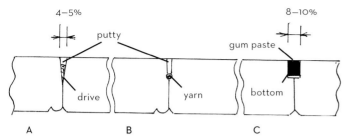

FIGURE 165 }

Ways of sealing solid plank decks:

A is caulked in a wedge seam; the caulk is then sealed with pitch, mastic, or elastic sealant. The depth of the seam is ⅓ of the plank thickness. The width is 4–5% of the plank width.

B is a version with yarn being pressed into a pre-manufactured groove.

C is modern elastic deck sealant. The depth of the caulk should be at least ⅕″ (5 mm), and then bond breaker in the bottom should be added to that. The width is 8–10% of the plank width.

FIGURE 166 } Guide bar for cutting tapered plank decks. The steel angle with many holes allows for nailing in a nearby seam rather than in the planks. The figure also shows movable distance guides that have the same dimensions as the distance between the side of the saw and the center of the circular saw blade, i.e., the distance that it should be between the guide bar and the center seam.

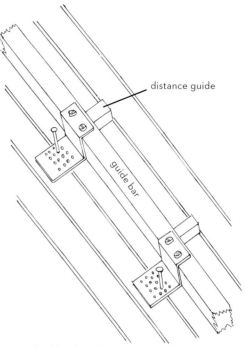

Teak decks that are kept neat with scrubbing (always across the grain), and even those left without care, wear quickly. There are several boats sailing around with their third teak deck. ¹⁄₃₂″ to ¹⁄₁₆″ (1–2 mm) in ten years is not unusual wear; after the first fifteen to twenty years, the plugs come off and it is time for new caulking and deeper re-fastening. If the deck is nailed at an angle (secret, or blind fastening), the nails can be visible after thirty years. The teak deck laid in the 1960s and 1970s made of 1/2″ (12 mm) of teak on plywood starts to be ready for replacement now.

Plywood decks from the beginning of the 1950s are often still in very good condition. The quality of the plywood and the design of the joints determine longevity. Pine plywood is rough on the surface, and the surface veneer cracks easily. Building instructions in some classes indicate that mahogany plywood can be painted but that pine plywood should be canvassed. Today, it is possible to "canvas" with fiberglass and epoxy glue.

The deck canvas is not waterproofed from the beginning, as it needs to be able to be stretched by linseed oil or shellac. This means that the fabric can rot under thick layers of paint. It is difficult to inspect the wooden deck under the canvas, and rot in cabin corners and hatches is common. The paint that canvas decks are painted with should be soft so it won't crack, and preferably also slip-resistant. Such paint sucks up dirt and must be scrubbed frequently; it needs to be repainted every year, and paint layers add up till the paint bursts. But it is possible to heat and take off thick layers of paint with a heat gun and putty knife.

RENOVATION TECHNIQUES

A plank deck in good condition and of adequate thickness can be re-caulked. Old hard putty can be cut out with a circular saw, preferably with the aid of guide bars that are nailed to adjacent seams. In an emergency, you can cut it freehand. Then you have to be able to aim for the saw blade's leading edge, and behind the blade you need to have a guide from the saws sole that follows in the new cut seam to prevent it from slipping on the deck. You cannot access many places along the superstructure and hatches with a machine, but different seam rakers are needed. This is a time-consuming task, and if you pay someone to do it you may make out better by just replacing the deck. If the deck is already re-caulked following all the rules of applying elastic sealant with bond breaking tape on the bottom, it may be enough to cut both sides of the rubber cord with a sharp knife and then pull the rubber out.

When the caulking is gone, the seam sides are sanded with coarse sandpaper wrapped around a scraper. (The actual caulking is in the section about replacing decks.) Canvassing the plank deck is an alternative to re-caulking.

The problem when you put new canvas on is that it can be difficult to reach to attach the canvas around the corner on the deck edge. It is common to attach the canvas with stainless steel staples along the cabin and hatches and on the edge between the covering board and plank deck. A trim is mounted over the joint there. You can mount a trim along the hatches and the superstructure, but if it is not done carefully, it will easily form moisture traps.

Adding a new deck of planks or plywood on top of the old makes for a heavy boat and is not particularly

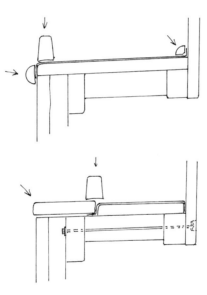

FIGURE 167 } Ways of making a canvassed deck. The top figure is the usual on, for example, Folkboats. When the boat is being built, the canvas is folded down around the deck edge before the cabin is mounted, but when redone, it is attached with trim. It is important that the dimension of the half-round guard rail is selected so that the row of screws doesn't end up in the middle of the joint between the deck and the hull. (It is unfortunately not uncommon for the trim to release and for moisture to find its way in because of this.) All trim should be laid with sealant. The lower figure shows a construction method common in boats such as Mälar boats in which the canvas is laid before the covering board. The toe rail is screwed to the seam between the covering board and the canvas. The figure also has a tie rod pictured.

durable, as you will have problems with condensation from the inside and with moisture migration from the outside. If you try this method, you have to start by stiffening the deck by screwing the old planks in the beams with stainless steel decking screws. The deck is sanded even with coarse sandpaper and coated with epoxy and canvas for diagonal strength and density. Then the new deck is glued with epoxy or elastic adhesive.

One option to save old mahogany sheet decks is to unscrew the old deck and put a marine plywood on the deck beams. Then the old mahogany is thinned out and is glued in place with epoxy and then it is plugged and sanded to ¼- to ⁵⁄₁₆-inch (6- to 8-mm) thickness.

REPLACING DECKS

Replacing a deck is a major project. Winter is short and a lot of steps require some warmth. To lay a glued deck outdoors at a yacht club requires launching to be postponed to the summer. The necessary prep work—replacement of damaged or rotten beams and other work on the framework, rusty chain plates, and any built-in tanks—should not be underestimated.

There are few things that feel as frustrating when I'm out on inspections as new decks, which require lots of work and expensive materials, that are laid on top of a framework that is ready to retire.

Choice of Method

The different types of decks are:

- Painted plywood, with or without covering boards of solid wood.
- Canvassed decks on planks or plywood, with or without covering boards of solid wood.
- Plank decks, solid or on plywood.
- Sheet decks, solid or on plywood.

Painted Decks

Plywood or canvas? A large number of our boats and mass-produced wooden boats from the 1930s onward have painted decks.

Until the 1950s, canvassed plank decks were in. Since then, it has mostly been about canvassed or painted plywood decks.

Some boats, such as Folkboats, have canvassed decks on planks or plywood, which end with a toerail and a guardrail. When the boat was built, the canvas was folded down around the deck edge and fastened with nails. Then the semicircular guardrail was mounted on the outside of the canvas edge. This was the fastest and cheapest way to deck a boat, and it produced well-sealed boats. Another way to lay canvas decks is seen in Mälar boats and Dragons. They have canvassed deck ends with varnished covering boards and sometimes a king plank. The covering boards can withstand a couple of canvas replacements, but then they are often so scraped down in thickness that they are ripe for replacement.

When it's time for a replacement, you need to determine if the deck is ready for replacement after the canvas, covering boards, and trim are dismantled. Check if the deck planks are still fastened in the beams; sometimes iron nails are more or less rusted off, and the planks must be fastened with screws instead. The planks can't be too torn at the side of the hull because then it's hard to get the new trim to attach. It is not uncommon for moisture to be drawn into the cabin and hatch corners and to cause rot in the deck. In these cases, you must consider whether it is time to replace the boards with plywood. The difference in material cost for new canvas and a new painted plywood deck is not that great. The plywood gives the boat added stiffness and reduces the leakage that occurs when the parts move relative to each other while sailing.

Another advantage of plywood is that the annoying trim toward the cabin, which covers the canvas edge and which is difficult to surface-treat and frequently creates moisture traps, can be omitted. The edge between the deck and cabin is caulked instead with paintable elastic sealant, such as Sikaflex.

If the boat has a plywood deck in good condition under the canvas, it is possible to coat it with epoxy instead of replacing the canvas. (More about replacing plywood decks under the title "Template and Fit Plywood" later in this chapter.)

Briefly on the Topic of Canvassing

Canvassing has been touched on in several places in this chapter. The most common method of canvassing today is probably where the deck is first sanded smooth

PLYWOOD FOR DECKS

The only plywood to use for decks is real marine plywood. The glue should be WBP glue (water boiled proof). The wood needs to be approved for marine use, be rot-resistant, and the density on the veneer should be above 0.5. Unfortunately, it's hard to come across marine plywood in Sweden. Ask your supplier to verify the quality of the wood. Plywood from the 1950s and 1960s is usually better quality than the plywood that has been sold recently. Before mounting, all end wood needs to be sealed with glue.

For a plywood deck to carry the weight of a person without the plywood bending between the deck beams, the relation between the plywood thickness and the maximum deck beam distance should be:

$\frac{1}{4}$" (6 mm) plywood	max 5.5" (140 mm) distance
$\frac{3}{8}$" (9 mm) plywood	max 8" (200 mm) distance
$\frac{1}{2}$" (12 mm) plywood	max 10" (250 mm) distance
$\frac{5}{8}$" (15 mm) plywood	max 12" (300 mm) distance
$\frac{3}{4}$" (18 mm) plywood	max 13$\frac{3}{4}$" (350 mm) distance

and oiled. Then, the nail holes are puttied, and the deck is coated with an oil paint. When the paint has dried, sometimes a paper is laid on the deck, sometimes the canvas is laid directly, but in both cases they aren't attached underneath. The canvas is placed in as large of pieces as possible without transverse joints. Any joints are hidden under a king plank. The canvas can be attached with stainless steel staples and stretched properly during assembly. After mounting, the canvas is shellacked then painted with a "soft" color that will not crack easily. The trick is to keep the paint layer as thin as possible, but it should still be thick enough that it is possible to sand the paint without damaging the canvas.

Another possibility is to apply linseed oil on the canvas rather than shellac. It won't tighten the canvas as well, but the oil waterproofs the canvas so that it does not absorb as much color.

What Type of Plank Deck Should I Lay?

Teak or Oregon pine? Teak or Oregon pine decks have long been a popular topic of discussion; there are pros and cons with both kinds, so I can't give you a definite answer.

Teak decks are slip-resistant and resistant to rot but difficult to keep clean. They don't need to be surface-treated, but to last longer the teak may be oiled, especially if the deck is made of modern teak, which grows quicker and is less oily and less rich in resin. Unfortunately, the oil usually binds dirt, and eventually the oiled decks become almost black. Untreated teak wears down fairly quickly and moves more, as a layer of varnish does not hinder moisture exchange.

Varnished pine decks are slippery, but anti-slip varnish can solve that problem. The deck requires sanding and varnishing each season so as not to flake off. The boat should also be on land, covered, by mid-October to avoid the varnish coming off the deck. I think it's easier to get a varnished pine deck to look elegant than to keep an untreated teak deck looking nice.

Teak decks can be screwed and plugged, but plugs in pine decks often become prominent because they break the grain, and the varnish releases easily from plugs as they swell. I therefore prefer to angle-nail pine decks.

Cost-wise, pine and mahogany are cheaper than teak, but sawn teak slats can be bought over the counter at competitive prices. They are short in length, and the grain is located all over the place in them.

Solid Plank Deck or Planks on Plywood?
There is a technical limit for solid decks. Usually, Swedish boats are built with a distance between the deck beams of 9–10" (225–250 mm). At a thickness of the plank that is less than 5⁄8" (16–17 mm), the loads will be such that the planks move relative to one another, the deck crackles when you walk on it, and the caulk is subject to large loads. I would be reluctant to put in a solid deck thinner than 3⁄4" (20 mm; this includes wear and tear). With tighter beam spacing, you could of course reduce the thickness. A solid deck will have a long life; there are no moisture traps, and leakage manifests itself in the right place. It becomes natural to fix dripping from a leaking seam.

Planks on a plywood deck, however, will make for a stiffer boat and horizontally stiffening knees can be excluded. There is no risk of leakage through the plywood. Leaking seams become apparent only when the moisture lifts the varnish. Unless all the planks are firmly adhered to or embedded in the rubber paste against the plywood, the water that enters through leaking seams

will spread. When water freezes to ice and expands, larger spaces are created. I have dismantled decks where there was water left between the planks and the plywood, even though the boat had stood on shore, under cover, for more than six months. Moisture between layers leads to delaminating of plywood and rot in the planks and plywood if it is not noticed in time.

Rubber Caulk or Epoxy Caulk on Plywood?
Today, two different varieties of plank decks are laid on plywood: planks in elastic bedding compound or planks in epoxy.

An example of a rubber deck is 1⁄4–1⁄8" (6–10 mm) plywood and 1⁄2" (12 mm) teak on top. 1⁄2" (12 mm) is the thinnest plank thickness for plugging a 3⁄16-inch (5-mm) plug. Pine decks that are nailed at an angle should be a little bit thicker. For planks laid in elastic bedding compound, the seams are approximately 3⁄16" (5 mm) deep and 3⁄32–3⁄16" (3–5 mm) wide and bottomed with bond breaking tape.

The corresponding epoxy deck may have two layers of 1⁄4-inch (6-mm) plywood glued together firmly in place and properly screwed. On top, a 1⁄4-inch (6-mm) plank is glued with loose spacers; the spacers are removed, and seams are filled with colored epoxy. The planks are chosen that thin for the glue to keep any moisture movement in the wood. Seams have no elastic function, but they can be narrower; I make them about the same width as old puttied seams (4–5% of the plank width). A typical width of the planks in the above examples are 1¼–1½" (32–38 mm). The varnish on the pine deck stays better on the epoxy deck; it easily cracks on soft rubber caulking. A deck that is built with two layers of plywood becomes rigid; the bonding between the layers helps keep the deck curvature instead of, as in other cases, when a thicker layer of plywood is bent by being screwed down to the beam shelf and thereby flattening the beams.

I have, for many years, glued the covering board to the sheer strake and the beam shelf; it creates an edge beam, which stiffens the corner between the deck and the hull. Sometimes you hear boat owners complain that the topsides cracks in the seams and ribs have broken when a boat has a new, stiffer deck. I have never encountered this. A crack in the seam should appear between the sheer strake and the next plank on a pine boat. Previously, the sheer strake has often been wet because moisture penetrated between it and the covering board; when things get tight there it dries the top plank, and since it is glued to the covering board the entire dry crack will develop between the first and the second plank.

The crack may be splined after one season. The cracked ribs may be the result of the lack of vertical knees that should be at the mast, in the front and the back of the cabin, and the deck hatches.

PROCEDURE FOR DECK INSTALLATION
Dismounting

Take pictures of the deck, especially of the details. Mark with a permanent marker on the deck where fittings are in relation to the coamings and hatches prior to taking the pictures.

Drill from the bottom up through the deck on both sides of the beams and repeat at both ends of the beams. Draw lines on top of the drill holes and get a grid pattern to cut off the deck after. Then, the planks on the beams are carefully removed so as not to damage the beams. The covering boards and the margin planks are removed in one piece, if at all possible, to be used as a template.

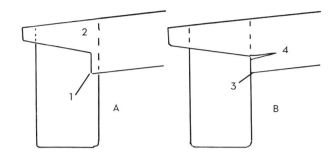

FIGURE 169 ⎰ Beam Ends

A A good deck beam.

  1 Support for the entire beam height.

  2 The beam ends are made thinner in order to not weaken the beam shelf.

B Common mistakes on the deck beams.

  3 Support missing.

  4 When loaded, the beam will crack here.

Do not forget to loosen the screws through the cabin and cockpit coamings before dismantling.

Repairing the Beams

Check across the deck and fix flaws, change rotted timber, and ensure that strength is retained in beam shelf and carlings. If large parts of the beams must be replaced, then the hull must be fixed in place in relation to itself during that time so that the boat is not skewed. Screw boards in the ribs across the boat under the beam shelf to keep the shape.

Hatch beams, i.e., beams fore and aft of the hatches, are often weakened by insets for carlings and by decay from leaks. As a result, these beams have become flatter than the other beams of the deck in general. Tighten up the beams to the correct the curve and reinforce them, or replace them.

The curve of the deck beams (the deck beam curve) often becomes flatter with time. An original drawing can give an idea of the shape. Beams at bulkheads and the top of bulkheads can also give an idea of the beam's original shape. The most common scenario has probably been that the deck gets a single deck beam curve across the deck. Another option is that the deck in front of the cabin is more arched than the aft deck.

FIGURE 168 ⎰ Make sure to replace decayed and weakened deck beams; it's a chance that you won't get again.

Some of the extremes in arched decks are boats built by August Plym, which often have so much deck beam curve that it may be difficult to walk comfortably on the planks at the sides of the cabin. Another is the 5.5-meter yachts that have flat decks so that the water almost collects amidships.

Fix the top of the planking—it tends to be bad—especially toward the stern and at the chain plates; on motorboats, the bow is also sensitive. If you replace the sheer strake, you have to consider that the beam shelf then is also loose and can change position as the deck sags. Attach the beam shelf firmly to the ribs while working.

The screw holes in the top plank from the covering board screws are filled with glue. The easiest way to do this is to press thin wooden sticks, dipped in epoxy, down into the holes. It is difficult and time-consuming to fill the small-diameter holes with epoxy; air pockets can easily form. With help from the sticks, the epoxy is easily placed in the bottom of the holes.

Take the time to do this work properly; the chance will not return. It is better to postpone work on the rails until next year.

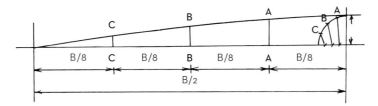

FIGURE 170 } Sketch showing how the deck beam curve can be splied out. The radius R is the height of the beam amidships and B is the boat's breadth. Points A, B, and C are obtained by dividing the radius and the circumference into equal parts.

The height of the curve is usually $\frac{1}{20}$ to $\frac{1}{30}$ of the beam length. If this curve is calculated on a single template for the entire deck, then the aft deck and, above all, the deck in the bow become almost flat. Actually, each beam should be reconstructed on the basis of its span. It means a time-consuming template job, and, in fact, a smaller number of curves is selected and faired with a batten and joiner into place. On racing yachts, the beams were made thinner at the ends than in the middle to save weight; the Square Meter Rule indicates 20% reduction of beam depth at the ends.

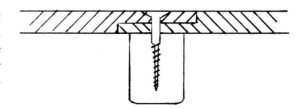

FIGURE 171 } Half a half-joint that is glued. Can be used on plywood, solid deck planks, and covering boards. Provides a large gluing surface. If the glue comes off so that moisture gets in, then the joint can be caulked; a regular, glued spliced joint creates an ugly diagonal stripe across the deck if it releases.

Check the Lines

Check the outline and the sheer line; if you are unsure, you can get help from a professional who can see if the outline is even. The carpentry and surface treatment can be as fine as any, but if the stern hangs or the boat is skewed, the results, in all cases, will be less successful. Shave off any dents or unevenness from the sheer strake and beam shelf so that the covering board will lie flat and will not crack when you screw into it. Larger imperfections can be corrected by dismantling the beam shelf from the top plank and adjusting its height together with the deck beams. Single straightened deck beams can be glued in on top to the correct curve.

Support the ends properly so that the boat won't lose its shape.

Making Templates and Installing Plywood

Make a simple drawing to scale (about 1:20 to 1:50) of the deck, with hatches and superstructure. Then cut out the scale in paper with the plywood board's sizes and place them on the drawing in the most economical way.

Avoid putting plywood joints by the forward and aft corners of the superstructure or other places where the deck is subject to large forces. With dual plywood layers, the joints are staggered between the two layers. In the case of a single layer of plywood, the joint can be jointed half and half on top of a deck beam, or the plywood can be cut with the proportions 1:10 and glued as a scarf joint.

On boats with covering boards, the plywood is cut $\frac{2}{3}$ out on the beam shelf. The edge can be routed in place or drawn with a guide and cut clean before the plywood is installed.

FIGURE 173 } Drilling a side deck screw with a guide.

Don't forget to transfer the position of the deck beams and reinforcements so that they appear on the plywood's topside before drilling. That's where all the screws and nails will be placed.

Place the plywood on the deck and fix it with a few screws; start with the largest pieces and finish by fitting in the smallest. When everything is in place, all the holes are drilled; then the sheets are removed and the drill shavings are cleaned off.

Oiling and varnishing beams and painting or varnishing the plywood are also easiest to do before mounting. Surfaces that need to be glued should not be coated in advance because it reduces the adhesive bond. Glue all end grains of the plywood. Either glue the plywood to the beams or place a string of sealant between the beams and the plywood to prevent creaking decks.

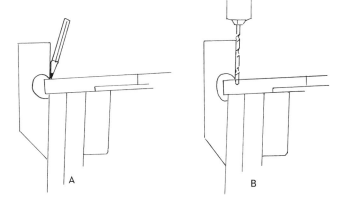

FIGURE 172 } Cat is a piece of plywood or wood with a notch for the side deck edge. Different shaped cats may be used for various purposes.

A Guide to mark the outer edge of the hull.

B Guide for drilling screws; it shows the angle and position.

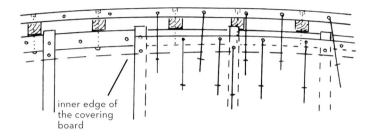

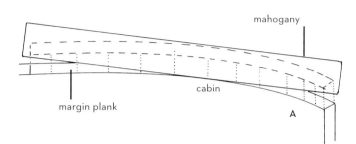

inner edge of
the covering
board

mahogany

cabin

margin plank

A

FIGURE 174 } Screw distribution in the covering board. At the right of the image the plywood is mounted. Shown here is a common way to transfer the positions of the screw holes of the beams, beam shelf and top of planking with spaced arrows drawn on plywood, and then transferred to the covering board's upper surface. The line gives the direction and the cross lines give the spacing, and the same distance is selected on all lines. A moderate spacing for the screws on the top of the planking is 4¾″ (120 mm).

If the boat is only to have plywood on deck, it should be laid out on the hull side with a little excess to be trimmed or milled off when the plywood is mounted. Joints in the plywood should be sanded out on the topside with a sander, and the joint should be sealed with a fiberglass tape laid in epoxy and then faired with filler. Then the whole deck should be coated with a coat of epoxy before it is painted.

Covering Board

One of the first things a professional looks at on a deck is if the planks are symetrical around to the king plank and the hatches and superstructure. When the plywood is mounted, the boat's center line is marked on it. If it's uneven, this can be compensated for by staggering the center line and by making the covering boards different widths. This is less visible than having the seams in the planks staggered. If you need to, you can also mark the insides of the covering boards on the plywood with smoother curves than the hull sides have.

You either make the covering board templates from the old ones or transfer the curve to the new material. Add an excess of material on the outer sides of covering boards for fitting.

It is better to cut the covering boards from a wide plank. Narrow covering boards can be bent; the hull shape determines how wide they can be. A variation I use is to cut the ends but draw the middle of the covering boards straighter. It's always hardest to bend the ends. The force needed to bend the plank at 10″ (25 cm) is eight times the force needed to bend the plank at 79″ (2 m).

When the covering boards are shaped, the bottom is milled for the plywood (the covering board goes over the plywood edge, see Figure 177). I tend to lengthen the covering boards with a half a lap joint.

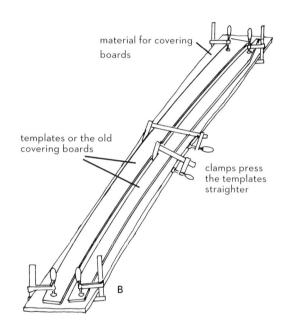

material for covering boards

templates or the old covering boards

clamps press the templates straighter

B

FIGURE 175 }

A Template for margin planks. If the curves are flat, you can set out the marks directly on the material with the help of a measuring stick. If the corners are sharper, it is better to sand in the templates for the shape; composite board is a good template material.

B Templates save material. Wood is not a homogeneous material; cracks and other problems in the grain can be avoided by using more accurate templates. If the old covering boards are in good condition, they can be used as templates. In direct copying as in A, it takes a 12-inch- (30-cm-) wide plank to get a piece for the covering board. With the help of templates that are pressed a little straighter as in B, it is possible to get two covering board pieces from an 18-inch (45-cm) wide plank.

Mark on the top of the planking and the beam shelf how the screws should be placed to give as even a screwing as possible but without them ending up in the old holes or in the middle of rivets and screws that go through the planking into the ribs. Then mark the placement on the plywood with distance arrows (see Figure 174).

It is easy to drill holes in the side deck edge too far out on the hull. A guide aligns the holes; another guide is used to plot the side deck's outer curve. First, drill a few locating holes for the covering board and then attach them provisionally. Then drill the other holes. Take off the side deck and clean the wood shavings. Glue and mount the covering board with all the screws to get good contact.

When the covering boards are mounted, the second layer of plywood for the epoxy deck can be templated; then proceed as above. Leave a recess for the king planks if they are to be screwed; they then become ½-inch (12-mm) thick; if they are placed on top of two layers of plywood, they will be ¼-inch (6-mm) thick and cannot be screwed and plugged.

Deck Planks

Draw the deck planks, margin planks and king planks on the plywood. Bend the plank with clamps or jacks that are attached to the side of the hull. If you have saved an excess of the covering boards, you won't have to be afraid of getting marks on the hull. When the plank installation approaches the center, it is wedged against the superstructure and temporarily bolted blocks.

It is most difficult to get nice curves at the joints. Take advantage of the natural curves of the plank and choose as long a timber as possible. If the plank is to be screwed, then seams are milled on both plank edges so that the plank can be bent along its natural curve. You can get pine in 18-foot (6-meter) lengths, but it's hard to get hold of teak over 9 feet (3 meters) in length. Hide as many joints as possible under the deck hardware.

If you nail pine planks at an angle, then mount one plank at a time. Drill properly. The nails we use today are usually stainless nails.

If teak planks are to be screwed onto plywood, it may be convenient to mount three to four lengths at a time. Screw the planks with mounting screws, drill all holes, mark the planks, remove and clean the shavings, coat the plywood with bedding compound, and screw the planks in. On plywood, the planks can be butt-jointed (end to end).

An epoxy deck requires heat when being glued (at least 55–59°F, or 13–15°C. The planks can be held in place with pins (see Figure 176). The distance between the planks is kept with plastic strips; the easiest way is to slice up a thin plastic cutting board; first, check to be sure that the glue does not stick to the material. Fitting and gluing the three plank lengths on each side will be a moderate day's work. It's good to have extra weights or sandbags to weigh down planks in the glue.

It is easiest to mount the king plank afterward. The planks can then be made a bit too long, and the recess for the king plank is cut or routed according to the guide bar when all deck planks are laid. Don't forget to taper off the king plank. The margin planks can be plotted directly onto the material with the help of a measuring stick (see Figure 175).

Seam Bottoms

Seams are bottomed with products recommended by caulk manufacturers. The bottom should be there to stop the caulking from attaching to the bottom of the seam groove; if it does, it won't have full elasticity. If the mass has 100% elasticity, the seam can then change its measurement from 3/32″–¼″ (3–6 mm) without the caulking coming out. If the caulking is attached to the bottom and the groove there is 0.003″ (0.1 mm), it can only change the dimensions to 0.008″ (0.2 mm) before the caulking starts to become overloaded.

FIGURE 176 Pins to hold down the planks during assembly. The pins are screwed through the plywood and the deck beams. If you tape the pins with packing tape, they will not get stuck in the glue. Plastic spacers are thrust into the seams; they are taken out after hardening.

A The heel presses the planks together. The pin has a gap at B in order to be able to press the planks down.

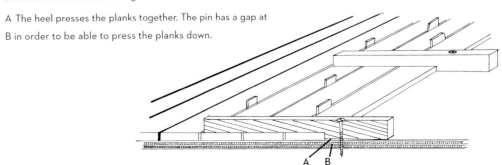

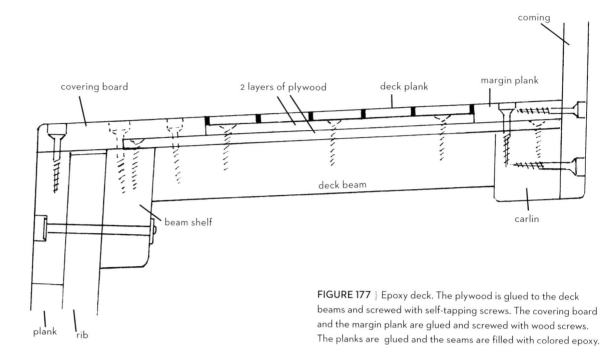

FIGURE 177 } Epoxy deck. The plywood is glued to the deck beams and screwed with self-tapping screws. The covering board and the margin plank are glued and screwed with wood screws. The planks are glued and the seams are filled with colored epoxy.

The bottom could be a round neoprene rubber band that also acts as a 0-ring seal in the seams, or narrow tape. The milled groove depth is determined by the bottom thickness; the rubber seam is usually estimated at around $\frac{3}{16}$–$\frac{1}{4}$" (5–6 mm).

Epoxy-caulked decks are not bottomed.

Caulking Rubber Seams

Use primer if the caulk manufacturers recommend it (especially on teak).

I prefer to do a rough fairing of the deck before the caulking. When the deck is ready, the planks are taped on both sides of the seam with masking tape. The caulking is placed in the seam with a cartridge gun. Fill from the bottom, and be generous. Allow the caulk to sink down for a while. Then remove the excess with a narrow trowel for a pine deck. On a teak deck, smooth out the splining with the back of a plastic spoon so that it is concave; it's the teak and not the caulking that you need to be attentive to.

The excess caulking is now on the tape. Pull the tape off before the caulking starts to set. As it cures from the surface, a teak deck is good to go after a few days. This way, it won't have any visible air bubbles. Pine decks must be allowed more time to harden before they are faired and finished.

Epoxy Decks

Seams are filled with epoxy mixed with pigment, usually black or white, and a little filler. If the pigment is mixed in the epoxy with which the planks are glued, you will have no problem with the color of the glue that comes up between the planks. Sand the deck roughly before the epoxy is put in the seams, and proceed as above with tape, cleaning up the excess epoxy. The end grain of Oregon pine should be coated with clear epoxy before assembly; otherwise the pigmented adhesive may penetrate the end wood and discolor it.

Caulking Compounds

There are many different caulking compounds. They will last anywhere from five to twenty years. There is something fishy about them, as manufacturers will periodically come up with "new" caulking compounds that finally resolve all leaking problems. The truth is probably that you will have to go in and touch up when necessary.

The requirements for caulking compounds are elasticity and adhesiveness, and it appears that the curves for these characteristics intersect. The better the elasticity, the poorer the adhesion, and vice versa. Silicones have the greatest elasticity but easily release from wood. The silicone causes silicone contamination when the varnish is sanded; silicone particles that remains on the surfaces to be varnished have so little surface tension that they create fish eyes in the varnish.

Polyurethanes have good adhesion but may crack over time when exposed to UV radiation. Because they are harder, they are easier to coat over without the varnish cracking.

In recent years, we have used caulking compounds based on silyl-modified polymers, SMPs; they are marketed as MS polymers, such as Samson Deck Caulking. They have worked well and can withstand both linseed oil and alkyd varnish.

Many manufacturers also recommend the use of a primer to improve adhesion. All caulking compounds except the most elastic ones demand bottoming the seam joint.

Solid Plank Decks

The previously described workflow applies fairly well even to solid plank decks, but the plywood is omitted. Make seams at both edges so that the planks can be reversed and the natural bend can be utilized. Nail in the deck beams at an angle, and lock the planks to

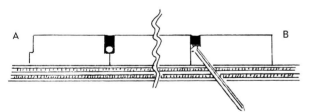

A   B

FIGURE 178 } A gum-caulked deck is laid with thicker planks on a layer of plywood.

A If the seam is cut on both sides of the plank, it will reduce the risk of tearing, and also the plank may be reversed along its natural curve. The seam in the image is so deep that a neoprene trim fits as a bottom.

B For angle nailing, it may be convenient to have the entire seam to nail in. The seam is bottomed out with tape.

each other with one or two nails between the beams to prevent any movement. The planks are jointed with half lap joints over a beam. Use tension rods acrosss the side decks. If you bead the plank on the bottom, it gives it a nice impression from underneath, and the differences in levels between the planks can't be seen as much. The deck could be caulked with caulking compound as described above; it can also be driven with yarn. The yarn of a deck can be driven in with a thin caulking wheel on a handle. The wheel rolls down the yarn on the bottom of the seam. Then you caulk with gum paste or putty.

Sheet Decks

Most of what has been described in the previous workflow applies to sheet decks as well.

The fact that mahogany is dimensionally stable allows it to be laid in wider sheets. An old sheet deck had weatherstrips or seal trim of the same wood, approximately ⅝–⅚" (15–20 mm) wide, that were screwed down between the sheets. The strips had beveled angles and flexed during installation. The planks were well-oiled and mounted in thick varnish. When the sheets, hopefully after many years, have moved and leak, then the trim can easily be replaced with wider trim. The same method can be used today when changing sheets. The mahogany in the sheets should have a moisture content of 9%.

Another method is to glue thinner mahogany panels on the plywood. Thus, in the same way you would an epoxy plank deck and with the same thickness, i.e., about ³⁄₁₆- to ¼-inch- (5- to 6-mm-) thick mahogany. If you are looking for a traditional look, you should include the trim, not with seams but rather with glue joints. Plugs should also be included, even if there are no screws under them.

Coating

A teak deck hardly ever needs to be smoothed afterward, but a pine deck that is to be varnished with high gloss varnish will mercilessly reveal any irregularities; you can forget about machines—this needs to be sanded by hand to make the deck look even. One trick that makes the roughness less visible is to mix anti-skid powder into the varnish; the surface won't reflect as much then, and in addition, the deck won't be as slippery.

Coat a small piece of pine deck or a test panel to verify that the oil doesn't dissolve the rubber compound.

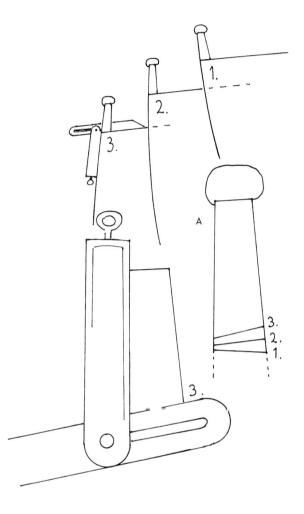

FIGURE 179 } Template of the railing. The corner angles vary between amidship (3) and the bow (1); this is where the railing also is slightly higher at the bow. The cap rail is easier to mount if it is given a rim, as in sketch A.

I find that traditional finishing with oil and varnish gives a more mature and deeper shade to the deck. Finishing with epoxy and polyurethane makes it more abrasion-resistant and provides a surface that does not age and turn yellow as fast, but it can look a little like plastic and eventually turn lightly milk-colored. Everyone chooses according to his taste.

Consider the location of hardware; a clean deck area is quick to maintain.

RAILING

The railing has multiple roles. First, the purely practical—not for anything is the low toe rail usually known in Sweden as the potato rail; it will help loosen objects such as screwdrivers and potatoes to remain on deck. Secondly, the aesthetic—the railing frames the deck with all its details into a whole. It also gives the hull its shape and highlights the deck's sheer-line.

The most complex railing is the one in which the bulwark follows the shape of the hull and basically is shaped like a plank; it often ends with a cap rail in a different timber. To further complicate matters, the bulwark is often higher in the bow than at the stern. It thus gives the boat a new outline. A boat designed and built this way has an exaggerated line on the deck from the cockpit and aft. It is sometimes called a "ducktail," and is used so the railing is less and less dominant on the transom.

One advantage of a railing of this type on an old boat is that it provides a means to adjust any deformation of the deck's sheer line.

The toe rail, which stands on the covering board or the canvas deck, may be placed in different locations, from the topside of the hull into the joint between the covering board and the deck. It is usually tapered—that is, thinner at the top than at the base (this also applies to true bulwarks). Sometimes the toe rail is divided into shorter pieces with room for hardware and water drainage between the pieces. Personally, I think the split type often makes it difficult to give the deck a harmonious appearance, especially if the parts have different lengths.

A railing must have water drainage for rainwater and spray water. The most common are oval cut-outs on the bottom of the railing. On white-painted boats, there are often dirt marks on the sides right by the drains. Deck scuppers are common on larger yachts. They are deck drains with grills that flow channel the water down through tubes to outlets along the waterline. In our climate, where the boats are on land half the year, it is important that boats with bulwarks are supported on stands so that a drain is at the deck's lowest point so all condensation water can drain out; otherwise the boat will easily get varnish and freeze damage on the covering boards and railing in the middle of the puddle that will form.

SUMMARY

Decks wear out quickly; when you buy a boat, you should find out if the deck needs to be replaced within a few years and decide if you want to take on the cost; it can be difficult to sell a boat with a bad deck.

The renovation of an old, scraped-clean deck is a pretty sad affair. The deck often gets worse the deeper you scrape.

With all the prep work needed for replacing a deck, it is difficult to find enough time to do it over a winter; you will also need warm weather for many of the steps.

Correct all defects in all nooks and any lopsidedness during a deck replacement; you won't get another chance.

Make sure the plywood is of Marine grade quality.

A tight deck increases the comfort onboard significantly, and, as with old houses, a sound roof is the best way to stop decay.

SUPERSTRUCTURE

When the hull was completed and the deck beams and the carlins were mounted, it was time to make the boat's main bulkheads and interiors. We are spoiled with good electric lighting, but when the old boats were built it was dark below deck after the deck was laid. With the main interior mounted it was time to add the deck, and then the boatbuilder started to think about the superstructure.

SUPERSTRUCTURES OF SAILBOATS

A low, slender hull was the ideal for a long time. It worked on day cruisers and on the really big yachts, but to make the boats sized in between habitable, they were outfitted with cabin trunks. The dominant species of wood in the cabins has been mahogany. From the 1890s to the 1920s, it was the fashion to have rounded fronts on cabins. During this period, there was often a skylight in the cabin top for extra natural light (see Figure 160).

After that, the plow cabin dominated, in which the side edging continued toward the forepeak hatch or ended with a plow in front of the mast.

From the 1940s on, the cabin trunk extended forward past the mast. In order to get bigger and more comfortable spaces inside, they began placing the mast on the deck or the cabin top. This required a construction that sent loads from the mast to the bulkheads and the hull sides. Figure 207 shows a coastal cruiser drawn by Iversen with a trunk cabin and the mast on the cabin top.

The different needs of headroom in the cabin and galley meant that the cabin was made with a step; the "doghouse" was created.

In the meantime, the freeboard was made higher. Around 1920, it took a ten-tonne boat to get standing head room in the cabin; by 1960, a three-tonne boat sufficed. The height of the cabin has varied more with the help of the camber of the top than with the height of the sides.

At the end of the 1940s, the whale deck was launched—a design that Arvid Laurin used on many of his Koster boats. An arched side deck raised the hull so that the cabin got more height all the way to the hull. Some of the Koster boats got such good height inside that cabins didn't need a trunk but were built flush to the deck. The international meters yachts have been built flush decked; the 6-meters have been built with open cockpits, and the 10-meters with a self-bailing cockpit and a skylight.

SUPERSTRUCTURES OF MOTORBOATS

The first habitable motorboats also had low freeboards, but the motorboat is shallower in the hull than the sailboat, so those superstructures were really high. A solid plank could not build such a high superstructure; it would crack or warp with moisture movement. Instead, it had to be made as framework in which the top and bottom pieces were out together with tenoned posts. Either glass or wood panels was mounted in the frame. The saloon boat has this construction on the saloon sides. To increase the seaworthiness and space in the forecastle, the foredeck was raised so the hull got a nonlinear outline when viewed from the side. See page 232: *Elisabeth* with framework saloon sides and elevated foredeck.

A small motorboat with berths under the raised foredeck was called a cabin boat. C. G. Pettersson has given his name to this type of boat, although boats of this type were constructed by most designers, and Pettersson drew many other types of boats. The living room of the motorboat was the open cockpit; from there, you would run the boat, cook, and eat. The cockpit could be open or partially roofed and provided with a cover, and was made as large as possible. The cabin and the aft cabin were mostly sleeping quarters. The Pettersson boat in Figure 206 is a boat on this theme, but it is seagoing, and the galley has been moved down below the deck, so it can be called a "long-distance cruiser." The aft corner—the "ear"—on the raised foredeck was exposed at moorings along piers and was even difficult

because of its construction, so it was common to get damaged both from accidents and moisture penetration.

In the late 1930s, the height of the topsides increased, so the need for the raised foredeck decreased. The increased height of the topsides also made it possible to make the superstructure lower.

Towards the end of 1950s, the "cabin cruiser" became common. The location of the controls was moved behind the superstructure, which now contained the main cabin. The wheelhouse was equipped with windscreens and sometimes with a roof. The cabin boat was also often made with framework with large glass panes.

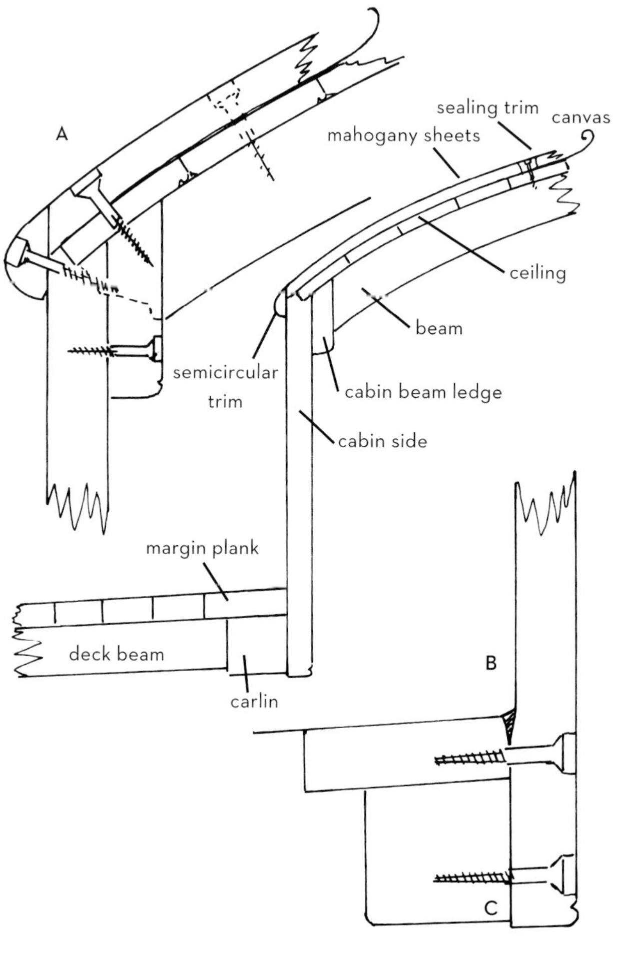

COMMON DAMAGES OF THE SUPERSTRUCTURE
Rot on the Edge of the Cabin Top

Fastening the trim to the top needs care, otherwise it is easy for the screws to wedge apart the different pieces of wood or for the tips of the screws to go through and become visible (see Figure 180A). In this corner it gets damp easily; either the moisture enters through the joint between the trim and the mahogany top or it comes off the canvas (which lies between the roofs) from dry cracks up on the roof. The moisture finds its way into the end grain in the roof beam, and if it's made of ash it soon begins to rot away.

Here, it pays off to nip it in the bud and fix leaks before they create permanent damage. Replace the semicircular trim and mount the new one in elastic sealant. Semicircular trim is a somewhat improper name, for it is formed as a continuation of the cabin top.

Dry cracks in the mahogany sheets are sealed with elastic adhesive or epoxy adhesive. You need to go about cracks above and below the waterline differently. Dry cracks below the waterline can be sealed with wax or other material that is not elastic; when you launch, the wood will swell, the excess sealant will squeeze out, and the boat will be tight. Above the waterline, the seal must be able to cope with repeated moisture movement. If the crack has opened up all the way through so water can drain away, then it may be enough to pour varnish into the crack and expect it to seal from the moisture when it starts to rain. If there is more wood below the crack where the moisture can collect, then it is necessary to make sure that the surface is sealed. Since wood can handle pressure across the grain better than a pull across the grain, the seal needs to be made when the joint or crack has dried apart.

FIGURE 180 } A common version of a superstructure with a mahogany roof.

Filling in cracks with glue works best if the crack is so new that there is no debris and old varnish in the crack. Old cracks can be opened so the joint gets some width, and then you can caulk it with an elastic adhesive. A crooked, dry crack can be cut clean at the edges with a sharp knife. Straight cracks can also be splined.

If the rot has spread in the cabin top, you will eventually need to remove it. You could possibly remount the old mahogany sheets when the rotten ends of the roof beams and the bad planks off the ceiling have been replaced. The roof is now thinner than it was in its original state. One way to enhance the strength is to add mat and epoxy to the ceiling and then glue on the thinned sheets; it can be provisionally fastened using the old screw holes; screws are then removed and the holes are plugged. It's probably quicker to change mahogany; the sheets are shaped to match the camber of the top so that they don't have be pressed down across the grain, which could easily cause them to crack. One trick the old boatbuilders used in the beginning of the last century was to lay the sheets above the hearth of the forge and let the bottoms dry a little extra, which make them shrink and bend; then they had to screw them in before they swelled flat again.

Moisture between the Carlin and the Cabin Side

If the margin plank or a possible quarter trim is leaking, the moisture will find its way down between the cabin side and the carlin (see Figure 180B). This is yet another damage that can be avoided if a boat owner is observant. Leakage during the sailing season is a clear sign and is usually addressed, especially if it occurs over the skipper's berth. Otherwise, the moisture reveals itself as the varnish darkens and begins to release along the screw lines on the inside; then you need to release the moisture by scraping off the varnish. The outside of the cabin of an old boat is often scraped clean, so the seams against the margin are ⅓–1/16″ (1–2 mm) from the side. Take out the caulking in the seam between the side and the margin with a hook (see Figure 39) and caulk the joint with elastic adhesive.

If the leak comes back, you have to go in deeper, pull up the caulking, and cut deeper into the joint with a thin saw blade. This part must be given a chance to dry out; heat the inside of the cabin side repeatedly with a heat gun.

With this procedure, the gap has created a smaller joint surface. Carefully bend the cabin side with a chisel; if it moves, the screws through the side are bad. Take out a couple and check their condition. When you are sure that the screws have a good holding ability, you need to stiffen the joint. This can be done by pouring un-thickened epoxy in the seam. If that is not an appealing option, you can pour mold protection in the joint and then caulk it stiff with cotton yarn. Then seal on the surface with a elastic sealant, regardless of whether it is glued or caulked with yarn. If the joint is sealed by C in figure 180, it will create a real moisture trap low down in the joint.

I'm not fond of the quarter trim; it easily becomes a new moisture trap and is difficult to maintain. I prefer a elastic sealing between margin and side.

Decay in Cabin Corners

On boats built before 1950, the cabin sides and the front were often joined only by screwing the front in between the sides and into the end grain of the front piece (see Figure 181A). This construction was used so that the direction of the grains would be consistent and the pieces would move equally when they swelled and dried. The screws, however, were not that great in the end grain, and water could find its way into the corner between the deck beam and the carlin.

On more recently built boats, the corner was usually made with a corner post (see Figure 181B). It was a sturdier construction, but when the cabin side moved from moisture it could crack by the screws in the post. In this design, the moisture finds its way into the joints between the post and the end wood of the cabin sides.

In order to prevent leakage in the first case, you can attempt to unscrew the screws in the end grain. Remove the screw, clean the hole with a drill, and glue in a wooden stick soaked with epoxy adhesive. Then drill the hole; in the end wood it is important not to drill too small of a hole as it can easily crack. Mount the screw soaked with epoxy adhesive. When the joint is assembled, it can be sealed on the outside with elastic adhesive.

In a cabin with a corner post, you can cut or saw the joint in the post to the depth of the cabin side. The end wood in the side is saturated with epoxy or primed, and then the joint is sealed with elastic sealant. Alternatively, the joint can be splined—the spline will glue well against

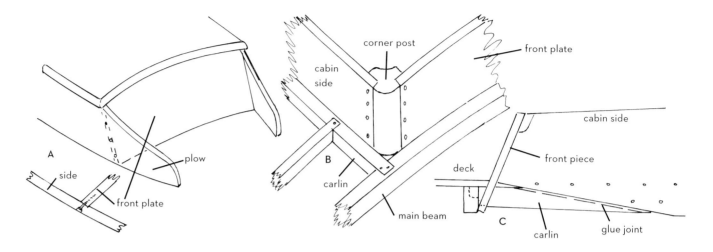

FIGURE 181 } C shows a patch where the lower part of the cabin side has been cut out so that you can place a glue joint in the carlin; the tenon in the new carlin is inserted in the main beam. It is important that the side and the carlin are supported while you work on them so that the deck doesn't slump.

the corner post, and the glue seals the end wood of the side. Cracks in the cabin side end from screw holes can also be splined; the joint is opened up with an router bit 1–4″ (5–6 mm) so that you can have new adhesive surfaces, and the spline is tapped in without being to tight. When the adhesive has hardened, drill a plug in the spline end to hide it.

If the moisture has had time to act, then the important corner between the carlin and the beam is often rotten. This is difficult damage to deal with while maintaining strength and structure. A main supporting beam has been damaged, which often means that the deck has become flatter. If it is on a sailboat, the rigging loads have not been capable of being held well. This is a typical example of damage in which the renovation is many times more time-consuming than it would be to build it in the correct order in the first place. Dismounting and deciding the new joint surfaces are a challenge. It is difficult to access the inside of boat, and the different parts with their new joints need to distribute the loads in a good way. When the new joint surfaces are made, it feels like half the job is done. The solutions will also vary from boat to boat. On a boat with a plywood deck, it is tempt-

ing to cut out a piece of the deck to get to certain areas, but in a boat with a planked deck or a canvassed deck, you have to work underneath. Most important that the glue joints should be 5 to 1 with the grain direction, and that the supports and tenons should be retained.

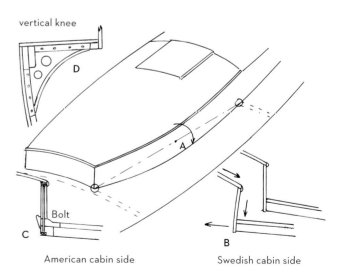

FIGURE 182 } Hanging cabin sides.

The Swedish construction method in which the cabin sides are attached to the inside of the carlin is adapted to Scandinavian protected waters. According to U.S. Coast Guard standards, the cabin sides of an ocean cruiser should be on the carlin and be bolted vertically through it as in Figure 182C. The weaker Swedish design combined with the sides being made with graceful curves gives the effect described in 182A and B. The cabin top swells and wants to flatten out, and the deck swells sideways while the side sinks obliquely downward and inward and the beams become flatter. The side has a tendency to rotate around a straight line through the attachments of the carlin in the main beams (see A), and the cross-section changes as in B. These defects, with a warping of the side and a dip in the deck towards the cabin, disturb the boat's outlines and harmony and make the boat weaker.

If you are aware of the problems you can choose to stop the decay and to restore the original lines. When replacing the deck or the cabin trunk. You should take the opportunity to correct the lines. To just stop the deformations, the sides may be pushed apart at deck level while they are lifted from below. As with any straightening of a boat, you should take it easy and give it enough time. Tighten with struts and jacks or wedges. The deck and the sides will not find their way back to their original shapes, but the lines will be better. Then lock the shape with vertical knees between the deck beams and frames and planking. Vertical knees could be plywood bulkheads in conjunction with lockers or metal knees. Knees of solid wood are hard to make stable enough in attachments. An elegant knee that takes minimal space from the bunk is shown in Figure 182D. It can be made out of stainless steel. The flange toward the boat can be made out of a tube so that there are no sharp corners.

Inferior Tenons

Saloon sides and windscreens were built with framework. In the upper and lower sides of the saloon, they made mortises for the tenons of the vertical pieces. The longitudinal pieces dominated for the sake of stiffness. The tenons were made long for the sake of strength. On the windshields, different builders varied between making the tenon in the vertical or the horizontal piece. The corner pieces were often fitted with a mortise.

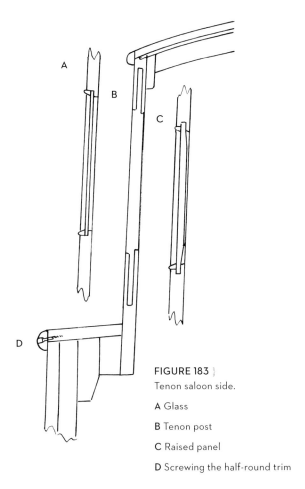

FIGURE 183

Tenon saloon side.

A Glass

B Tenon post

C Raised panel

D Screwing the half-round trim

The tenons had to be sealed so as not to be filled with water; they were tapped in with oil or varnish in the joints and locked with screws. In the mass construction of the fifties, the tenons were glued.

Raised panels are the solid pieces of wood that are mounted within the frame of a saloon side or a raised panel bulkhead. The raised panel could be mounted in slots in the frame during assembly of parts. Sometimes, raised panels were mounted on the wood afterward, in the same manner as a windowpane. The raised panel was mounted with oil or varnish with a little slack so that it could dry without cracking and swell without pushing apart the framework. The same method can be used for renovations, or you can take plywood, attach a thick veneer to it, and glue it into the framework in order to provide increased strength.

Moisture damage resulting in rot or freeze damage in the lower mortises is common. The damage first appears as the varnish starts to come off right by the mortise. The simplest method to deal with this is to seal with an epoxy adhesive using a syringe. Scrape clean and dry out the wood and drill small holes into the mortise and inject epoxy. The holes are crammed with wooden sticks as the mortise is filled. If the tenon and mortise are screwed in, the screws can be removed and the holes used for injecting epoxy.

The lower pieces are usually bad on the outside, where the wood is also depleted after having been scraped bare over and over again. If the wood is in good condition otherwise, the outer half of the bottom piece can be cut away and the tenon can be dried out and repaired before a new outer piece is glued on. Thin down the tenon so that the new piece of wood isn't too thin right in front of it (see Figure 184).

If the tenons and mortises are so rotten that the framework needs to be replaced, it is better to begin by making exact MDF templates off the framework before the windshield or saloon side is dismantled. When the framework is detached, the joint surfaces of the tenons are so short and wobbly that it isn't possible to glue the new framework based on them. Draw the shape of the different pieces

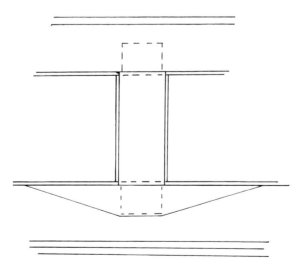

FIGURE 184 Repair of the bottom part of the saloon side right in front of the lower post. This vertical piece has a shorter, visible part on the inside to match the rebate of the glass.

of the template and cut them out. The mortises were usually made with a mortiser. A mortiser basically looks like a deep end drill and is rigged up to a drill press. Nowadays, you can make tenons and mortises with a router boss with different attachments. If the mortise is glued with epoxy, the holes don't need to be so deep. The final shape of the opening for the glass pane is cut when the frame is glued.

Decks below Windshields

On many motorboats, the windshields are standing on deck or on the cabin top. Condensation and leakage from the panes makes the deck rot, particularly where the windshield posts stand with their end grain towards the deck. The canvassing on the deck could also have been replaced, except for under the windshield, so here is an opportunity for moisture to find its way down. Holes for cables may have been drilled in the deck, so water will follow the cable holes into bulkheads below. Space below windows, even below deck, may be considered an outdoor environment due to condensation drip. Check to see where the water goes and drill drains to lead the water to places where it does not do as much damage. When it comes time to replace the deck, I recommend dismantling the windshields and redoing the whole deck instead of cutting it flush with the outside of the windshields like you see sometimes. A renovation like that won't last very long.

Rounded Cabins and Laminated Corners

Rounded corners are often steam bent, either in solid wood or with thinner laminates. Mahogany isn't as easy to steam as oak. The front of a cabin in single mahogany plank with a thickness of ⅞" (22 mm) and a radius of 29.5" (750 mm) is a piece that will be hard to steam-bend. Sometimes it was bent in two layers, which were then assembled with varnish or oil in between; that solution often results in the varnish coming off since the moisture will be trapped. I usually steam this kind of front out of three ¼- to ⁵⁄₁₆-inch (6- to 8-mm) layers. The mould is made as an inner mould made by wood or particleboard. When the mould is built, you have to remember to make a lot of room for clamps and install it so there is access to put clamps on both sides. The newly bent laminates are strapped with blocks crossways and double clamped. A few days after bending, the laminates are loosened and mounted with thin strips of wood in between so they can dry. When the laminates have dried, they are glued together over the mould. The reason that I choose to have the layers so thick is to not risk going through the surface layer when trimming out the side or when scraping it clean.

Corners with a smaller radius need to be made from thinner laminates. A simple rule of thumb is: the radius of the corner divided by 100 is equal to the maximum thickness of the laminate. There is a high risk of sanding through laminates thinner than $\frac{3}{32}$″ (3 mm); with smaller radii the veneer needs to be steam bent. Wetting them with glue also makes them more pliable.

It is common to have glue come apart at the rounded corners, especially in the aft edge of the cockpit sides. Previous designs (in the forties and fifties) were made with thick steamed layers, and more recently (in the sixties and after), the corners have been glued from thinner veneer. The veneer corners are difficult to renovate, but the sides with thicker layers can often be re-glued. Usually, there is trim on top of the side to hide the glue lines; the trim is removed so that the glue joints can be inspected. Dry the wood, try to wedge the layers apart as much as possible, and try to roughen the bonding surfaces with sandpaper or a hacksaw blade; heat, dry out, and clean the surfaces with acetone. When you are satisfied, seal beneath it with tape and pour epoxy down the joints, letting the glue soak in and adding more glue if necessary, then clamp the corners. To avoid the clamps making marks, you need to use pressure-equalizing wooden blocks, and so the blocks do not get caught in the adhesive they need to be taped with packaging tape (plastic tape) that the glue won't stick to.

Semicircular Trim

Trim is sometimes used to seal edges; however, it is not unusual for the trim to become a moisture trap in the long run. In a lot of the quality construction during the 1900s they did not use outside trim at all. The edge between the covering board and the top plank was sealed, and any canvas just went up to the covering board's inner edge. The trim that might be left was the trim on the cabin roof. On motorboats, they used more trim to emphasize the boat's lines.

This kind of trim is often bent both laterally and vertically. If the trim follows the deck edge on the bow of a

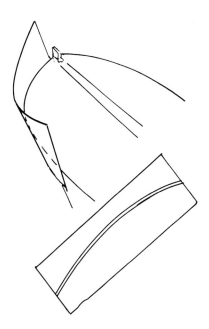

FIGURE 185 } The curve on the semicircular trim at the bow of motorboats is often highly curved in the vertical direction. The trim is stiffer vertically so the curve can then be templated and then sawn up.

motorboat, then it tends to be mounted flat to the planking. If you bend a piece of MDF so that it gets flat toward the planking, the traced deck edge becomes very crooked (see Figure 185). It is difficult to bend such a trim on both levels, so we usually cut out the shape height-wise from broader material; then we only have to bend the trim in one direction. The trim is cut out uniformly for the width, and the rounding is made with an ogee cutter; it is often better to route the upper round when the trim is installed. If the bend sideways is sharp, the trim may be bent in place by letting it lie in water a few days and then bending it with heat using a hot air gun while keeping it wet with a sponge. The trim is screwed in without the plugholes drilled (it breaks easily from the weakening that plugholes cause) and with washers under the screw heads. When the trim has acclimatized for a few days, it is taken off and then mounted with sealant and plugs.

When a semicircular trim is screwed on, the ambition is to screw it onto the piece at the top of the joint (see Figure 183D). A semicircular trim that is screwed to the top plank instead of the edge of the covering board moves with the top plank, resulting in a gap between the trim and covering boards.

I prefer to set trim with glue or elastic adhesive. The glue should be gap filling (epoxy). The elastic adhesive should be a structural adhesive (one-component polyurethane, such as Sikaflex). On an old boat, there is often damage to the wood behind the trim from previous careless screwing that needs to be filled and sealed.

HATCHES AND COAMINGS

Hatches are often rebuilt on old boats, and when you replace them it helps if there is an original drawing to go by. Otherwise you can look at boats from the same era and choose a solution that is true to that time. An inspection below deck will often reveal where the hatches were in the beginning, as the beams in the forward and aft edges of the hatches were thicker than the other beams. Old hatch tops were made of solid wood, so they move a lot with moisture. This can be a problem, because if the hatch is loose it leaks in dry weather, and if it is made hard it swells and gets stuck in wet weather. One could say that if a flat wooden board manufactured from straight-grained wood is varnished with the same number of layers of varnish on both sides of the wood, the wood will be flat when it swells and dries. If a reinforcement is glued to the back of the hatch top, it will bend upwards in the middle as it swells, and if it dries out further there is a risk that it will crack. To avoid this, the reinforcements can be screwed on using loose screw holes that allow a little movement, or you can cut a dovetail into the wood (see Figure 187). A hatch of solid wood that is taken home to a hobby room or boiler room over the winter will dry and crack.

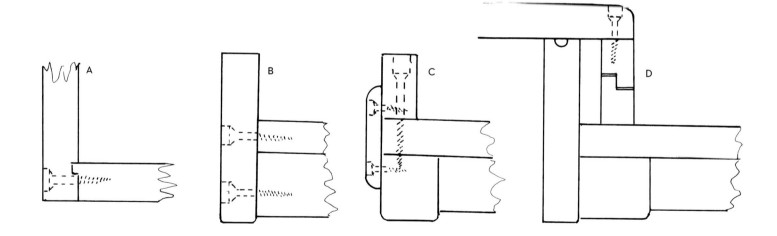

FIGURE 186 Hatch coamings.

A Corner of the coaming; the track fixes the corner in place.

B and C The two most common ways to mount coaming.

D Hatch for an ocean cruiser from a 1950s model; the space between the coamings will take care of splashing water and is drained at deck level to the lowest point. The image also shows a water channel on the inner coaming and a folding of the outer coaming; rarely were all three methods used simultaneously.

The older hatch types were seldom particularly tight, so seawater came in, but they were outfitted with a canopy when the boat would be used in rough weather. A folding hatch with inner and outer coamings in the style of the fifties is the driest variety (see Figure 186D). One way to seal a forepeak hatch of traditional type is to install a canvassed piano hinge along the edge rather than overlying hinges that allow water on the hatch top to flow down into the boat when opened.

The sliding companionway hatch on the cabin top is usually mounted on brass slides which are screwed onto the coaming. In order to be able to lift off the hatch, the slides need to be unscrewed. The runners are made of bent sheet metal strips (see Figure 188). For a companionway hatch to be reasonably dry, the trim on the leading edge of the hatch must fit reasonably against the cabin roof. An arched hatch is given its curvature with a plane; it is not bent into shape.

A flush deck hatch that has its upper surface "flush" against (on par with) the deck should be fitted with a water channel that drains overboard. Otherwise, rainwater will shorten the life span of the hull below.

SUMMARY

Sealing from above is more important for the boat's life than sealing the bottom. The decay process in hot humid joints is fast. Only apply sealant from the outside so that water does not get trapped in the construction.

If you watch out for signs of moisture lifting the surface treatment, you may prevent costly repairs.

Moisture damage on tenons is common. When windshields are replaced, their shape needs to be templated before they are dismantled.

Do not bring home doors and hatches of solid wood for renovations. They will crack in the heat and dry air.

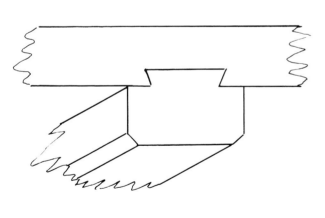

FIGURE 187 } Cutting in the reinforcement that allows the moisture movements of the hatch.

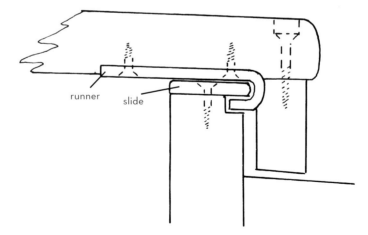

FIGURE 188 Mounting the cabin hatch; usually the hatch has four runners.

INTERIOR DESIGN

Interior design is a huge topic that could be covered over several chapters. This is a brief overview. In the old days, there was a distinction at the larger shipyards between boatbuilders who built the boat and the carpenters who built the interior. At the smaller yards, the boatbuilder had to do everything, from manufacturing to sweeping the shop floor. The interior of a small boat represents a small part of the construction period, while it represents a large part of the construction period for a bigger yacht.

FLASHBACK

The classic interior of a boat from the beginning of the 1900s was built of framework with panels. Large, solid wooden sheets were not used "as they wouldn't last" and moved with moisture, swelling and bending. The bulkheads in these furnishings do not stiffen the hulls too much. Tenons and mortise could be filled with glue, but they were just coated with linseed oil a lot of the time, and the panels were loosely tucked in, so they could swell without pushing the frames apart.

At that time, it was not uncommon to have bulkheads of tongue and groove—made out of quarter-sawn pine that was screwed into frames and deck beams—and then had a mahogany framework screwed to the visible side.

During the twenties, bulkheads also made as raised panels came into fashion; they were double-sided with a beautiful appearance on both sides. See the image on the previous page: the interior of the 10 meter Itaka built by Plym in 1934. Framework and panels of mahogany, trim of walnut.

The art deco period influenced the thirties, and smooth bulkheads made by glued wood covered with veneer became common.

In the fifties, plywood was in vogue. Then the boats were built with glued wood planking on laminated frames. Plywood bulkheads were screwed and glued to the frames and thus became a stabilizing part of the hull.

The fronts of the bunks and the lockers were screwed in between the bulkheads. Floorboards and cabinet bottoms were just laid in without being attached afterward. Building an interior on a finished "floor" has never been considered particularly serious, creates many inaccessible nooks, and makes it difficult to maintain the boat.

In more modern interiors, it is not uncommon for the interior to be built after the sole and ceiling have been mounted; that type of furnishing will shorten the life span of the hull now. Often the ceiling and sole are made of plywood, which is untreated on the backside. Sometimes mold and mildew that cause bad odor will collect there.

The early interiors were symmetrical, especially on yachts; the interior on the starboard side was the same as the port—only reversed. The forepeak had a galley and a bunk for crew. In the thirties, the crew moved out and the galley moved aft. The strictly symmetrical interior was replaced with a more functional interior design for more comfortable recreation.

MAINTENANCE

The interior doesn't need the same kind of annual work as the outside surfaces do. Sanding and varnishing is done whenever needed; the cabin sole and countertops get the most wear. Scraping the interiors bare is most common during major renovations. There are many fifty- to sixty-year-old boats that have never been scraped clean on the inside. It's nice if signs of the old boat owners are still there; worn ladders and thresholds gives the boat patina.

The furnishings were often varnished with pure oil varnish. If a cabinet door or other piece of the interior is put in the blazing sun, the oil varnish may bubble, and you will be forced to scrape it clean.

You may want to remove the ceiling and clean behind and possibly oil at intervals of every five to ten years. Protect against rot and give the ceiling a thin coat of varnish on the back to eliminate one reason for bad odors.

On larger boats there are fixed tanks, which are difficult to access. There, it may be good to rinse behind them periodically. Tanks under the cabin sole should be lifted out at least every five years to make it possible to clean underneath them. The chain locker should also be accessible for cleaning. It should also be easy to clean beneath the heads.

This is something to keep in mind when renovating: Do not build interiors that are hard to take apart in front of the tanks. Build removable beams for the sole over the tanks. Make a box for the chain that is easy to take apart, and build a sole and ceiling that are easy to dismantle in the heads.

Leave a clearance of a coin (2 mm) around for floorboards, cabinet doors, and drawers that should be able to stay in the boat year round. Drawers are varnished throughout and waxed with a candle to slide easily.

COMMON DAMAGES

- Bulkheads that are bolted to steel frames are often damaged; the wood has retained moisture that has caused the frame to rust. In that case, you can often strengthen the post towards the center of the boat so that it holds up the bulkhead, and a bunk bracket or a shelf bracket, can be made a bit sturdier and be bolted securely to the bulkhead so that the damaged part can be removed. This also creates better ventilation.

- Laminated wooden bulkheads were seldom glued with waterproof glue. If they are in a "foot bath" or if there is a pane of glass above that leaks or provides moisture from condensation, the bulkhead is often delaminated with rot and mold inside. These bulkheads are difficult to take apart, as the longitudinal interior is screwed into them. They were also so large that they were assembled before the cabin trunk, which means bulkheads can be permanently bolted between the deck beams and cabin trunk. These are time-consuming

and costly renovations, which may be useful to know before purchasing a boat. The interior along the sides can be used for many years as long as it stays in place, even if it is worn, but when it is removed in conjunction with replacing a bulkhead, it has probably been more damaged by the handling, and you will not want to mount it back again.

- Berths have often been re-built; originally there were usually chain bottoms in the bunks and sometimes springs. Even folding Pullman berths were common (in a Pullman berth, you sleep on a mattress that is attached to the rear side of the foldable backrest). The bench they sat on during the day was narrower and sat lower so there would be enough head room below deck. Today, this is usually converted into plywood bunk tops that are mounted higher and provide storage underneath. During a renovation, it is often possible to find traces of the original design after a careful inspection of old brackets and plugged holes in the bulkheads.

- Over the years, people have probably sawed into the beams that support the bunk base and floorboards. The boards are loose and wobble, and the front of the bunks and lower parts of the bulkheads shuffle towards the center of the boat. Take out the floorboards, bunk tops, and the bottoms of the lockers. Inspect the old beams; try to level them and see if the bulkheads that they are screwed to are still plumb. Decide where you want the bulkhead to stand and align it. Lock it in with new beams. Level a beam underneath at each end of the space and align the other beams with the help of a straightedge leaning on the first beams. Apply surface treatment on the new beams all around before mounting. Once that's done, the old floorboards can be fitted; they usually need to have new wood glued on some side. Original floorboards are often made of teak and are worth renovating.

- The screws in hinges release frequently. Remove the hinge and see if it works well; the pin could be bent or there could be old varnish in the joint surfaces. There are certainly no replacement hinges that fit in their place (believe me, I've looked). Take it as a challenge and part of your hobby to grease and get the old

FIGURE 189 } A The interior can be sparse in order to emphasize the shape of the hull.

one going. Fill up the old screw holes with small sticks covered in epoxy, and then drill the screw holes.

SUMMARY

Interiors could have a book of their own; they involve a kind of carpentry that is different from the rest of boatbuilding. Renovating the interior is a very time-consuming and detailed hobby craft. Major renovations done today include new interiors; there are few people who can afford to have someone renovate the old ones. In this situation, you could copy the old or build an interior that is functional but true to the era and adapted to modern times. Fortunately for the boatbuilder, it is the boat owner who must make that decision.

MOUNTING HARDWARE

What is missing in renovations today is access to the skilled blacksmiths and foundry men who once made hardware for boat building. A set of original hardware may be what determines whether a boat will be renovated instead of being cut up. Today's stainless steel hardware won't fit well on vintage boats, but they are liked by the owners of sailing yachts from the thirties and forties who race for medals in the Championships. The wooden boat hobby has many different branches.

Hardware made of bronze, red brass, and brass shines for visitors at vintage boat meets; it is beautiful, but when the boatbuilders want strong hardware, they choose galvanized steel. If you want that look today but feel more at home with Marine grade stainless steel, then glass-blasted and varnished stainless steel hardware has a nice patina.

Chromed brass and bronze hardware are not always chromed. Up until the thirties, they were nickel-plated, which gives off a bit more of a yellow sheen.

DOCK CLEATS AND HARDWARE FOR HOLDING LOADS

Equipment for docking needs to be well attached. Besides it being dangerous, it is sad if a cleat disappears with a piece of the deck when you are being towed. The cleats should be mounted with bolts that go all the way through. The space on the underside of the deck between two beams is filled with a block of wood, a so-called filling. Underneath, place a backing plate that is large enough to reach over the beams and is attached to them with wood screws. The cleat is bolted through the deck and these pieces of wood and is fitted with large washers under the nuts.

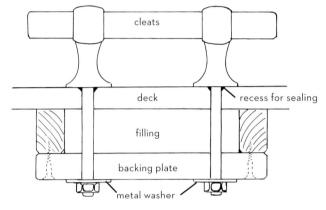

FIGURE 190 } Attaching docking cleats. This type of assembly is also used for winches and similar hardware to withstand large loads laterally.

Protect from rot and waterproof the blocks before mounting. Countersink ⅛″ (4 mm) or so of the deck around the bolt holes to provide a space for sealing. The upper side of the deck should be painted before mounting hardware. This kind of hardware, which won't be dismounted for a long time, can be mounted with an elastic adhesive. If a winch is being installed, it needs to be able to be removed for servicing. Seal around the bolts with sealant, but place the winch on a (approximately ⅛-inch-, or 4-mm-thick) gasket cut out of a piece of rubber.

OTHER DECK HARDWARE

Deck hardware that does not take on such large loads can be mounted with wax or a bedding compound for hardware installation that does not glue as well. Make a recess for the seal here, too. Do not use silicone on wooden boats. Chrome hardware can be fitted with stainless, oval, countersunk metal screws; they have better threads than brass screws and can stand being assembled and disassembled repeatedly. When a screw is reinstalled, do what you would do with a machine screw: turn the screw slowly backwards until it feels like it is sinking down a little and setting in, then screw it in.

When mounting hardware, you should also consider maintenance. Can the hardware be easily moved so that it is easier to varnish around it? Is it possible to paint between the sheet track and toe rail?

On canvassed decks, you may want to mount the hardware on a plate to distribute the pressure and not make holes directly into loose fabric.

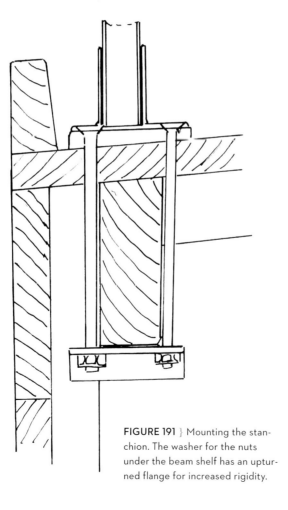

FIGURE 191 } Mounting the stanchion. The washer for the nuts under the beam shelf has an upturned flange for increased rigidity.

STANCHIONS

Stanchions are a source of chagrin on wooden boats. It is hard to apply any coating around them. If they are assembled with wood screws, they are often loose, so moisture can find its way into the beam shelf and deck beam ends. You can often see this from the inside where the guardrail is located; this is where the beam shelf is dark and damp.

When you tackle this damage, you need to start by removing the foot of the stanchion. The covering board is scraped clean and allowed to dry out. Holes for screws are dried out and drilled so that the edges can be healthier and better; then they are glued shut with sticks dipped in epoxy. Holes for bolts are plugged. Decide where the foot should stand; it may be possible to bolt it with bolts that straddle the beam shelf. Do not weaken the beam shelf with holes; it has a stiffening function in the hull. Glue on a wooden plate (⅜–½″ or 10–12 mm thick) to the deck so that the holes in the foot are above the water that collects on deck. Water must have room to flow between the plates and the rail or else the water that will be collecting by the plates will find its way under the covering board. Drill for the bolts of the foot; if you can't use bolts, then use fully threaded screws, as this needs to withstand thrusting. Varnish the covering board and plates and mount the feet with elastic adhesive. Hopefully, the stanchion will bend in the future. To reduce the risk of freezing, there should be drainage holes in the guardrail feet.

CHAIN PLATES

The accuracy in mounting the chain plates affects the life span of that section of the boat. Leaking chain plates lead to rot in the deck, beam shelf, and deck beam ends. The covering board also tends to wear out here.

The classic way to mount the chain plate is to mount it on a plate of metal or wood and bolt it through the planking. Chain plates are made out of flat steel, either galvanized or stainless. Since flat steel is not pliable on the flat side, there is no reason to take it down further than the bilge where it will straighten out in between the bolts and not transfer any loads. If there is a problem with deformations in the hull, this can be solved with a few strong-laminated wood frames instead. Four to five bolts may be just right through the chain plates.

FIGURE 192 } Chain plate mounted on wooden plates. To the right are wood frames that have been sistered.

If you use fully threaded bolts, they should be dipped in epoxy so the thread is filled out; otherwise they have too much room and "saw" the holes. To get a stronger bond, the wooden plates should be bolted or riveted to the planking. On laminated mahogany topsides, you could also glue the wooden plate.

On many racing yachts, the chain plates were moved onto the deck to give the foresails better sheeting angles. On meter-yachts with deep V-shaped hulls, this worked fine. In the shallower, flatter bow of Skerry cruisers, this led to deformations. The shrouds often attached directly to plates bolted to the steel frames. The frames were straightened out, and this created dents in the hull. During a renovation, you need to try to push it back into shape and build sturdier frames. A common way to restore these boats is to set up the mast on the deck on a mast beam where the chain plates also are attached; the forces will then come down through the hull by means of vertical knees mounted in reinforced frames. In a system where the mast is on deck, the chain plates are often mounted with eyebolts to the beam. They should not be putting more loads on the hull in this case, but the mast beam should be a separate entity in terms of strength, and it should hold the forces of the mast downward and the shrouds upward.

The seal of a traditional chain plate to the deck is made in two stages. First, a little bit of wood is chiseled away laterally around the chain plates and down along the chain plate through the covering board. Then, the bottom is caulked tightly and epoxy is poured into the cavity to a level of about 1/16" (2 mm) below the deck. This provides lateral rigidity. Then the top is sealed with elastic sealant formed with a slope from the chain plate to make it dense.

On racing boats with shrouds that go all the way through, to turnbuckles below the deck, the shrouds go down through the deck in pipes that open so far under the deck that moisture does not get into beams, sheer clamp or stiffeners made of wood.

VENTILATION

It is easy to arrange the outgoing ventilation of a boat so that vents in the deck suck out warm air that rises to the deck from inside the boat. It is harder to take in air; when renovating, you need to try to make room for a pair of vertical shafts that flow under the floor boards, and they can easily be fitted in a double bulkhead. The ventilation cowls provide a means to control the air flow by turning them toward or away from the wind. To keep rain out of the ventilators, they can be equipped with water traps, or so-called dorade boxes.

The engine room requires a lot of ventilation for the engine to run well. Here, it is perhaps about 35 cubic feet (1 cubic meter) per minute of air that the engine intake sucks in. It may not leave much air to cool off the engine and other installations. When the engine is shut off it will stop taking in air, and the temperature in the engine room will go up; this can be remedied with an exhaust fan that starts when the engine is turned off. A gasoline engine should always have an engine fan running for a few minutes before starting the engine. All this takes a lot of room; boatbuilders were often good at equipping boats with ventilation from the start, but sometimes the systems are out of function because of rebuilding over the years. On a sailboat, ventilation around the motor is often worse—mostly due to the fact that ventilation on sailboats must be sealed against seawater spray.

This is something you need to include at an early stage in planning a renovation because then the solutions are easier to implement.

THROUGH HULL CONNECTORS

The number of through hull fittings or seacocks grows rapidly with the size of the boat. A small boat with an outboard might have one on the topsides for the bilge pump. The large ocean racer we worked with recently had twelve through the hull fittings under the water and another ten in the topside.

In Sweden, almost all through hull fittings are threaded, while abroad bolted fittings are more common. The most common material is brass, and there are several grades; the higher grade ones are approved by the EU. Marine grade stainless steel fittings have been sold in recent years. The fittings are either surface mounted or recessed; the recessed ones make annual maintenance easier.

Today, we use ball valves, while slide valves were more common thirty years ago. The ball valves should be opened and closed a few times when the boat comes up on land so that they are drained of water.

When you install through hull fittings, it's best to make the hole with a hole saw; if the hole size is wrong, you can always file it to size. The hole should be so wide that the hull connector won't hang on to the threads but will flatten against the hull. When using a recessed one, you make the recess with a chisel and a sharp knife. Install the fitting with elastic adhesive; the nut is threaded on and the valve is screwed on with okum sealing. When the valve is fully threaded the handle is turned to the correct position, and the nut on the inside of the hull is tightened.

SUMMARY

When renovating, you need to plan the hardware installation and design of the ventilation at an early stage while there is still some space left in the boat.

Install the hardware that will handle heavier loads with bolts that go through all the way. Other hardware can be installed with wood screws.

The type of sealant to be used depends on how often the hardware needs to be dismantled.

Fix leaky chain plates before the wooden parts underneath rot.

Well-functioning ventilation provides a better climate in the boat and extends the boat's life span.

Inspect the through hull fittings, and check if the seacocks work; drain the ball valves in the fall so they do not freeze.

MASTS

In the old days, masts were planed from solid tree trunks. Lengths were therefore limited, and topmasts and gaffs stretched the sails upward. Drilled masts were used on racing yachts even before the turn of the twentieth century. The hollow masts, booms, and gaffs were imported mainly from the United States. August Plym also made hollow masts; it is said that he used a method of drilling out the masts by having the material rotate around a stationary drill. Already, the 1904 edition of the KSSS rule book talks about different dimensions for solid and hollow masts. Around 1915, the Bermuda rigs (triangular mainsails) began to emerge for larger boats, and by 1920 the Bermuda rig was the dominant rig type. A requirement for larger Bermuda masts was the technique for bonding it. In Gustav Plym's book *En seglare minns* (A Sailor Remembers), you can read about the gluing of *Miranda*'s mast (see the chapter on gluing). In the end of the 1920s and during the 1930s, they began to use different cross sections from the round mast.

FORCES ACTING ON A RIG

The force of the wind in the sail bends an unstayed mast, thus the mast has to be designed so that it doesn't break from the bending. To simplify it, you could say that on a wooden mast with rigging, the force of the wind on the rig is taken up by the stays, which are subject to tension and specifically designed for that. The mast, on the other hand, is subject to a downward directed pressure force by the stays and the halyards and is designed for pressure and buckling (deflection). With the same compression and cross section of the mast, the risk of deflection increases if the distance between the attachment points of the shrouds is increased.

On a gaff sail rig, the attachments for the shrouds were placed high up so that the gaff jaws or horns could be raised along the mast, and the sail was attached to the mast with mast hoops or mast lacing. This caused the buckling length of the gaff rig mast to be significant and similar along and across it. So it was natural for the mast to have a round cross section, and it was made thicker in the middle of the lower shroud mount and the deck where buckling forces were greatest.

In the beginning, the straight or slightly bent Bermuda rig was designed in the same manner. The spreader and the lower shroud sit high up, often at the same height as the shrouds of the *Boja* (see Figure 193). A special type of rig during the 1920s and 1930s was the Marconi rig. The mast was constructed with a curved top. There were probably several reasons for this rig becoming popular. When knowledge of aerodynamics increased, people knew that a sail that is wider and more elliptical at the top is more efficient than a sail that is pointed. On a boat such as the Skerry cruiser where the sail area is limited, it can be an advantage to have more sail area higher up where the wind is steadier and stronger (if the boat is stiff enough). In the first years that the new rig type was around, they only measured the triangle that was formed by the corners of the sails, and they had an unmeasured roach contribution to the sail's surface area, so they soon changed the rule, and the sail area in the rounding was measured. The disadvantage of a curved mast is that the sail gets the wrong shape when it is reefed. The mast was expensive to build, and the style was retired. The type of forward spreader on the *Rival* was common in the rigs of the 1920s but was later replaced with the jumper stay.

When the transverse buckling lengths were divided with multiple spreaders and the forestay was raised, other demands were put on strength, and masts were given an oval shape, which made them more rigid in the direction where they have longer bulking lengths.

FIGURE 193 } *Rival* (S 10) and *Boja* rounding "Kanholmens" during the Sandhamn regatta in 1922. Photo by B. Nordberg from the archives of SSHM.

The bolt rope of the mainsail made it necessary to have new mountings with bolts attach the stays, instead of the previously hoop-spliced stays that were laid over the shoulder blocks on the mast. The block was a rounded piece of wood that was fitted to the mast and attached with screws; on larger masts, the lower part of the block would be folded into the mast so that the forces from the stays would not cause the block to slide.

After World War II, the square, box-shaped mast came into fashion; it was less expensive to manufacture. The rigging hardware for it was formed along the mast in the direction of the force, and it was screwed with many thin wood screws so as not to weaken the mast.

By the 1960s, cruising offshore was in vogue, and boats were spacious and had a lot of interior, which made them heavy; there was not as much weight left over for the keel (low keel-weight percentage). This resulted in boats with low rigs with large head sails. These rigs had good stays in the transverse, but buckling longitudinally was considerable. The boats were provided, therefore, with double lower shrouds and a wide spread in the longitudinal direction of the chain plates. At this time, the aluminum mast was introduced.

The hollow mast has been the most common in the 1900s. Massive masts are used in some classes to keep the price down, i.e., with M30s, M22s, Folkboats, Neptune cruisers, and Dragons. These masts are glued in several parts in order not to warp or crack. An unglued massive mast in which the pith remains in the center almost always has cracks from drying and bends easily.

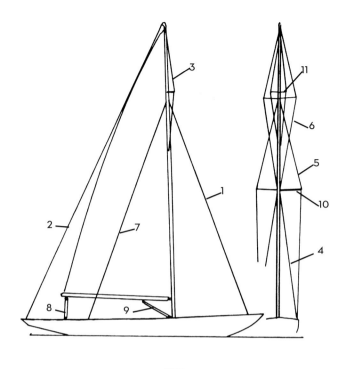

FIGURE 194 } What is what?

Standing rigging:

1 forestay

2 backstay

3 jumper stay

4 lower shroud

5 cap shroud (upper shroud)

6 diamond

Running rigging:

7 running backstays or runners

8 mainsheet

9 vang or kicking strap

Other:

10 spreader

11 jumper

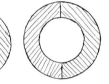

Weight 100%   Weight 71%   Weight 68%

FIGURE 195 } Mast sections with equal strength. The image is from the book *Bygg båten själv* (Build the Boat Yourself) and clearly shows the advantages of hollow masts and the savings on labor and material costs of building a boxed mast of planed wood. The wall thickness is $\frac{1}{5}$ of the diameter. Increased diameter quickly adds stiffness while the surface of the cross-section center has little effect on the stiffness.

SOME RULES OF THUMB

Per Brohäll writes about the design of masts in his excellent book *Bygg båten själv* (Build the Boat Yourself), written in the fifties:

> Because of the many unpredictable forces that a sailboat is subject to, it hardly pays to make any strength calculations for the rig. Instead, you have to use values of material dimensions that others have had good experience with. You might compare the estimated strength of a new mast with one that is known to be suitably dimensioned.

- Both the Skerry cruisers and 6-meters have ¾ rigs; the forestay is located approximately ¾ of a mast height from deck to masthead.

- The largest diameter of the mast should be at ⅓ of the height above the deck; the diameter could be reduced to 95% by the deck, to 85% at the attachment of the forestay, and to 50% at the masthead. If a forestay is raised when the rig is redone, you need to check that the cross section does not drop below 85% at the new attachment.

- The diameter of a massive mast in relation to the length is approximately 1 to 1.1% (meaning for 33 feet or 10 meters) of a mast 4 to 4⅓" (100–110 mm) in diameter; for a hollow mast, it is approximately 1.2–1.3%.

- The wall thickness of a hollow mast has, ever since they drilled masts at the turn of the century, been set to ⅕ of the diameter.

- The angle of the stays in relation to the mast should not go below 10°. If the intention is to keep the mast as straight at the small angles of the shrouds as it is at the wider ones, then the loads in the shrouds will increase and the strain will become significant; the downward forces on the mast will also increase and the risk of breaking will be greater. In addition, the loads on the hull between the chain plates and mast foot will increase.

- During the 1900s when writing about the sail area of a boat, it was always referred to as the "internationally measured sail area." This can be written as:

Luff of the mainsail = P, foot of the mainsail = E, height of the foretriangle = I, base of the foretriangle = J, sail area = SA.

$$SA = \frac{P \times E}{2} + 0.85 \times \frac{J \times I}{2}$$

It is usually this area that has been listed and not the actual surface area of the sails. For example, a 6-meter yacht has more than a 430-sq-ft (40-sq-m) measured sail area, but it seldom sails with less than 645 sq ft (60 sq m) of sails.

An approximate value of the relationship between internationally measured sail areas and the displacement can be 108-sq-ft (10-sq m) sail area per tonne of boat.

BOOM

Older booms were often round and had roller reefing. When the jiffy reefing came into fashion and sheet points moved in on the boom, the forces were greater height-wise than sideways, and it was made oval or rectangular with a cross section that was higher than it was wide. When the boom was fitted with a kicking strap or vang, it became even more important for the boom to be stiffer in the vertical direction. A way to ensure that the boom or mast won't break by the kicking strap is to provide it with an undersized shackle, which will break first.

MATERIAL

Masts are made of coniferous wood, which has longer fibers than deciduous wood is are therefore tougher and more elastic; it is also lighter in comparison to its strength.

Spruce has always been the main mast material; it is light and strong for its weight, and it's available in long, knot-free lengths. Spruce places special demands on hardware, as screws won't attach well in the soft wood; sometimes harder wood such as ash is spliced onto the mast, where the hardware is attached.

Norwegian spruce is a domestic alternative, but it is harder to get in knot-free lengths. It darkens easily from mould.

Oregon pine is sometimes used for masts for cruisers; it is heavier but able to withstand impact and damage better.

Scots pine is sometimes used, but I can't see any advantage over Norwegian spruce.

Below is a table showing the properties of different woods. The values of flexural strength are for the same area; the values of flexural strength versus weight are favorable in lighter woods.

The table shows the difficulties in sizing wood constructions. Wood is not a uniform homogeneous material such as steel. The table shows 10–20% variations in density and

TYPE OF WOOD	DENSITY	FLEXURAL STRENGTH	FLEXURAL STRENGTH/ DENSITY	SURFACE HARDNESS
Spruce	390–450 (kg/m³)	60–80 (Mpa)	0.13–0.2	1.2 (Brinell)
Norwegian spruce	390–480 (kg/m³)	66–84 (Mpa)	0.14–0.21	1.2 (Brinell)
Scots pine	480–530 (kg/m³)	83–89 (Mpa)	0.16–0.18	1.9 (Brinell)
Oregon pine	500–550 (kg/m³)	80–93 (Mpa)	0.15–0.18	2 (Brinell)
Compare to:				
Mahogny	500–560 (kg/m³)	74–84 (Mpa)	0.13–0.17	1.4–2.3 (Brinell)
Oak	690–760 (kg/m³)	90–100 (Mpa)	0.12–0.14	3.4–4.1 (Brinell)

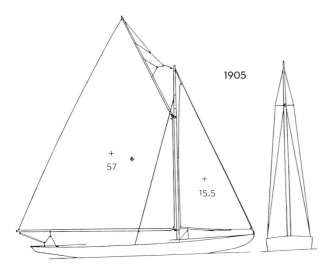

FIGURE 196 }

push from the wind in its bulging cotton sails, she would cut into the broach, sometimes uncontrollably, instead of the heeling, and possibly end up in distress at sea.

Note the long and low boom. The running backstay has a small angle, and it does not sit at the height of the forestay, which was otherwise most common (the intention was probably that it would hold the forward forces of both the forestay and the gaff jaw on the mast). The gaff was weak and was kept straight by bridles of wire; the halyards were also made of wire with a double end of the rope. The jib was on a weak boom. The mainsail had battens but small roach. The lower shroud has bad angles, just 8.5° to the mast. It provided significant buckling loads on the mast which therefore needed a generous cross section. When switching from Bermuda to gaff, the old mast cross section is often not enough to handle the forces from the gaff rigging.

20–30% difference in flexural strength for the same kind of wood. The boatbuilder's knowledge and experience in material selection was of great importance for the result. Quick growing timber—with a greater distance between growth rings—is stronger in proportion to its weight and is not as prone to wrapping as denser wood might be.

COMING FULL CIRCLE—COMMON TYPES OF RIGGING

The boat in the drawings (Figures 196 to 198) is a 5-tonne cruiser with a 2.5-tonne keel (50% keel weight), 41 feet (12.5 meters) long, 9 feet (2.8 meters) wide, and with a 5.5-foot (1.7-meter) depth. She was built in 1905.

1905: In the beginning, she got a gaff rig of 74 sq m. The gaff rig had a low center of effort, and therefore she could carry such great sails. C of E is the center of sail area where the gathered strength of the wind can be said to attack. The reality is more complicated than that; wind blows with greater strength at higher altitudes, and the high rigging is affected in practice by even greater wind forces). In the longitudinal direction, the C of E was far aft; it gave weather helm—a half an hour with brisk winds needed people that were up to it. In those days, you would really feel it when you were wrestling with the elements and the tiller. The weather helm was good in itself, even if the rudder angel worked as a break bit. If the boat got a good

1916: She was rigged with a triangular main; she raced sometimes and therefore had more sails than she would normally have had for cruising. This rig had, for its time, a common sail set up; the relationship between the luff and the foot was 1.7:1—in other words, a low and wide mainsail. The mainsail had battens but still a very small roach. Because of the length of the boom

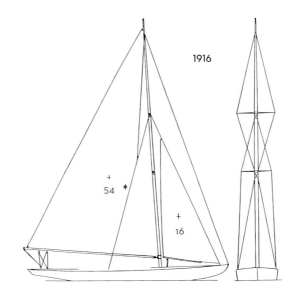

FIGURE 197 }

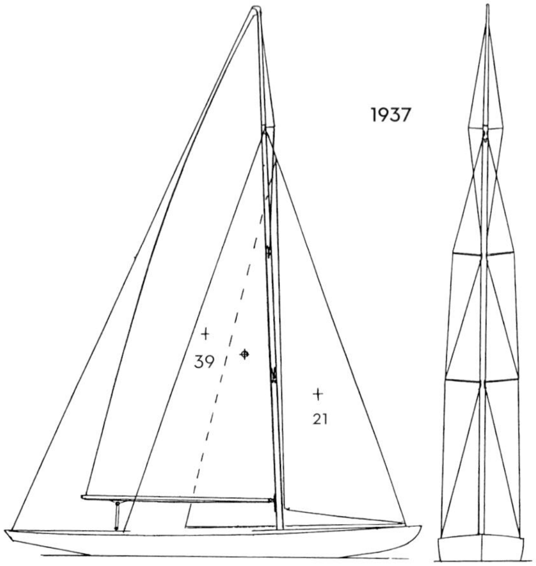

1937

FIGURE 198 }

was thin, only 2¾″ (70 mm). The sail area was reduced slightly, but the C of E had moved up so that the boat had become somewhat weaker; the C of E had moved forward but still required a strong man at the helm when the wind was strong.

1937: She was rigged over again with a modern rig from one of the most famous shipyards. It was quite unusual for this kind of old-fashioned boat to get a new rig. More common was that the boom in the drawing from 1916 would be shortened so that the boat would become more stiff, with less windward helm, and could then use the back stay; otherwise, the mast (without having been shortened) from 1916 could still be used today.

The rig from 1937 was not much higher than the previous one, but since the forestay had been raised and the mast lacked stays at 38 feet (11.5 meters), longitudinally the mast was built with an oval cross section and thereby increased in stiffness. The mainsail has a boltrope with a groove in the mast. The boom was significantly shorter; the ratio between luff and foot was 2.55:1. The mast had a jumper instead of the outer forestay to ease the use of the spinnaker. The shrouds passed over two spreaders for better angles (approx. 15°); both the top shroud and the middle shroud went over the lower spreaders down to the deck. The runners had been moved aft on deck to hold up the forestay without causing too large of loads on the rigging and mast step (larger angles = smaller loads).

there was no backstay; the top of the mast was held only by an upper part of the runners, and the thin mast top must have bent forward going downwind. The side riggings were modern for their time, with double spreaders. It had lower shrouds, intermediate shrouds over spreaders, and a diamond (the shroud on the upper spreaders that connect to the mast by the lower spreader). The top

SOME MEASUREMENTS OF THE RIGGING PARTS IN FIGURES 196 TO 198	GAFF IN 1905	1916	1937
Sail area	796 sq ft (74 sq m)	732 sq ft (68 sq m)	646 sq ft (60 sq m)
Length of mast (from deck)	31 ft (9.5 m)	49 ft (15 m)	50 ft (15.3 m)
Luff	19½ ft (6 m)	44 ft (13.5 m)	46 ft8.7 (14 m)
Boom	28½ ft (8.7 m)	26 ft (8 m)	18 ft (5.5 m)
Gaff	20 ft (6.2 m)		
Height of C of E	17 ft (5.3 m)	18½ ft (5.7 m)	5.9 m
Foretriangle: height x base	30½ × 13 ft (9.3 m × 4m)	30½ × 12 ft (9.3 m × 3.6 m)	38 x 12 ft (11.5 m x 3.7 m)
Distance deck to lower shroud	23 ft (7.1 m)	19 ft (5.8 m)	15 ft (4.5 m)
Boom height	19½″ (0.5 m)	25½″ (0.65 m)	33½″ (0.85 m)
Mast diameter	6⅓″ (160 mm) solid	175 mm hollow	7½ x 6⅓″ (190 x 160 mm) hollow

The weakest point in the rigging was where the jumper met the upper shroud, but here they chose less strong rigging in order to get the leech of the *Genoa* to sneak through, so that the boat would point high.

This rig is timeless and could just as easily have been from the 1980s. Compared with the rapid development between 1905 and 1937, very little has happened over the last forty years.

The C of E has been moved forward, and she can be easy on the leeward helm with a jib in light weather, but with the *Genoa*, she balanced well even then. The boom was long enough for her to run in the downwind; a higher rig with a shorter boom would have required a spinnaker for fun downwind sailing.

2002: Today, the sails are a bit tired, and the new owners are considering switching to a gaff rig when they can afford new sails.

For those who are interested, I have to mention that this story is not true, but it is credible, and the original constructors of the rigs are Axel Nygren, Tore Herlin, and Tore Holm.

MAINTENANCE AND REPAIR OF MASTS

This section of the chapter will deal with maintenance and repair of the mast. I feel a bit hesitant to write about repairs; mast failures are so serious that a professional should do the repair for safety reasons. Repairing a broken mast is like renovating a diesel engine; you should have the skills and the equipment needed to make it meaningful to even try it.

Take care of the mast; a new wooden mast is more expensive than the equivalent aluminum mast, and there are few mast builders. Today, the Mälar-22 is the only boat of Swedish Championship status where all boats need to have wooden masts. The Folkboat Association approved aluminum masts a few years ago; the fewer wooden masts built, the fewer mast builders are left. So maintenance is important; without proper handling, the wooden mast ages quickly.

Maintenance

The mast should be in a mast shed over the winter; if it is not possible keep it on trestles with the butt end down. The mast should be covered, not wrapped in plastic. Make sure the mast is straight so that it won't be permanently deformed.

A hollow mast is untreated on the inside and must be kept dry inside; there can't be any leaks through cracks or holes left by old hardware. To avoid moisture collecting and causing rot, there should be a drain from the hollow part of the mast to the bottom of the mast so that the water can drain. Usually, masts are built hollow down to just above the boom attachment and solid from there down; rot in the bottom of the cavity is not a rare cause for breakdowns.

A coat of varnish a year might not be enough; a mast is heavily worn by both sun and abrasion. I usually forget to take out the spreaders in time for varnishing, but the top of them is where the sun will hit the hardest.

If you scrape a mast clean, it should not be out in sunlight because then the surface will dry too quickly and crack the wood. Nor should it be left untreated in the rain, as mast glue is just water resistant and not boil proof. It also means that a glued mast should not just be oiled, as the glue joints will be exposed to too much weather damage. Too much oil can also impair the stiffness of the mast (compared with linseed oil bending).

An unglued solid mast (tree trunk), still has its pith in the center and almost always has drying cracks from the surface into the pith along the grain; these should be oiled and waterproofed but not filled with putty, as it will just wedge the mast apart more as it swells in humid weather. This kind of mast is better to oil than to varnish; the cracks allow the moisture to become trapped behind the varnish.

It is the chain of long cells that makes masts strong; avoid drilling the fibers to make tiny bungs or plugs. You are better off with discoloration or a small dent than a mend that cuts more fibers.

Watch out for halyards that bend; a slapping halyard can wear a hole in the paint in a week.

Hardware and Rigging

Slack off a bit on the rig when the boat is not used for a while, especially the backstay, and use boom gallows; if the wood is bent for a long period of time, it easily becomes permanent (compare to steam-bending).

When hardware is screwed on, the screw holes are treated, either with oil, wax, or glue. Given that the mast walls are often thin, you need a fully threaded self-tapping screw (metal screw) with its powerful symmetrical thread for best results.

Hardware is prevented from slipping along the mast by means of bolts and straps. If the mast is hollow where the hardware is mounted, the hole is fitted with a pipe that has the same length as the diameter of the mast. The hole in the hardware gets the diameter of the bolt, so when bolts are tightened, the tube prevents the mast from getting squeezed and possibly cracking. Another great way to hold loads is to equip the hardware with straps that are screwed with many screws in the direction of the pull.

Today insurance companies recommend rig rivets with cotter pins instead of nuts and bolts for the rig. Shackles in standing rigging are not popular either.

Replace rusty wires and bent turnbuckles; make sure that the rigging screws won't break in the chain plates (replace with toggles). Make sure the chain plates aren't corroded.

The halyard sheave should have as large a diameter as possible and spin well; otherwise the loads when you set the sails will be unnecessarily large, and the wire will wear out excessively fast.

Adhesives

The earliest adhesive was bone glue that had to be heated in order to be used. We have repaired eighty-year-old masts that have had intact bone glue joints.

After World War II, carbamide glues were introduced after having been developed in the aircraft industry. The most common brand was Aerolite. Carbamide glue is the most common mast glue to this day.

Phenolic resin, such as Cascofen, was used in the sixties, but the joints became glass-hard with time and could not maintain the elasticity of the masts, and it has been involved in many rig failures.

Epoxy adhesive is also used, but it is disputed as a mast adhesive. However, I have repaired masts with epoxy for forty years without seeing any drawbacks, and epoxy is the most readily available adhesive today.

REPAIRS

Mast breaks often occur when the rig isn't set up correctly or when a shroud, a stay, or their attachments break. It

could also be adhesives that give up or rot in the wood. The mast is a glued construction from the beginning, and if only the remainder of the mast is in good condition, don't hesitate to glue it back together again.

SPLICING PROCEDURES

If the mast has broken at one end, the new end can be made out of the two halves joined to the old mast with long glue joints with a ratio of 1 to 12 (thus 2″, or 50 mm, thickness requires at least a 24-inch, or 600-mm, long glue joint).

1   Place the mast flat and straight across several trestles.

2   Put the remains together and try to take the important measurements of length.

3   Cut off the mast with a 90° cut above the break; mark the center, which is often the original glue joint.

4   Mark the joint's other end, i.e., where on the mast it should end, selecting the same length joints on both sides of the mast.

5   Make the mast pointy with a saw and a plane or planer; sharp tools and good support are the most important for good results.

6   Then make two pieces from the same kind of wood as the mast; turn the heart side out so the growth rings will be directed across the mast's curvature. Make sure

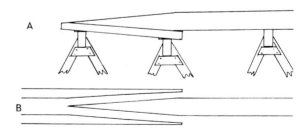

FIGURE 199 } Splicing the mast.

A Planed mast with supports under joint, so it can be planed straight.

B Splice ready to be put together and glued. The sidepieces have been planed slightly concave at the ends for better control of the glue pressure.

that the joints have the same length and thickness as the planed mast joints; if you try to be accurate, the joints will fit and create a straight splice. To get some glue pressure in the tips of the joints, you need to plane the joint of the splice so it is a little concave.

7 Freshly shaved adhesive surfaces are important for good results. Wet the joint firmly with glue. Don't be stingy with clamps. Use a string to check that the mast is straight.

Spliced Mast Repair

If a mast breaks in the middle, it can be spliced back together. This kind of splice is not done with flat joint surfaces, but rather the mast is planed out in a smooth curve to which the joint pieces are strapped down with clamps.

SUMMARY

Take care of the wooden mast; a new wooden mast is more expensive than the equivalent aluminum mast.

Masts glues are not boil proof and therefore require to be surface treated (varnished).

Do not wrap the mast in plastic over the winter as it will easily suffer from rot and mold damage.

Since the mast is usually a glued construction from the start, it is only natural to repair masts this way.

FIGURE 201 } Mast clamps are inexpensive and easy to make; all it takes is planed timber, 2⅓ × 1⅓" (60 × 40 mm), and a threaded rod with a nut.

1 Glue the mast on a provisional basis at the break; make sure the length is correct and that the mast is straight.

2 Plane down to the cavity on the two opposite sides. Shave a maximum of ¾" (20 mm) deep per 3 ft. (1 meter) of mast length. Let the plane do the work by setting the blade so that only the front and rear edges of the plane, along with the blade, lie against the wood and provide a concave joint surface. A planed board is clamped down in the cavity on each side and glued in place.

3 Turn the mast and plane the other two sides. Make sure the joint lengths are different than the ones from before. Otherwise, it's easy for the mast to be too stiff in the mended area and bend unevenly when trimming. Bend and glue the new pieces.

4 Shave the spliced area first in a square, then an octagon, and then a circle.

5 The most common mistake when using a plane is when too much wood remains in the middle of the splicing; when you then fair the mend with the old mast, a pit will easily form in the old mast just outside the spliced area.

FIGURE 200 } Spliced mast repair.

FIGURE 202 } One piece of wood is slit from the edge into the hole so that the clamp can be opened without the nuts being completely removed.

ENGINE INSTALLATION

Engine installation includes the entire chain of operations, from the construction of the engine bed until it's time to turn the ignition key. This chapter is mostly about the first part—getting an engine and drive train in place (drive train = shaft, bearings, and propeller).

MOTORBOATS

The Engine Bed

The frame of the boat is made up of a lattice consisting of the floors and the longitudinal beams—the engine bed. This device is an important stiffening component of the hull. When changing engines and exhaust pipes on the boat, it is important to not weaken the frame. Many boats have an inner engine bed to which the engine mounts are attached; the bed is bolted to the side of the outer bed. Primarily, changes should be made on the inner bed.

A replacement of the engine should begin with acquiring dimensional drawings of possible new engines. It is possible to measure and compare the alternatives with the old one in place. The main measurements are:

- the vertical distance between the output shaft and the bottom of the tray
- the vertical distance between the output shaft and the engine mounts
- the height of the engine above the output shaft
- the width of the engine and the width between the engine mounts
- the length of the engine

FIGURE 203 } External engine bed and steel floors forming the truss that holds the shape of the bottom. The inner engine bed is not mounted yet. The hole for the propeller shaft is visible, as well as holes for the exhaust pipe in the aft floors. The image is from *Segel och Motor* (Sail and Motor), 1936.

It's easy to replace the engine if the measurements correspond.

If it is impossible to mount the engine with the outgoing shaft in the same position as before, the propeller shaft needs to be re-angled. The solution is a deflection of the shaft by means of an intermediate drive shaft provided with flexible coupling being connected with a thrust bearing mounted to a bulkhead astern of the engine. The propeller shaft is connected to the thrust bearing, which will relieve the engine of propeller thrust forces. This solution can be used even if it is not necessary to address an angular error. When the thrust doesn't stress the engine, the elastic engine mounts can be softer with more vibration damping. If the boat is also a bit soft at the bottom, the system with a trust bearing between the propeller shaft and the drive shaft will create less bending in the propeller shaft bearings. A common brand of flexible joints with thrust bearing is Aquadrive. A thrust-bearing bulkhead is placed just forward of the inner shaft bearing with its shaft seal. The bulkhead is made out of a thick metal sheet bolted to the engine bed and possibly to the keel. If the bulkhead is wide, it may be reinforced with bracing or stiffening flanges (see figure 205). One complication of the installation may be that the thrust bearing will have a radius of at least 2″ (50 mm), which must fit under the floor boards.

The width of the engine and the width between the engine mounts will determine if the bed needs to be rebuilt. If the boat has already had a couple of different engines, then a lot of times a saw and an axe have been there and weakened the boat. It is then best to remove additions and the inner bed if its size is no longer correct. Thereafter, the outer bed is checked and repaired if necessary. If the weak parts are in the middle of the inner bed, it can be used as a stiffening backing block. I prefer to do these pieces out of oak, which is hard, stiff, and heavy, so it dampens sound and vibration. Distribution beams past floors and the brackets for the feet can be made of galvanized steel. The biggest problems arise if the engine block and the tray won't fit between the beds. Then the bed must be strengthened on the outside before it is possible to remove material.

The engine mounts should be mounted with nuts and bolts; if that's not possible, you can use studs with wood threads at one end. If the engine needs to be dismantled, then just loosen the nut.

The floors under the engine are often weakened by cut-outs for the tray. If the new engine has more clearance at the bottom, you should take the opportunity to restore the structure and strength.

In Figure 203, you can see holes for the exhaust pipe in the floors at the top right of the photo. When replacing the exhaust pipe, it is important for the bottom transverse strength that the floors remain intact. If you have to cut the floors, then you need to restore the strength of the upper flange of the floors.

Switching to a Larger Propeller Shaft

Increased engine power may require an increased shaft diameter. It brings with it a new propeller, new sleeve pipe, new cutlass bearings, and possibly a new strut. The most practical thing to do is to choose a shaft with a standard attachment and a suitable propeller; those who choose a special attachment on the shaft to make it consistent with the old propeller usually regret it when the propeller is damaged by grounding.

The stern tube and its bearings were mostly threaded together when assembled; thread off the inner bearing (or seal) and try to loosen the stern tube. If it was attached with tar, then the best way to detach it is to heat the pipe with propane till the tar softens. The hole can be widened with a drill made of a tube with the old hole diameter with one or two cutters welded to it. The cutters can be made of a plane blade. The pipe is centered in the old hole, and the cutters will cut off the wood; just keep your fingers crossed that there are no bolts in the way at the side of the hole. The old keel must also have sufficient width for the new pipe. This is described in more detail in the chapter on keels. If you assemble it with a thrust-bearing bulkhead close to the sleeve pipe, the inner bearing can be replaced with a flexible propeller shaft seal. Externally, you usually mount a water-lubricated cutlass bearing on the sleeve pipe.

The bearing of a strut has to be replaced with a thicker bearing. Remove the strut and replace the pipe attaching the bearing with a larger pipe, or have a new strut made. Mount the strut when the shaft is mounted and centered. One way is to attach the foot of the strut to the hull with fiberglass putty between the plate and the hull; the bolts are tightened so that the bearing gets centered and the shaft is easy to turn around. The excess putty is squeezed out and what remains is an exact distance block when the putty has hardened.

FIGURE 204 } Hole in a sailboat rudder for a propeller. The rudder is made of plywood and is coated with epoxy and matt. The height curves in the plywood make it easier to cut out the rudder to accurate shape.

FIGURE 205 } Engine mounted with a thrust-bearing joint with a bulkhead (shaped like steel floors in this case). This sort of shoehorn assembly requires that the motor be used as a template.

SAILBOATS

New Motor Installation

A sailboat shouldn't need an engine. In the old days, you had to paddle home when the wind was gone; sometimes you wouldn't make it to work until Monday afternoon. These days, that doesn't work for everyone. It's crowded at ports, which puts greater demands on maneuverability. It is also crowded at the most popular natural harbors. If you want your own anchorage for the night, you need to find a spot in the lee of the prevailing wind; if the wind turns at night, you risk damage to the boat without a reliable engine. On a beautiful wooden boat, an inboard engine disturbs the looks less than an outboard one that weighs down the stern.

Where the propeller is placed has varied over the years. The boat will have the best control under engine

if the propeller sits in a recess in the rudder. The rudder will then work in the water stream from the propeller. However, the hole in the rudder causes swirls around the rudder when sailing. A shaft assembly in which the propeller ends up askew and aft of the rudder makes for a boat that turns better in one direction when the motor is on and in general makes it more difficult to maneuver in tight spaces. It's become common for cruisers to use a set-up with the propeller in the rudder, while boats of higher performance types select a mounting with a shaft and a strut, or a solution in which the shaft is exactly on the side of the rudder stock just above the rudder. The hull shape is also critical for the selection. A Skerry cruiser or similar boat with a flat bottom and a lot of bottom aft of the rudder can choose a shaft and a strut; the shaft will then be mounted through the planking besides the counter timber but relatively parallel to the midline. A V-shaped boat may get an arrangement with the engine deep in the hull. Here, the choices are to have the propeller out of the rudder, or via a side-mounted shaft with strut and the propeller forward and to the side of the rudder. Mounting it on the side of the rudderstock could also work well (Fingal and Vega assembly, see Figure 207; the Iversen cruiser has that solution). If the shaft is to come out of the rudder, you have to make sure not to weaken the rudderpost too much. For good maneuverability, it is an advantage if as much of the recess as possible is made in the rudderpost. If the boat has a weak rudderpost, this method is not used.

A drill bit for the shaft hole may be made of a pipe; large ⅜-inch (10-mm) teeth cut faster. The teeth are cut with an angle grinder. Fold every other tooth out and every other one inward, just like a saw, and file the teeth like a serrated saw. One option is to cut off a hole saw and splice it with a pipe; then you get both the teeth and the attachment to the drill.

If the hole is made in the stern post, you will use bearings and a sleeve pipe as previously described. In an assembly through the planking, the shaft will have its bearings externally in a strut and internally in the engine or a thrust-bearing. The hole in the hull is just a seal. We usually make the fitting of a stainless steel tube welded to a plate. The plate must be on the outside and the tube extended through the planking, and fitted with a shaft seal of some kind. The angel between the pipe and the plate is often small, and it is often best to make the first welding with the pieces temporally mounted on the boat. A fixed propeller slows the boat down while sailing, a folding propeller is a good solution for sailing ability. Unfortunately, it won't fit in a rudder recess, so you have to choose between a fixed and a feathering propeller.

Weight Distribution

I have previously described a development where the weights in the boat moved astern over the years. For the yacht to have a nice trim that matches the lines that the designer once put on paper, the engine should be mounted as far forward and as far down as possible. Take advantage of the possibility of the best compromise by making a template of the engine or putting it in place before the final placement is determined. It is always snug so the exact dimensions may cause a minor part of the interior to be rebuilt. A thrust-bearing flexible mount can take up an angle of up to 16° and can provide the opportunity to place the engine under an existing cockpit. Batteries and tank can be positioned forward to offset the weight. In general, a moved weight is worth twice as much. If it is 44 pounds (20 kg) from the stern to the bow, it should be compared with the same weight in the stern, compensated by 88 pounds (40 kg) in the bow of the boat, to get the same trim.

Water in the Engine

Sailboats often have their engines below the waterline and sometimes sail with great heel. This means that there is a risk that the engine gets filled with water either through the cooling water intake or through the exhaust pipe. The strainer on the intake of the cooling water is turned backward to reduce the risk that water will be pushed in while sailing. (On motorboats, it is turned forward, as the engine needs coolant as soon as it is running.) An anti siphon or check valve is also mounted on the water hose between the water pump and the engine to prevent the engine from filling. The anti-siphon should be installed on the centerline and at least 12.5″ (300 mm) above the waterline. The exhaust pipe is aft in a bend close to the deck so as to minimize the risk of water coming in that way. The cooling water flows with the exhaust gases in the exhaust hose to cool it. When the engine stops running, the cooling water in the hose before the bend flows back toward the engine. A water trap placed 10″ (250 mm) below the engine's exhaust outlet needs to be the correct dimensions to handle that water. Often, it may be difficult to achieve this when the engine has been squeezed with a shoehorn into its best position. Sometimes the trap needs to be placed under or in front of the engine. Fresh-water cooling does not reduce the risk of flooding. Sea water flows through the heat exchanger and into the exhaust pipe, which is filled, and water goes into the engine through the back.

Spill Tray

Should the engine be equipped with a spill tray? Older engines leaked oil and were fitted with a spill tray of sheet metal; it was often attached to the engine bed lengthwise and equipped with some form of draining device. It is virtually impossible to clean under the tray. Today's diesel engines hardly leak at all, so there is a reason to consider the need for an overflow trough when changing engines.

SUMMARY

Making engine changes is a time to tidy up under the engine and to check and reinforce the bed.

A thrust-bearing flexible coupling makes it possible to eliminate vibration and bends in long shafts. It also provides the ability to tilt the engine and thus reduce the need to rebuild the interior.

The choice of propeller arrangement for the sailboat is a compromise between maneuverability under power and sailing quality. Avoid weakening the rudderpost if it is weak from the start.

Anti-siphon and water traps reduce the risk of flooding of the engine.

Think of the weight distribution in relation to the motor installation; moving weights results in the most effect in the boats trim.

PURCHASING A WOODEN BOAT

A beautiful wooden boat attracts many people's attention; the outline pleases the eye. There is a special feel for the material and craftsmanship in the construction. The image of a boat elicits a nostalgic flashback; maybe your first experience at sea was on a wooden boat. You wonder if it could be something for you and if it needs a lot of maintenance. A well-maintained wooden boat requires roughly the same annual maintenance as a well-maintained plastic boat, but it requires continuous care in order not to deteriorate and become more difficult to manage; a plastic boat is more forgiving. If you are interested in purchasing a wooden boat but have limited time, then buy a good boat with good equipment. A less expensive boat in poor condition is more time-consuming and ultimately more expensive.

Save most of the questions about the renovations until after owning a boat for some years. However, many people are fascinated from the beginning with the desire to save an old, worn piece of cultural heritage. The challenge to create and renovate becomes the driving force for buying a boat. Renovation projects will be costly, so here this is a decision based on interest in a hobby that can easily become a passion.

INSPECT THE BOAT CAREFULLY BEFORE PURCHASING

How can a prospective purchaser assess the condition of a wooden boat? Bring a friend who knows boats; four eyes see more than two, and you will have different perspectives. Always look at the boat when it is out of the water before making the deal.

It is best to hire a surveyor who knows wooden boats. It will cost a bit, but it is not uncommon that notes in the inspection report enable discounts on the final price that are more than the cost of the inspection. Insurance companies usually require an inspection and assessment in order to insure a wooden boat.

It's also possible that the inspector, at an early stage during the survey, identifies problems that make a deal uninteresting.

Sometimes an ad will say that the boat has been cared for by a shipyard as something positive, but if this is the case, it depends on what services the boat owner ordered at the yard.

RENOVATION PROJECTS

If you are looking for a fixer-upper, it is best to look for a boat in decent condition with limited renovation needs. Broken ribs or a bad deck is better than a totally rundown boat. Thin planking is difficult to fix. The boat's outline should be attractive from the beginning; new pieces of wood alone are not enough to create a beautiful boat. Proper documentation of the boat is important from a historical perspective.

If you are handy but have a limited budget, it is important that there is equipment for the boat. When the hull is finished, it is usually difficult to get motivated to invest in accessories. For sailboats, the equipment is in the form of mast, sails, and winches. For motorboats, it is a good set of original hardware—such as window frames—that is worthwhile. Hardware was often made for a particular boat from scratch, and there is nothing like it to buy today; it has to be specially made. If there is a motor on the boat, that's great, but engines are more of a consumer item.

What the amateur has trouble understanding is that during construction of a four-ton boat, the construction cost of the hull and deck is only a third of the cost of a finished boat, and the bigger the boat, the smaller the part of the cost that is attributed to the hull and deck. People often think that everything is done just because the hull is renovated.

As a wooden boat enthusiast, you can rejoice at this lack of understanding, as it has saved many seemingly hopeless projects, sometimes another enthusiast had to take on and complete the work.

SURVEY OF THE BOAT'S CONDITION

Walk around the boat and get a general sense of it; this provides a good basis for what each inspection should be focused on. Is it in intact and clean, or dirty and lop-sided? Does it smell fresh inside the boat, or does it smell like an old wooden boat? There is an old wooden boat smell if the bilge is dirty, there is poor ventilation, or there are leaks in the deck that cause bad odor in the cushions underneath. A well-maintained boat should not smell musty.

It is difficult to assess a newly painted boat just before launching in the spring. Flaws may have been filled and painted over; the boat owner will be reluctant to let you scrape or put a knife in suspicious places. You have to confine yourself to tapping with a hammer along the stem and keel and the butt joints. Rotten and freeze-damaged wood gives off a duller, more hollow sound.

In the fall and winter, it is often easier. You can easily see where the wood is bad, as the paint has come off there. In particular, the varnish will show clear signs of where moisture has penetrated.

The Hull

1   *The lines.* Did the hull keep its shape over the years? Try to get a look at it from the furthest possible distance. Look along the hull, keel, and covering board and try to see unevenness. On long, narrow boats, the aft tends to hang down. On broader-hull sailboats, it can be uneven by the chain plates. Motorboats may have damage along the keel from resting on the trestles. The keel is at its weakest at the point where the outer keel ends and the propeller shaft exits, and there may be indentations in the planking. On cruisers, this often coincides with the place where the cabin ends and turns into the sides of the cockpit, where there will easily be deformations of the side deck.

2   *Frozen plank ends.* Freeze damage is noticeable as a more muted tone when tapping on the planking. The planks are usually also swollen and extend beyond the stem. This is more common in boats made of African mahogany. The damage usually occurs where there is end grain, as in hood ends and butt joints. Freeze damage is rare in the middle of the planks but exists where stems, knees, butt blocks, and wood keel hold moisture and prevent drying.

3   *Broken ribs.* The hull has swollen and pushed out the planking in the bilge; this is most common in the bilge at the stern. The wooden frame has cracked where the radius of the bend is the smallest. It is difficult to restore, but it is possible to stop further deformation by sistered ribs besides the cracked ones.

4   *Poor floors under the mast.* Mast pressure is distributed along the centerline by the mast step that rests on several floor timbers. If the mast step is cracked or too weak, the load becomes too heavy on the floors by the middle of the mast. If they are pushed down, the planks can open up a little and start leaking if the boat is pressed hard going to windward. That may also happen if the boat has wooden floor timbers with corroded screws. Then mast pressure will turn the floors into a wedge that pushes apart the stem and the planking.

5   *Steel frame and steel floor* begin to rust when the hull leaks or if they are below the bilge water level. The ends of the steel frames are also usually attached with a screw between the stem and planking. Corrosion of visible steel can be fixed. But if the rust grows between the frame and the planking a $\frac{3}{32}$-inch-(3-mm-) thick frame flange can grow into a rusty $\frac{3}{8}$-inch (10-mm) thickness and push out the planking. Damage to steel inside the bilge is probably the most common and is the worst to repair.

6   *Bad butt joints.* As stated previously, moisture penetrates most easily into the end grain. Butt joints where the moisture has penetrated to the end wood will freeze and rupture, and if the backing block is made out of steel, the moisture will make it rusty. This is a common damage, but if you're observant and get to it in time, you can save the plank ends and you may only have to replace the butt blocks.

7   *Replaced planks with poor staggering of the joints.* Joints in adjoining planks may not be closer together than $3\frac{1}{3}$–4 feet. (1–1.25 meter). On a sailboat, there should be a minimum of joints in the mast area. For motorboats, that goes for the areas where the outer keel ends (where the propeller shaft comes out) and in the topsides directly in front of where the cabin ends and the deck or cockpit begins. In these areas, the hull needs to be extra strong to not become deformed.

FIGURE 206

(The numbers in Figures 206 and 207 refer to the list that begins on p. 222.)

A motor sailor with supporting rig, designed by C. G. Pettersson in 1935. Length 29.5 ft (9 m), width 7.8 ft (2.40 m). Displacement 3.6 tonnes. Sail 148 sq ft (13.75 sq m). Lead keel 660 lbs (300 kg) Motor Pentad A-4 25 hp. Cruising speed 8.25 knots. Fuel 74 gallons (280 liters)

Construction principle: "The boat is being built of Honduras mahogany on steel frames with steam-bent oak frame on a keel of oak. The covering board is teak, and the rest of the sheet deck is Honduras mahogany; teak floor boards and furnishings of mahogany."

Steering quadrant and spinlocks are clearly visible. A strong boat like this should not have had any problems keeping its hull shape. A canopy over the open part of the cockpit saves a lot of time on maintenance and will keep the underlying engine room dry. The risk of electrical problems and corrosion damage will decrease drastically. The sunken garboard strakes make it possible to keep the bilge water level within a small portion of the boat, which protects the steel floors and the backbone.

The portion of the transom and its frame that lies below the waterline is a moisture collector. The stem and knee underneath the chain locker at the bow are hard to clean, and mud from the chain can block the limber holes so that water collects and freezes. This type of connection for the propeller shaft won't cause the same problems as one with a shorter outer keel and strut.

C. G. Pettersson drawing from the magazine *Med Motorbåt (The Motor)* in 1935.

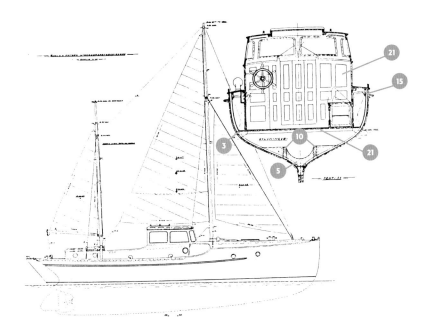

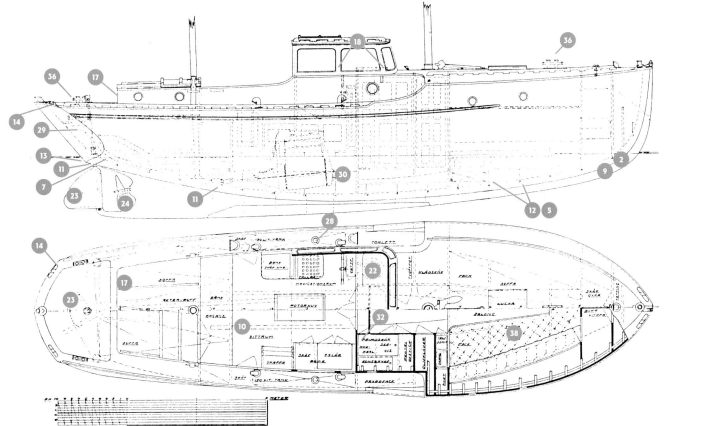

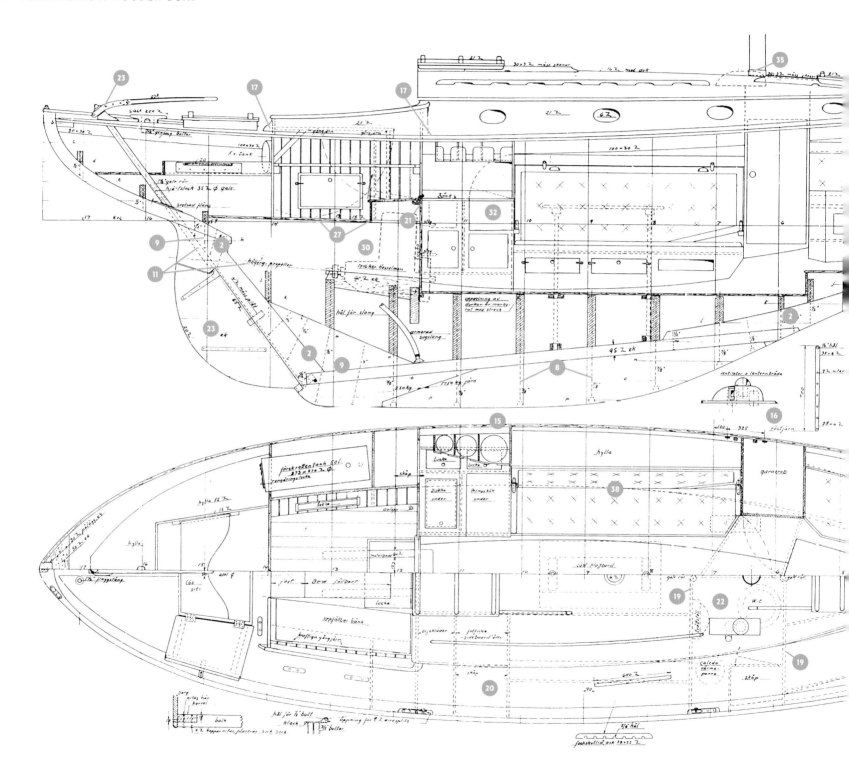

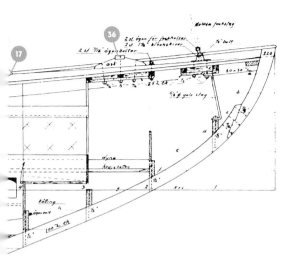

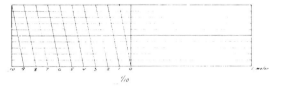

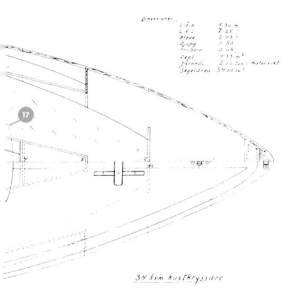

FIGURE 207 ǀ Canoe-stern coastal cruiser designed by Jac M. Iversen in 1941. Length 30.5 ft (9.30 m). Width 8 ft (2.43 m). Depth 5 ft (1.5 m), Displacement 4.33 tonnes. Ballast keel 2 tonnes. Sail area 366 sq ft (34 sq m). Hesselman engine 13 hp.

The mast is stepped on the cabin roof; the construction of the mast beams are not shown in this drawing. This is a construction to relieve the floor timbers, but it can cause leaks in the cabin and subsidence of the bulkheads.

The propeller shaft is taken out completely on the side of the rudder shaft pipe above the rudder. This is a place where there is a high risk of freeze damage, both in the plank ends and the rudder stem. The cockpit is designed as a self-draining well and has cockpit drain, but the well is too deep for the drain to drain outboard. At least the construction allows for a dry engine compartment. The helm's man's cockpit is complete with folding hatchtops a common construction method in Norway.

Drawing from Jac M. Iversen Collection at SSHM.

8 *Keel bolts.* Keel bolts are difficult to inspect. Steel bolts rust, and bronze bolts can wear out. In less salty water, this is rarely a problem with stainless steel keel bolts if the steel is Marine grade. Check for deformation and signs of movement in the joint between the wood keel and ballast keel. If the boat has been in the water, you can often see rust around the bolts in the joint. If there are no signs of cracks or rust in the paint by the joint, then there's no problem. For a newly painted boat in the spring, this is something that is difficult to see; if the bilge is newly painted, then it will be difficult to inspect. It is possible to x-ray keel bolts, but it is expensive and quite complicated. It might be better to remove a keel bolt and replace it, then you at least have an intact bolt. The wood keel with keel bolts cannot just hang in the planking, but the forces of the ballast keel must be spread throughout the hull through the floors. A common damage of this type is that the bottom of the metal floors has rusted apart.

9 *Backbone.* The first place that the wood gets bad is by rusting bolts. The acid from oak speeds up the attacks. The wood turns black and becomes more prone to absorbing moisture, which leads to frost damage in the form of cracks. The wooden keel below the knee and the rudder post is the most sensitive place on sailboats. On powerboats, it is the joints in the wooden keel. Knots and the residue of ingrown branches also cause cracks and leaks in the long run. Frost cracks are heard as dull sounds when you tap on the hull with a hammer.

10 *Engine bed.* The engine bed on motorboats has a stiffening function. On racing boats, they go from the most forward floor all the way to the transom. The designer has taken them into account for hull strength. You have to make sure that the bed hasn't been weakened by sawing for engine replacements, or been cut off when the bulkheads were moved in the interior.

11 *Propeller stern tube and rudder shaft tube.* Vibrations and loads on the bushings can cause leakage between them and the wood. Moisture that enters is difficult to get out again and leads to freezing and eventually rotting. Rudder tubes of steel tend to rust, leading to damage to the counter timber.

12 *The plugs in the planking* are worth a closer study. On varnished topside, it could be that the rivets are showing because of many scrapings down to bare wood; however, that means that ⅕ to ¼ of the planking is scraped away with a corresponding loss of hull strength. By the next scraping, the rivets will need to be removed from the planking, the holes will need to be countersunk, and the rivets will need to be replaced in order for them not to be sanded off or for the hull to be dented. On the bottom, you can usually see which frames are made of steel as the rust on the rivet heads has pushed out the plugs. It is possible to maintain, but is time-consuming.

13 *Transom.* The bottom of the transom is often below the waterline on motorboats. A transom constructed with exterior and interior sides and also a frame on the inside is difficult to dry after the boat has been taken out of the water, and freeze damage is very common. The damage can spread to plank ends. Tap on the outside and check on the inside; there is often a need for renovation.

Deck and Superstructure

14 *Transom.* This brings us back to the transom. In a transom, the wood meets in a variety of directions. The pieces swell and dry differently, and this creates gaps. A common damage is for the mitered joint between the covering boards of the side and the transom to open up and allow moisture to find its way into the transom and the end wood of the frame. These damages are relatively complicated to fix in a professional way. They are discovered when paint and varnish come off and the wood eventually becomes discolored and black. The same philosophy for old houses is also true of old boats: start your renovation with a tight roof to stop the moisture damage. Seal the top, so the moisture cannot find its way down into the underlying structure.

15 *The top planks.* Another place where dank, moist air remains sitting is between beam shelf and planking; rot is very common in this area. If the rot is allowed to spread to the sheer clamp, deck planking, covering boards, and deck beam ends, you will need a very expensive repair job. On motorboats, the damage shows up first on the side planking just below the guard rail. Are there any cooking damages? The steam from boiling water can lead to rot in the beam stringers and deck beams over the galley.

16 *Chain plate*. Inadequate sealing at the chain plates also leads to rot in the hull and beam shelf. If the wood goes bad here, the chain plate bolts may come undone with a dismasting as a result. Inspect both the inside and outside. Chain plates of steel can rust so bad at the covering boards that they will brake. Tap on the chain plate on deck and hear if it sounds muted.

17 *Cabin corners* are sensitive; you have to look for decay and discoloration in the cabin side, beams, and carlin from the inside of the boat. It is the most common damage on the deck and cabin trunk, and it is often difficult to access and replace the pieces with new ones of the same structure and strength.

18 *Windshield frames* tend to rot in the tenon joints, changing them is almost more maintenance than restoration.

19 *Delaminated bulkhead*. A damage that is complicated and that has come up quite often in recent years is bulkheads made of plywood or laminated wood that have released their bonding due to leakage from the deck and condensation from the windows. These moisture damages will quickly lead to rot and mold. The bulkheads are often supports for the cabin roof and the longitudinal interior and are difficult to replace without dismantling large parts of the interior. Also, look at the bulkheads from inside the lockers and closets.

20 *Planked decks* wear down more quickly than other parts of the boat. Teak decks are literally scrubbed away, and pine decks are often scraped to remove dents and flaking varnish. The deck is something of a disposable product, and I know some boats that are on their third deck. Prior to purchasing, you must decide if you want to commit to a job as big as replacing a deck.

21 *Interior and cockpit*. What is original, and what was added on afterward? Has there been rotting in the bulkhead in line with the cabin sole? Has the frame under the cockpit benches rotted? Are all the joints in the paneled framework of the bulkheads intact? Have the bulkheads rotted where they are attached to the frames?

22 *The heads*. There are boats in which the hull is more or less corroded under the toilet. A lot of time, there have been renovations done in this area, and all renovators have not been as good as the original

boatbuilders. The part of the boat that ought to be easiest to keep clean is often the most difficult to reach. Pipes, solid soles, and toilet hardware prevent cleaning and inspection.

Equipment

23 *Rudder*. Try to feel the gaps in the rudder and rudder pintles and gudgeons. Does the rudder risk being lifted by grounding? Is there a rudder stopping function that prevents the motorboat rudder from extreme travel in reverse? Is the quadrant safely attached to the rudderstock? Are the blocks for the fairleads firmly attached to the hull? Is there rust damage to the rudderstock where it goes into the rudder pipe? Are the screws in the tiller fitting intact?

24 *Propeller and shaft*. Does the propeller sit rigidly attached to the shaft? There must be no movement. Is it easy to turn the propeller shaft around? It should be if the bearings are aligned and intact. Is there just enough room for the shaft in the bearings? Remember that boats change shape depending on whether they are on land or in water; the shaft of a motor boat can be hard to move if the boat has been on stands under the keel just in front of the outer stem bearing.

25 *Struts*. A lot of times during grounding, the skeg pushes up the struts in the hull. On the inside of the hull, there has to be a robust floor that can take this load. This floor timber retains moisture in the same way the keel does, and often there is also a bad limber hole below it. Both grounding damage and moisture and decay may have led to the planking having been repaired in this area, and with varying success. The worst version has short spliced planks and many new butt joints. Then if the strut is just attached to the planking, it's really bad.

26 *Through hull connectors*. The security inspection that is performed at the yacht clubs by SBU's (Svenska båtunionen, Swedish Boat Association) inspectors is sometimes jokingly called by club members the "counting of hose clamps." Anyone who has owned a wooden boat for a few years knows that there should be double stainless steel hose clamps fastened in the opposite direction on all hoses that flow under or less than 4″ (100 mm) above the waterline. The inspectors do a good job, and inspections have raised safety awareness, even if some of the rules are diffi-cult to implement on old wooden boats. The hoses to the connectors should be in good condition and be checked regularly. But sometimes the flange for the hose is so short that there is only room for one hose clamp. Through hull fittings will corrode and should be replaced every now and then; however, older con-nectors are usually of better quality than newer ones. If a boat owner has had his boat for many years, a lot of times there are certain hull connectors that have been opened and closed regularly while others have not been touched for years. Do not close or open one of those connectors on the boat in the water during an inspec-tion; it may end up breaking or leaking. Check it on land instead.

27 *Self-bailing cockpit.* One change in boating during the 1900s is that sway anchoring has decreased and that sailboats have been equipped with engines. The boats used to be designed and the weight calculated with-out the motor with chains and anchors in the bow. Nowadays, when the boats have engines and stern anchors, they are rebalanced and sit on the stern. If the self-bailers are on the forward end of the cockpit you may have rainwater collecting on the aft part of the sole with rot and decay as a result. Many self-bailing cockpits have been fitted with hatches in the floor dur-ing engine installations. If the hatches aren't attached and sealed, the boat can sink quickly if a rising bilge water level affects the floating position so that the cockpit sole is under the water level. The water will come in through drains, and it will flow into the boat through the hatches.

28 *Fuel system.* Hoses and tubes for fuel must be in good condition; bend the hoses and make sure that the fuel doesn't wet out. The fuel will be pumped from a tube opening on top of the tank; tanks from which the fuel is extracted from underneath are not approved. This can be a dilemma on vintage boats, because the origi-nal tanks are of this type and some older fuel systems don't have a pump or ability to draw out the fuel. We are talking about vintage boat installations, and every case is different. Tank openings on deck, vents, tanks, and the motor must be bonded to each other. Gasoline engines should have an engine fan.

29 *Exhaust pipes.* Older installations often have doubled exhaust pipes; this means that the emissions are dry in an inner pipe while the cooling water goes into a larger, surrounding tube. Water and exhaust are mixed just before they exit the through hull connec-tors. In this system there was less risk of flooding the engine through the back and less chance of rust on the engine's exhaust valves. Today, the exhaust hoses are made of rubber; they offer a faster, cheaper instal-lation and are quieter. The cooling water is mixed with the exhaust already in the exhaust bend by the motor, and they are combined through the hose. The system must be fitted with a water trap that can col-lect water contained in the pipe when the engine is turned off. The top edge of the trap should be at least 10″ (250 mm) below the exhaust bend on the engine. The hose is pulled up to the deck so that a gooseneck is formed just before it flows out through the hull (at least 14″ or 350 mm above the waterline). Sometimes the supporting portions of the hull, such as engine bed and floors, have been cut when the exhaust pipe has been repositioned, with deformations of the hull as a result.

30 *Engines.* What does it look like in the engine room? Is it clean, and are the hoses and wires clamped? No signs of gray from water mixed with oil on the dip-sticks from the engine? No oil leaks from the engine? Are the level wires fastened securely? Are the engine mountings intact? Gum dissolves from leaking oil. The engine room insulation should have a foil cover so that it cannot absorb oil and ignite as easily. It is dif-ficult to see how much property is left in the cooling channels of a salt water–cooled engine; after twenty years, the value cannot be set very high. Batteries must not be stored in the engine room unless they are held in confined boxes that are vented outboard.

31 *The electrical system.* The electrical system should be properly clamped, fused, and marked. But here it is common for the system to have expanded out of con-trol because of the increased electricity demand, and to most closely resemble a ball of yarn that the cat found. It is difficult to renovate an existing electrical system; it's better to just replace it. In a reliable elec-trical system, all users should be connected directly to the center without junction boxes and branch devices. In a 12-volt system, the cables should have an area of 2.5 mm.

32 *Propane and stove.* Bend your propane hoses and see if the rubber has a tendency to crack; in that case they must be replaced. The gas cylinder, regardless of size, should be in a tight container that is drained outboard. This may be difficult to achieve in a sailboat with low topsides; the risk is that the container will flood when you heel. Even the spare cylinder should be in a drained area, and installation should be of the low-pressure kind. If you cannot meet these requirements, you can switch to a galley with a different fuel.

33 *Heads.* The days when the toilets may be emptied directly into the sea will soon be numbered. During renovation you should consider a storage tank (septic tank) with the ability for suction.

34 *Heater.* The two main types of heaters are air heaters and hydronic heating systems. An air heater with a fan system dries out the boat and may function as a dryer that stresses the wood to crack. Water-based heating is gentler as it doesn't cause as great of temperature differences. If the convectors (radiators) are fitted with a reflective panel against the planking, it will help with not heating up the hull in vain, and the heating effect of the convector increases. The heater must be of a type suitable for use in recreational boats, the combustion air should come from the air outside, and the exhaust should be discharged into open air.

35 *Mast and rigging.* Check that hardware hasn't slipped on the mast; screws that have begun to capsize in their holes are a sign of that. Locate cracks and cracked adhesive joints. If the mast has a groove in the wood, make sure it is not too wide, as the boltrope can be torn from the mast. Rot in the mast can occur behind hardware and the mast root end if it is shod and poorly drained. The hollowness of the mast usually stops just above the boom and allows water to stagnate if the mast is leaky above. Galvanized wire rusts over time, and you can tell when it is time to replace it. A forty-year-old stainless wire looks like new, but when it first came into use it was said that it should be replaced every ten years. The most likely place to find evidence that it is getting bad is in the splicing and in the transitions to the end pieces. Spreaders in ash can start rotting behind the tape on the ends.

36 *Deck hardware.* Make sure that mooring cleats are fastened securely with nuts and bolts and that the loads are distributed over a backing plate on the underside of the deck beams.

37 *Winches.* Winch blocks are often so poorly anchored in the deck that the loads can cause the cockpit coamings to crack at the deck level. The self-tailing winches that we have today can be mounted lower as you do not need to tail the halyard by hand.

37 *Cushions and canopies* are consumable products; a cover will last for about ten years and cushions for about twenty. Proper maintenance can add another ten years to that. They are often undervalued in sales.

SUMMARY

I hope that this has not deterred all readers from buying an old wooden boat. A surveyor's job is to find problems and shortcomings; at a valuation, they then have to be weighed against the positive sides. The positive factors other than the purely technical ones are ones such as finish, appearance, comfort, originality, and documentation. In this chapter, I have not touched on the subject of finish. For some buyers, it is important that the finish is newly made; others would rather do it themselves. My personal opinion is that pricing in Sweden is too level. There should be a greater difference in price between a boat in good condition with good equipment and a boat that needs renovation and has poor equipment.

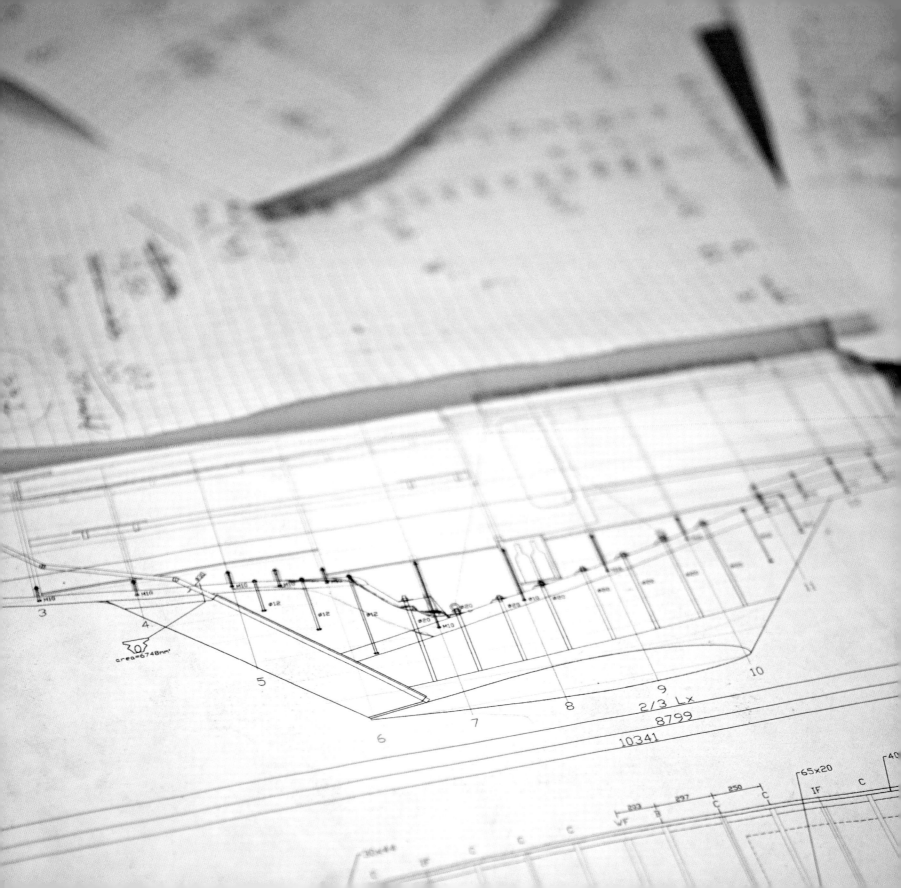

DRAWINGS AND SPECIFICATIONS

Good documentation of the boat is important. It gives an added dimension and conveys a cultural heritage. Plans and construction manuals provide insight into the crafts tradition, and the register of owners will be a link to former owners and their aspirations. An old wooden boat with a history has a greater chance for a second life than a boat without a history.

It is easier to do a restoration of the original appearance if there is a drawing. The maritime museum in Stockholm has drawings and documentation from many designers. Clubs for wooden and vintage boats can also supply contacts and give advice in the search for the origin and history of a boat. A drawing says a lot, but a specification says, if possible, even more. A specification may be harder to find; former owners are your best bet.

Here are drawings and excerpts from construction manuals for the motor cruiser *Elisabeth* that was constructed by the company *Motorbåtsbyrån*, which consisted of C. G. Pettersson and Einar Runius. She was built at the Fröberg shipyard in Kyrkviken on Lidingö in 1925. Fröberg's shipyard was one of the best in terms of quality construction, and *Elisabeth* remains in very good original condition; the current owner has had the boat for thirty years. The former owner found the original drawings, contracts, and the construction manual in the attic of the Fröberg shipyard.

The specifications shows the requirements that the designer and the client had. This kind of construction manual, with requirements and specifications, makes it easier to understand why there are so many boats that are still in very good condition.

DESCRIPTION

Over 43.5 ft (12.95 meter) motor cruiser in accordance with drawing no. 658A and 658B. For civil engineer Stellan Carlberg, November 6, 1924, Stockholm.

Dimensions

Longest length	42.5 ft (12.95 m)
Width of outside planking	8.2 ft (2.5 m)
Deepest draught	2⅔ ft (0.82m)
Lowest topside	2⅔ ft (0.83 m)
Lead keel	551 lbs (250 kg)
Displacement at LWL	4.9 tonne (4.9 tonne)

Specifications

Stem: Swedish self-grown oak 4⅓″ (110 mm) thick, width as per drawing, 1″ (22mm) at the leading edge and shaped fair with the planking. All stem bolts will have elongated heads so that they lie well-hidden under the bow rail.

Sternpost: Swedish self-grown oak 4 × 4″ (100 x 100 mm), well bolted to the keel and enlarged for the rudder sleeve.

Keel: Swedish oak, lined inside 5½ × 2″ (140 × 50 mm). The lower part 3¼″ (80 mm) wide at the rabbet and 1½″ (40 mm) wide at the bottom. Height according to the drawing. The keel is thinned carefully in the aft part to accomplish a good water drop. ½-inch (12-mm) galvanized iron bolts for all keel and stem joints. Screwed on sidepieces for the rabbet are not to be used. All oak should be well dry, without sapwood, rot, cracks, or significant knots.

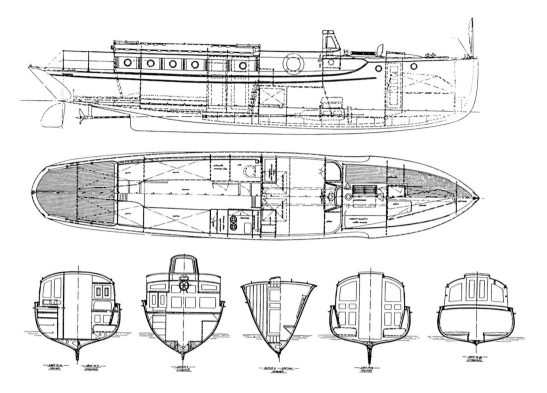

FIGURE 208 } *Elisabeth.*

Transom: Swedish oak 1″ (25 mm). Fastened to the planking with a ¹¹⁄₄″ (32 mm) angel bar of galvanized iron. Three 1 × ³⁄₁₆-inch (25 × 4.8-mm) galvanized flat irons will be outside the inner transom and countersunk, of which the lower ones are riveted into the interior angle irons to prevent bursting apart. Outer transom of ⁵⁄₈-inch (15-mm) Honduras mahogany mitered to the planking and attached with brass screws and plugs.

Planking: Carvel built out of Honduras mahogany. Garboard strake 1″ (26 mm), thinned down with ¹⁄₁₆″ (2 mm) at the waterline. Above the waterline a little less than an inch (24 mm), thinned down with ¹⁄₁₆″ (2 mm) at the railing. Completely dry materials without knots, cracks, sapwood or pith and of uniform color. The maximum plank width 6″ (150 mm). The joints are staggered at least three iron frames. The planking is riveted to the iron frame with ¼-inch galvanized iron rivets and to the wood frame with ⅛-inch copper rivets. Bolts and rivets

are plugged above the waterline and filled with red lead underneath. The planking must be fully tight and the seams tight on both sides.

Iron frame: Galvanized frames with 20-inch (500-mm) space with the laying flange screwed to the groove and the standing taken out so it makes a ¾-inch (20-mm) limber hole.

Wood frame: American grained oak 1⅓–1½ (33–35 mm), two between each iron frame, of non-dried material with the grains longitudinal.

Floors: ³⁄₃₂-inch (3-mm) galvanized sheet metal. The floors are riveted at the top with a 1¼-inch (30-mm) angle iron that will function as a support for the sole, and on the bottom with an angle iron attached to ⅜-inch (10-mm) lag bolts into the keel. Holes for ventilation are made according to the manual and the drawing.

Engine bed: Swedish oak 2″ (50 mm). Length according to the drawing. Inside bed of oak bolted together to the outside. The steel floors are carefully attached to the beds by angle irons bolted through the engine beds. The beds lie close against the ship's side with spacious limber holes on the frame sides.

Beam shelf: 4¾ × 1½-inch (120 × 40-mm) mahogany, riveted with ¼-inch (6-mm) copper and 5⁄16-inch (8-mm) galvanized iron rivets through the ribs to the upper planking and then plugged.

Deck beams: Ash 2⅓ × 1⅓″ (60 × 35 mm) at a (225 mm) spacing.

Carlin: Honduras mahogany 2 × 1⅓″ (50 × 35 mm).

Covering board: 1-inch (23-mm) Honduras mahogany.

Deck: ⅞″ (22-mm) Oregon pine 2″ wide (50 mm), light and fine with the grains on the edge, shaped along the covering board with decreasing width. Attached with galvanized nails and diagonally to the deck beams. Caulked with cotton yarn and seams filled with marine glue.

Coaming: For navigation room of mahogany in 1³⁄32-inch (28-mm) frames and ⅝-inch (15-mm) fillings. Shield of 0.1-inch (2.5-mm) galvanized painted white metal, fitted with 1 × 2⅓-inch (26 × 60-mm) rounded mahogany trim.

Saloon: Top board, coaming, and pilasters of 1-inch (28-mm) mahogany. Fillings according to the drawing.

Roof of the saloon: First class ½-inch (12-mm) wainscoted pine in small widths. Covered on the top with thick oil-coated canvas. Sliding hatches of 1¹⁄16-inch (17-mm) mahogany with 1¼–1½-inch (32–38-mm) semi-round overhang on 1⅛-inch (28-mm) runners with waterproof rebate.

Then the description continues with two pages of interior. Here's a sample:

Forecastle: Outfitted with a foldable berth of galvanized steel tubing with a chain and string bottom and a side of canvas with suspension brackets. Aft wardrobe of ¾-inch (18-mm) wainscoted pine with doors of mahogany in ¾-inch (18-mm) frames and ⅜-inch (10-mm) fillings. Bench of ¾-inch (20-mm) pine with mahogany trim. Ceiling against the hull 5⁄16–3-inch (8 × 75 mm) mahogany at ½-inch (12-mm) intervals.

Floorboards: Teak ⅝″ (16 mm) with brass fitted lifting holes in the gaps that make the bottom well accessible everywhere.

A half page like this follows:

Fender trim: 2–2⅓-inch mahogany with profile according to the drawing is fastened with thick galvanized iron screws with rounded heads and ditto washers. Attached from the inside next to each wooden rib and without the washer through each iron rib. The trim should be shod with Svenska Metallverken (Swedish Metalworks) brass profile no. 455.

Oars: 2 made out of ash, leather fitted, and the blades with copper bands at the end.

Followed by three pages of hardware in different categories: Nickel-plated bronze hardware. Copper hardware. Galvanized-iron hardware. Metal hardware. Miscellaneous furniture. Electrical lighting. Engine installation.

The construction manual ends with painting.

Painting: The entire hull is oiled twice with raw linseed oil and twice with boiled linseed oil. Red lead is applied twice under the floor boards and on the inside and outside of the boat up to the waterline and twice underneath the floor boards. The canvas on the saloon roof and the metal bridge railing is painted white, as well as bulkheads in the forecastle and engine room, as well as the forward tank room bulkhead in the engine room. Everything else is varnished repeatedly with Noble & Hoare surface varnish or equivalent, with sandpaper and water sanding in between until a completely hard and smooth surface is obtained. The last coat is with Noble & Hoare Outside Yacht Varnish. The exterior is coated with Knob Jens antifouling coating according to the customer's choice. The water line is painted, drawn up 4″ (100 mm) in the front, 3½″ (90 mm) in the aft, and 3³⁄16″ (80 mm) higher amidships over CWL.

Sources

Borgenstam, *Curt: Min motorbåt: på ritbordet, på varvet, i sjön (My Motorboat: On the Drawing Board, At the Shipyard, In the Water)*, Norstedt, Stockholm 1954.

Boutelje, J. B. & Rydell, R.: *Träfakta 44 träslag i ord och bild (Timber Knowledge: 44 Wood Types in Words and Pictures)* Trätek, Stockholm 1986.

Broch, Ole-Jacob: *Trebåten, (The Wooden Boat)*, Univesitetsforlaget, Oslo 1993.

Brohäll, Per: *Elektrokemiska angrepp på båtvirke (Electrochemical Attack on Boat Timber), Till Rors (At the Helm) #8*, 1955.

Brohäll, Per: *Bygg båten själv (Build Your Own Boat)*, Teknik för alla, Stockholm 1964.

Gougeon: *The Gougeon Brothers on Boat Construction*, Michigan 1985.

Henrikson, Janicke: *Plymepoken (The Plym Era)*, The Museum Association for Swedish Pleasure Boat's Yearbook, 1982.

Hernlund, Göran: *Båtbyggarens receptbok (The Boatbuilder's Recipe Book)*, print out from the Skeppsholmen college.

Keaton, John, *Merseyside Maritime Museum: Nail Sickness, Classic Yacht*, Sept. 1992.

Kinney, *Skene's Elements of Yacht Design*, A&C Black, London 1981.

KMK: *Bestämmelser samt råd och anvisningar för motorbåtars byggnad och utrustning (Rules and Advice and Guidance for the Building and Equipping of Motorboats)*, Häggström Book Printing and Publishing House, 1929.

Liewendahl, Ingvard et.al.: *Sexornas jakt* (The 6-Meter Yachts), Finland's 6m Club, Helsinki 1992.

af Malmborg, Andreas & Husberg, *Ola: Träbåtar (Wooden Boats)*, Prisma, Stockholm 1999.

McIntosh, D.C.: *How to Build a Wooden Boat*, Wooden Boat Publ. Maine 1987.

MYS register 2001.

Nordens Båtar (Scandinavian Boats) eds. Otto Lybeck, Lindfors publisher, Stockholm 1939–1942.

Nordisk båtstandard (Nordic Boat Standard) 1990.
Fritidsbåtar under 15 m (Pleasure Boats under 15 M), The Swedish Maritime Administration, Norrtälje 1990.

Plym, Gustav: *En seglare minns (A Sailor Remembers)*, Nordsteds, Stockholm 1972.

Rules and Regulations for the Classification of Yachts and Small Craft, Lloyds, London 1979.

Rydholm, Yngve: *Sjösportens ord (Terminology of Sailing)*, Bonnier, Stockholm 1967.

SSKF: *Bestämmelser för skärgårdskryssare (Requirements for the Skerry Cruiser)*, 1996.

Svensson, Tore & Trägårdh, Kurt: *Handbok i båtvård (Manual for Boat Maintenance)*, Norstedt, Stockholm 1955.

Thelander, Per: *Alla våra skärgårdskryssare (All of Our Archipelago Cruisers)*, The Square Meter Association, Boat and Sea, Stockholm 1990.

Wahrolén, Hans: *Kryssare och kappseglare (Cruisers and Racers)*, Ateljé Måsen, Stockholm 1980.

Warren, Nigel: *Metal Corrosion in Boats*, Adlard Coles Nautical, London 1980.

Yearbooks from Föreningen Allmogebåtar (The Association for Utility Boats).

Magazines: *Till Rors (At the Helm)*, *Segel och Motor (Sail and Motor)*, *Seglarbladet (The Sailing Post)*, *Med Motorbåt (Motorboat Owner)*.

PHOTOGRAPHS

Thomas Larsson: Figures 2, 4, 5, 7, 8, 9, 10, 11, 13, 15, 16, 17, 38, 42, 44, 48, 49, 51, 71, 76, 77, 82, 83, 86, 90, 91, 95, 96, 97, 98, 103, 104, 105, 106, 114, 130, 138, 141, 143, 144, 149, 150, 15, 157, 159, 168, 173, 189, 192, 201, 204, 205

Niklas Skärlund: Figure 3

Christer Ulvås: Figures 14, 23, 24, 26, 30, 31, 37, 40, 41, 52, 53, 80, 100, 128, 131, 132

Björn Widström: Figures 72, 73

Malcolm Hanes: Figures on pages 10, 14, 18, 24, 30, 42, 50, 62, 74, 82, 90, 94, 100, 110, 126, 134, 145, 166, 184, 194, 198, 204, 214, 220, 230

ILLUSTRATIONS

Thomas Larsson

Glossary

0-line also datum line. Dashes drawn across two or more pieces to enable them to be assembled into position again, a reference line.

A

Alkyd The most common artificial resin for paint.

Angled nails Also secret or hidden. To angle nails means to attach them on the diagonal. A nail that goes diagonally through a deck plank into a deck beam.

Anvil An anvil is needed to take up the vibrations when hammering, also called a doll, bucking iron or holding.

Askew An edge or surface that changes the angle is askew.

B

Backbone The assembly of the backbone, ie., keel and its attached stem and transom.

Ballast keel is used to increase the boat's stiffness, an exterior keel made of lead or iron.

Beam shelf Longitudinal stiffening beam along the hull that supports the deck beams, see Stringers.

Bending to soften the wood with heat, usually with steam.

Bilge Where the hull transitions from side to bottom, the bilge can be hard or soft depending on whether it has a large or small radius, There is also a lower part of the bilge where the planking is concave on the outside.

Bilge stringers Longitudinal stiffening beam in the bilge, see also Stringer.

Bilge water The term Bilge is also used for the lowest part inside the boat, where the bilgewater is standing.

Bolt rope grove A grove on the mast where the mainsail luff is attached.

Boxed mast A mast built with a rectangular section.

Bull-nose rabbet plane A plane with knives as wide as the plane, it means that you can shave the inner edges and the sides.

Bulwarks A high edge of the deck out to the hull, see also Railing.

Bung repairing of wood, see also Cut.

C

Cabin Really refers to the superstructure, but is often used for interior spaces of the cabin or saloon.

Canvassed deck Deck planks can be covered with canvas that is painted, the canvas keeps the deck watertight.

Cap The top piece of a toe rail or a bulwark.

Card scraper or cabinet scraper. A piece of metal for smoothing and scraping wood.

Carlin Similar to a beam, except running in a fore and aft direction, such as cabin carlin, hatch carlin.

Carvel planking Where the planks are placed edge to edge so the hull is smooth, see also Clinker.

Central punch A pointed steel tool that you strike with a hammer to make marks in metal.

Chain plate The shroud mount in the hull.

Clinker planking or lapstrake where the planks are overlapped and riveted together, old Nordic planking method, see also Carvel.

Coaming A vertical board forming the side around the cockpit and cabin (cabin side).

Cold-baked Cold moulded veneer glued over a mold.

Copying ring A guide for milling after a template.

Countersink drill bit A drill for countersunk screws.

Covering board or gunwale. A board that follows the side of the hull from bow to stern, it stiffens the deck edge.

Cut To cut in a piece of new wood, see also Bungs.

D

Deadwood sometimes called false keel. Timber that is bolted between the wood keel and the ballast keel to increase the draft or to fill out between the ballast keel and the rudder.

Deck beam Transverse beam that holds up the deck.

Drain plug A screw or a plug in the keel's deepest point to drain water when the boat is on land.

E

Electrochemical attacks Attacks on wood caused by galvanic corrosion.

Engine bed Longitudinal beams at the bottom on which the engine is attached.

Epoxy also called epoxy resin. A plastic material used for bonding and coating.

F

Fairing Using a plane or a long sanding board to make the surface fair.

Fall wood The slow-growing, resin-rich part of a ring, see also Growth rings and Springwood.

Feeler gauge is a tool used to measure small gap widths.

Female mould A concave mold or template.

Filling The pieces of wood that are used as reinforcements, for example in hardware they are fitted between deck beams or ribs, and also fillings in framework, see also Raised bulkheads.

Fitting Shaping work pieces to fit tightly to each other.

Flange The lips of pipes, shafts, and motors are joined with flanges. An angel bar has two flanges.

Floors connect the keel and the planking. If they are made of wood they are called floor timbers.

Frames The boat's ribs. Transverse stiffineners of the hull.

G

Garboard strake or planks attached to the keel.

Glueing table Is for clamping the work piece, adjustable workbench for glueing

Growth rings Also referred to as tree rings and annual rings of wood.

Guard Rail A protection strip along the hull.

H

Heartwood. The mature inner part of the trunk that has stopped transporting nutrients. It is the heartwood that is used for boatbuilding.

Hog The inner part of the keel.

Holding tank Septic tank, sewage tank.

I

Interlocked grain Spiraled wood that reverses direction regularly.

J

Joint A splice on the wood.

Jointer Plane A long plane for alignment of the wood.

K

Keel bolt The bolt holding a ballast keel.

Keelson Lies parallel to the keel but above the transverse members, such as the floors and frames for additional longitudinal stiffness.

King plank An actual strengthening plank amidships on the deck, often as a board of different wood between the planks of the deck.

Knee Stiffening of corners: vertical knees from deck beam to the frame, horizontal knees between deck beams and beam stringers, stem knees between keel and stem.

L

Laminates Thin slices or strips that are glued together into frames or for other purposes, see also Veneer.

Lap Seams in the planking of a clinker-built boat.

Leak A crack or a joint in which the wood is deformed by repeated swelling and drying.

Limber holes Hole for the bilge water in the floors. For the boat to have a long life, you must have limber holes performed with care and kept clean.

M

Male A convex mold or template.

Margin The boards of the deck that follow cabins and coamings.

Mast partner Reinforcement in the deck for the mast hole.

Masthead rig The forestay that goes all the way to the masthead.

Mildew Mold fungi stains; this was common on cotton sails that had been wrapped up moist.

Mitered joint A joint where two boards meet by dividing the angle.

O

Open-hearth steel making This is a method to create steel out of pig iron.

P

Pith Center of a log. The pith rots and cracks easily.

Plank deck Deck made by planks or strips, often caulked, sometimes canvassed.

Planking is the shell of the hull; planks go from stem to stern.

Plug Seals the screw holes.

Power train The transmitting power from engine to propeller: shoulder, joints, flanges, bearings, propeller, and strut

Primer Prime coating.

Propeller shaft pipe Around the propeller shaft. It is attached to the keel and usually has a seal and a bearing.

Punch mandrel with a cylindrical tip is used to take out bolts,

Q

Quadrant mounts the steering wire to the rudder stock.

R

Rabbet A recess in the stem and keel in which the planks are mounted.

Rabbet line The edge between the planking and the stem or keel.

Railing A low bulwark.

Raised bulkhead A bulkhead made up of frames and fillings (raised).

Red lead Lead oxide, an orange, tight, heavy pigment that is toxic.

Rivet punch A tool to attach the washer on the rivet when riveting.

Rivet tool tidies up the riveting.

Rudder stock The shaft of the rudder, can be made of wood or be a shaft or a tube of metal.

S

Sealing trim The strip between the sheets in a sheeted deck.

Seam A joint between two planks or two deck planks, see also Lap.

Shaft strut Bracket mounted for the outer propeller shaft bearing.

Shearing displacement Forces that are involved in cutting and punching.

Shoulder Piece of wood on the mast, in which hooks for the stays are the bracing attached.

Skeg Sternward projection from the keel in front of the rudder. Protects the rudder from damage during grounding.

Smoothing plane (No 4) A plane that gives a smooth surface.

Springwood The rapidly growing part of a growth ring.

Steering It consists of a steering wheel or tiller and the transmission by wire and quadrant or other methods to the rudder stock and rudder.

Stem the forward part of the backbone.

Stringer Longitudinal stiffening, such as bilge stringer. Also common in plywood boats and cold moulded boats.

T

Talmeter A tape measure with which it is easy to transfer measurements and take internal dimensions.

Tapered To become smaller or thinner at one end.

Tenon The projected part in a mortice and tenon joint.

Tiller Tiller lever by which the rudder is operated.

Toe rail A low railing.

Toggles A joint for a turnbuckle. Is used so the screw isn't subject to buckling and bending.

Topsides The planking above the waterline.

Transom The aft transverse section of the hull.

V

Veneer Thin slice of solid wood; veneer can be joined to plywood and cold-moulded constructions.

Ventilation hole A hole in the steel floor, to save weight and improve ventilation.

W

Wood keel. The center part of the backbone to which the floors and the garboard strake is attached.

INDEX